D0419859

Professionalism Reborn

Sheffield Hallam University
Learning and Information Services
Withdrawn From Stock

OP Purchase

3 0 JAN 2013

ASSBK

PROFESSIONALISM REBORN

Theory, Prophecy, and Policy

Eliot Freidson

Polity Press

Copyright © Eliot Freidson 1994.

The right of Eliot Freidson to be identified as author of this work has been asserted in accordance with the Copyright, Designs and Patents Act 1988.

First published in 1994 by Polity Press in association with Blackwell Publishers.

Reprinted 2004

Editorial office:
Polity Press
65 Bridge Street
Cambridge CB2 1UR, UK

Marketing and production:
Blackwell Publishers
108 Cowley Road
Oxford OX4 1JF, UK

All rights reserved. Except for the quotation of short passages for the purposes of criticism and review, no part of this publication may be reproduced, stored in a retrieval system, or transmitted, in any form or by any means, electronic, mechanical, photocopying, recording or otherwise, without the prior permission of the publisher.

Except in the United States of America, this book is sold subject to the condition that it shall not, by way of trade or otherwise, be lent, re-sold, hired out, or otherwise circulated without the publisher's prior consent in any form of binding or cover other than that in which it is published and without a similar condition including this condition being imposed on the subsequent purchaser.

ISBN 0 7456 1280 6
ISBN 0 7456 1446 9 (pbk)

British Library Cataloguing-in-Publication Data
A CIP catalogue record for this book is available from the British Library.

Typeset in 10 on 12pt Garamond Stempel
by Graphicraft Typesetters Ltd, Hong Kong

Printed and bound in Great Britain by
Marston Book Services Limited, Oxford

This book is printed on acid-free paper.

WL
305.553
FR

*For
Molly*

Contents

Contents

Acknowledgments

The essays in this volume appear as originally printed, though in some cases text and references were cut to minimize repetition, and brief text added to link papers to one another. Their original substance (as well as the references they relied on at the time) has been preserved.

"The Theory of Professions: State of the Art," appeared in Robert Dingwall and Philip Lewis (eds), *The Sociology of the Professions: Lawyers, Doctors and Others* (London: Macmillan, 1983), pp. 19–37. © 1983, Eliot Freidson. Reprinted by permission of The Macmillan Press Ltd.

"How Dominant are the Professions?" appeared in Frederic W. Hafferty and John B. McKinlay (eds), *The Changing Medical Profession: An International Perspective* (New York: Oxford University Press, 1993), pp. 54–66. © 1993 Oxford University Press. Reprinted by permission.

"The Division of Labor as Social Interaction" is reprinted from *Social Problems*, 23, 3 (1976), pp. 304–13, by permission. © 1975 by the Society for the Study of Social Problems.

"Professions and the Occupational Principle" is reprinted from Eliot Freidson (ed.), *The Professions and Their Prospects* (Beverly Hills: Sage, 1973), pp. 19–38. © 1973, Sage Publications. Reprinted by permission.

"Occupational Autonomy and Labor Market Shelters" is reprinted from Phyllis L. Steward and Muriel G. Cantor (eds), *Varieties of Work* (Beverly Hills: Sage, 1982), pp. 39–54. © 1982 Sage Publications. Reprinted by permission.

"Professionalization and the Organization of Middle-Class Labor in Post-Industrial Society" originally appeared in *Sociological Review Monographs*, no. 20 (1973), pp. 47–59. Reprinted by permission.

"The Futures of Professionalization" originally appeared in Margaret Stacey, Margaret Reid, Christian Heath, and Robert Dingwall (eds), *Health and the Division of Labour* (London: Croom Helm, 1977), pp. 14–38. Reprinted by permission.

"The Changing Nature of Professional Control" is reproduced from the *Annual Review of Sociology*, 10 (1984), pp. 1–20. © 1984 by Annual Reviews. Reprinted by permission.

"Are Professions Necessary?" originally appeared in Thomas L. Haskell (ed.), *The Authority of Experts: Studies in History and Theory* (Bloomington: Indiana University Press, 1984), pp. 3–27. © 1984 Indiana University Press. Reprinted by permission.

"Professionalism as Model and Ideology" is reprinted from Robert L. Nelson, David M. Trubek, and Rayman L. Solomon (eds), *Lawyers' Ideals/Lawyers' Practices: Transformations in the American Legal System* (Ithaca: Cornell University Press, 1992), pp. 215–29. Copyright © 1992 by Cornell University. Used by permission of the publisher, Cornell University Press.

"The Centrality of Professionalism to Health Care" is reprinted by permission from *Jurimetrics: Journal of Law, Science and Technology*, 30 (summer, 1990), pp. 431–45.

"Nourishing Professionalism" is reprinted from Edmund D. Pellegrino, Robert M. Veatch, and John P. Langan (eds), *Ethics, Trust, and the Professions: Philosophical and Cultural Aspects* (Washington: Georgetown University Press, 1991), pp. 193–215. Reprinted by permission.

Introduction

This book brings together a selection of the essays I have written about the professions over a period of twenty years. Both my preoccupation with the topic and my writing about it extend back even further, however, for when I undertook intensive study and analysis of the medical profession during an earlier decade, the larger problem of understanding professionalism[1] as a general phenomenon was never out of my mind. But with the exception of a recent paper that argues an important policy issue for the professions in general by analyzing efforts to control the cost of American health care in particular, nothing of what I have written about medicine and health care is included here.[2]

The papers address a number of different topics and are arranged in several broad categories. The articles in Part I are concerned with appraising the state of the field, the reasons for some of its inadequacies, certain of the methodological issues it must face, and the complexity of the phenomenon it addresses. In Part II I advance some of my own efforts to develop a theory, beginning by establishing my choice of occupational control of work as the guiding concept for the theorizing, and then elaborating its implications. The essays in Part III turn to the more topical matter of evaluating the present position of professions in advanced industrial society in the light of recent shifts in public opinion and state policy. I analyze forecasts of professional decline in the light of available evidence, and indicate what I believe is happening to the professions today. In Part IV the tenor of the essays shifts from descriptive analysis to an attempt to inform social policy, which must inevitably judge and choose among alternatives and cannot be neutral. I argue that, on balance, professionalism is preferable to alternative modes of organizing the work of professionals (and others) and suggest how its virtues can be reinforced.

THE EARLY POSTWAR PERIOD

At any given time, much of what is chosen to write about reflects not only the stage of development of one's own thinking but also a response to contemporary issues and interests. Thus, these essays must be seen in part as a product of the development of the field of the sociology of professions during the second half of the twentieth century. Let me briefly sketch that development in order to provide a context for them.[3]

As I note in Chapter 1 and other essays in this book, the professions have been considered worthy of special attention in the English-speaking world for at least a century. Herbert Spencer dwelt on their special importance in English society, as did Beatrice and Sidney Webb, R. H. Tawney, A. M. Carr-Saunders, and T. H. Marshall, each for different reasons. But the concept of profession was largely taken for granted, and there was little systematic thinking about it until academic sociology in the United States expanded after World War II. The most widely known American theorist, Talcott Parsons, had been perhaps the earliest to address the professions in theoretical terms. In a prewar essay (Parsons, 1939) he sought to make sense of the ostensible contradiction between the idea that professions manifest altruistic rather than self-interested behavior and the assumption on the part of economic theory and utilitarianism that all behavior is self-interested. In postwar work (Parsons, 1951, 1964, 1968) he theorized about both the medical and the legal professions, and claimed special importance for the professions in advanced industrial societies. In a lower key, outside the then-dominant functionalist tradition, Everett Hughes (1958) wrote a series of provocative essays that cut through the mystique with which professions attempt to surround themselves, analyzing both what they had in common with far more humble occupations, and what distinguished them.

In addition to those pre-eminent sociologists, many other well-known writers made self-conscious efforts to develop a concept of profession that would distinguish it from other occupations, and to discover regularities in the historic process by which an occupation attains professional status (e.g., Wilensky, 1964; Goode, 1969; Moore, 1970). By the 1960s,[4] a number of British sociologists had joined in the enterprise (e.g., Jackson, 1970; Elliott, 1972). A literature of considerable size had begun to accumulate.

THE CRITICAL PERIOD

Until the 1960s, the tenor of writings by scholars on the professions was, by and large, neutral. If it was not critical of the professions, neither was it laudatory. Only Talcott Parsons (who was himself hardly an apologist for the professional status quo) singled them out for a position of special importance in his vision of modern society. As for other fields, however, the 1960s were an intellectual watershed for the study of the professions. Under the ideological influence of that period, historians and sociologists began producing "revisionist" histories of the professions and their institutions, emphasizing their economic self-interest and concern for their status in the policies they pursued, and analyzing how their activities facilitated control of the poor, the working class, and the deviant (e.g., Platt, 1969; Rothman, 1971; Auerbach, 1976). Influential sociological essays warned against the adoption of the professions' own self-advertisements and, denying the possibility of neutrality, urged both a more critical stance and taking the side of the deviant and the client.

By the early 1970s, two writers reflected the intellectual ferment of the previous decade and shifted the emphasis of subsequent theorizing about the professions away from their role in holding society together and toward issues of conflict and power. My books *Profession of Medicine* (1988 [1970a]) and *Professional Dominance* (1970b) were focused on the medical profession and the organization of health care, while keeping in sight the implications of the analysis for understanding professions in general. They emphasized the ideological character of professional claims, unjustified aspects of monopolistic privilege, and the way organized professional institutions create and sustain authority over clients, associated occupations, and the very way we think about deviant or undesirable behavior. Shortly afterwards Terence Johnson (1972) defined profession as a method of controlling work – one in which an occupation, rather than individual consumers or an agent or agency mediating between occupation and consumer, exercises control over its work. And he emphasized the role of power in establishing and maintaining such control. Subsequent literature from both the United Kingdom and the United States was described by commentators as taking a "power approach" rather than the "trait approach" of earlier structural-functional writers. Later in the decade, Larson's *The Rise of Professionalism* (1977) brought both Marxist and Weberian theory to the fore in her analysis of professions, studying them as interest groups linked to the class system of capitalist societies and analyzing professionalization as a "collective mobility project" in which occupations seek to improve not only their economic position but also their social standing, or prestige. The broad historical orientation of her work also stimulated greater interest in historical studies of professionalization, which I shall discuss shortly.

The revival of Marxist analysis in the United Kingdom and the United States from the 1960s on also made its mark on studies of professions.

Marxism, of course, emphasized the ultimate importance of economic relations. But so, too, does economic liberalism, which was also revived. The intellectual consequence was that those otherwise mutually hostile ideologies joined in attacking the social standing and economic privilege of professions, arguing that professionalism represents unjustified elitism that reinforces the class system, and that its exclusionary "social closures" limit opportunity (Collins, 1979) and interfere with the operation of a free and putatively efficient labor market. Similar criticism was implicit in the more neutral-sounding academic work of those adopting the "power approach." It remains the dominant theme in evaluating professionalism today, perhaps because in virtually all capitalist democracies the high cost of health, legal, education, welfare and other professional services has become a critical policy issue.

In the early 1970s, the primary target of most of the British and American writers criticizing the professions was medicine – how it dominated social policy, the other occupations in the health-care division of labor, the institutions in which its members work, and patients or consumers, and how it has "medicalized" personal and social problems (e.g., Berlant, 1975; McKinlay, 1973). But later in the decade, under the influence of Marxism, the emphasis on medicine's power (and the power of the professions) began to shift. The literature turned to predicting the decline of medicine, law, and professions in general. A considerable literature has since grown up that speculates about the consequences for the professions of financial and administrative policies being undertaken both by private corporations and by the state. In addition, attention has focused on the possible consequences of changes within the professions themselves, such as increasing numbers of practitioners and greater internal stratification and fragmentation into specialties, not to speak also of the influence of consumer movements. All analysts agree that in virtually every industrial nation the professions are going through important changes. Marxist analysts predictably forecast proletarianization; others prophesy considerable reorganization of the professions, if not actual loss of their status.

THE EMERGING COMPARATIVE APPROACH

Until the 1980s, medicine served as the primary model for conceptualizing professionalism. An early essay by Rueschemeyer (1964) pointed out that there are major differences between law and medicine even though both are recognized by everyone as true professions, and he warned against generalizing from medicine alone. But since it was medicine and paramedical occupations that were familiar to most writers, his warning fell on deaf ears and had little influence at the time. By the 1970s, sociologists in Canada, Australia, and New Zealand had joined British and American sociologists in studying the professions – concentrating on medicine and related occupations in the English-speaking countries (e.g., Larkin, 1983; Willis, 1989), but beginning to pay some sustained attention to the legal profession (e.g., Dingwall and Lewis, 1983).

By then, however, an increasing number of historians were undertaking studies of professions that began appearing in print in the 1980s. Indeed, histories of professions became, in the words of one review-essayist (Ramsey, 1983), a cottage industry for historians. Furthermore, they did not restrict themselves to health-related professions in English-speaking nations (e.g., Geison, 1983a, 1983b; Frieden, 1981; Peterson, 1978; Gawalt, 1984; Cocks and Jarausch, 1990; Ramsey, 1988). Typically, they turned to sociology for concepts and theories to use either as a guide or as rhetorical straw men for organizing their exposition. Many of those studying professions on the continent found those concepts wanting (e.g., Gispen, 1988). But sociologists had also become dissatisfied with concepts that were developed more for analyzing medicine than other professions, and, even then, in English-speaking countries with relatively decentralized and passive governments.

Strong interest in the professions grew on the continent as well as in English-speaking countries during the 1980s. Previously, European scholars had seemed to consider the concept of profession to be of little pertinence to their own societies. This is not to say that they ignored medicine, law, and other educated, middle-class occupations, or that they were unaware of the increasingly conspicuous role of experts in their societies. But they did not use the Anglo-American concept of profession to organize the way they dealt with those topics. Their neglect of the concept was no doubt due to a number of causes, such as their intellectual propensity to think in terms of class rather than occupation, the absence of a term with similar implications in their own languages, and, perhaps most important, the fact that European professions in general are more closely bound to the state than their English-speaking counterparts.

For whatever the reason, during the 1980s French, German, Swedish, and other historians undertook studies of physicians, lawyers, engineers, secondary school teachers, and others (e.g., Burrage and Torstendahl, 1990; Torstendahl and Burrage, 1990). Stimulated primarily by the work of Larson, they sought to analyze how the modern professions emerged in Europe during the nineteenth and twentieth centuries – that is, the process of professionalization. In doing so, they were quite critical of the way the process had been conceptualized by earlier Anglo-American writers and sought to distinguish the different paths of different professions in different nations with different cultural and political traditions. In most, the state played an active role in initiating the institionalization of some professions and reorganizing others. Furthermore, in many cases it served as the professions' prime employer. This obviously made for a different course of professionalization than occurred in the English-speaking countries and will no doubt lead to new theories in the future.

Interest in comparative studies of the position of contemporary professions also developed during this time. Medical sociologists (Hafferty and McKinlay, 1993), sociologists of education (Clark, 1987), and scholars concerned with the bearing of public policy on the various professions (Freddi and Björkman, 1989; Jones, 1991) brought together volumes comparing the position of a number of different professions in the same nation, or comparing the position of the same profession in different nations. Abel and Lewis (1988a, 1988b) published a massive compendium of studies of lawyers in both civil and common law countries, as well as a volume of essays (1989a) exploring some of the theoretical implications of that comparative study. By now a considerable literature of comparative transnational studies has begun to accumulate, with many more likely to come well before the end of the century.

Parallel with growing interest in transnational comparative studies has been the growth of a marked emphasis on the role of the state in the affairs of the professions. No doubt this is due in part to having to explain the position of professions in nations on the European continent (and elsewhere), which had different kinds of state traditions, but it also reflects an intellectual shift in emphasis and interest that has taken place in the larger disciplines of political science and political sociology. Elements of that shift have begun to appear in the literature, as in my own exploration of the legal and other state-supported institutions that sustain professionalism in the United States (Freidson, 1986a), Rueschemeyer's proposal (1986) to compare professions by adopting a state-centered rather than profession-centered approach, and Halliday's invaluable appraisal (1989) of the pertinence of corporatist theory to understanding the position of professions in various nations.

THE STUDY OF PROFESSIONS IN THE FUTURE

It is far too early to tell where growing interest in comparative studies and in the state will take us. We can assume that historians' interest in professionalization will continue if only because the study of how institutions develop over time is intrinsic to their discipline. Nor can there be any doubt that Abbott's recent (1988) brilliant analysis of the role of jurisdictional claims and disputes in the changing fortunes of professions will force us to pay closer attention in the future to the interaction between occupations in contiguous positions in a division of labor. In both cases, the role of the state is almost certain to be explored more thoroughly than was the case in the past. My guess is that the emphasis on professional monopoly that has dominated the literature for many years is in decline, due partly to its own intrinsic limitations, and partly to a shift in intellectual interest that has little to do with the limitations of what is abandoned. Similarly, "revisionist" histories are likely to decline, and it may be that greater attention will be paid in the future to aspects of professionalization that cannot be explained easily by reference to material self-interest. Who knows? Whig history may yet return! Whatever else, I have little doubt that cross-national comparisons of particular professions will thrive, and I hope that the systematic comparison of different professions will also do so.

In addition, I hope that sociologists will answer Abel and Lewis's call (1989b) to study the work that professions do and to make greater efforts to grapple with conceptualizing the influence of differences in the kind of knowledge and work on the process of professionalization (see Halliday, 1985; Abbott, 1988, pp. 33–58 and 177–211). And certainly more can be done to trace the influence of professional knowledge on both social policy and everyday life. One intellectual current that has already contributed to that topic, though not always in a comprehensible fashion, stems from the writings of Michel Foucault (e.g., 1975, 1979). While neither he nor his French followers appear to have examined closely the institutional forms through which those disciplines are exercised (see Freidson, 1986a), it is clear that he was in fact concerned with professionalism, for the professions are the agents which create and advance the knowledge embodied in disciplines, and their members project that knowledge into human and state affairs. By and large, the major exception being Magalí Larson (1989, 1990), the question of the influence of the knowledge and concepts of professions on human consciousness and state policy has been given too little attention by sociologists.

Finally, I might mention the most serious deficiency of the field today – namely, its lack of an adequate theoretical foundation. At present, the sociology of professions stands as a topical field, loosely affiliated with class theory by some, but essentially without any clear theoretical roots. I believe it should be grounded in a theory of occupations, for a profession is generically an occupation, and certainly not a class. What distinguishes occupations from each other is the specialized knowledge and skill required to perform different tasks in a division of labor. This is a distinctly different criterion than location in a class system or in a firm.

As I note in Chapter 5, neither class theory nor organizational theory can
account adequately for the self-organizing potential of occupations. What
is needed to ground theorizing about professions is the development of
a genuine sociology of work that deals in a systematic fashion with such
topics as the nature and varieties of the specialized knowledge and skill
that are embodied in work, the role of that specialized knowledge and
skill in the differentiation of work into occupations, and the varied ways
by which that differentiation becomes organized.

Apart from developing a theoretical foundation for a true theory of
professions, it is essential to establish a guide for their empirical study.
As I note in Chapter 2, the more comparative studies there are, the more
likely is it that they will be incomparable if they are based on different
conceptions of profession. I believe that a fixed standard is most useful
for that purpose – namely, an ideal type. But an ideal type that can serve
as a standard cannot merely define the substantive essence of some historic
form of occupation. As European criticism of Anglo-American efforts to
define profession has correctly shown, there is no single, invariant historic form. Success in creating a standard that can guide a wide variety
of comparative studies can come only from an ideal type that is constructed systematically out of basic concepts of work, the ways by which
it can be organized and controlled, and the institutions necessary for
gaining and maintaining that organization.

PROFESSIONALISM REBORN

Having provided the historical and intellectual context for the essays
in this volume by briefly reviewing the development of the field of the
sociology of professions, I wish to note the way in which its title, *Professionalism Reborn*, is intended to draw them together. My efforts to
conceptualize professionalism in these papers owes much to the work of
earlier, now often criticized or ignored writers such as R. H. Tawney,
T. H. Marshall, Talcott Parsons, Everett C. Hughes, and William J. Goode,
Jr. I have tried to use their substantive insights and arguments in a manner
intended to avoid the European charge of Anglo-American particularism.
I propose professionalism as a logically distinct and theoretically significant alternative to currently received models for conceptualizing the
organization and control of work. Thus, in a number of the essays of this
volume much of the work of those earlier students of professions and
professionalism becomes reborn to shape an analytic concept.

In other chapters I focus on the empirical forms of professionalism,
addressing the fact that, in all major advanced industrial nations, the

position of professionals and the nature of their practice are changing. My papers discuss others' efforts to conceptualize those changes as evidence of the decline and future disappearance of professionalism. I argue, to the contrary, that the essential elements of professionalism are not disappearing, but rather are taking a new form. Professionalism is being reborn in a hierarchical form in which everyday practitioners become subject to the control of professional elites who continue to exercise the considerable technical, administrative, and cultural authority that professions have had in the past.

The essays in Part IV of this volume represent my considered response to the torrent of criticism to which professions in the United States have been subjected over the past two decades by both radical and free-market ideologues. My past work on the medical profession has been cited often to support both positions, but I believe that both are ill-considered, especially in light of the practical question "What are the alternatives to professionalism?" I try to redress what is now an extreme imbalance of intellectual opinion. The evaluative tradition of Tawney, Carr-Saunders, and Marshall is reborn in my argument that professionalism is both necessary and desirable for a decent society.

However, that argument, and the analysis of professionalism throughout this book, is grounded in the historic conventions that govern the labor market. Insofar as those who perform complex, discretionary work must gain their living by it, then professionalism represents the more desirable method of organizing their position in the labor market. The connection of professional work with income, however, is a constant stimulus to self-interested exploitation of the sheltered autonomy that professional institutions provide, so we may hardly consider professionalism to be the optimal solution to the problem of organizing work; it is merely the better of the three alternatives I discuss. Are there any other ways of organizing work by which the professional spirit can be reborn in a new and even more desirable form?

Bearing in mind my belief that a truly adequate theory of professions must be rooted in a generic theory of work, a *conception* of work is required that encompasses all forms of productive labor, not merely those that take place in the conventional labor market. Many kinds of work and workers do not appear in the official statistics of the modern state on which most sociologists rely. Close study of those *unofficial* forms of productive labor expands our conception of work beyond the official economy. Furthermore, it provides us with resources that can expand our conception of professionalism beyond the historical conventions with which this book is primarily concerned. When we look for productive labor outside the market, we find in fact many empirical circumstances in which skilled, creative work is performed for sustained periods of time largely without pay (see Freidson, 1986b; Stebbins, 1992, pp. 1–19). Such work is performed primarily for its own sake, for the love of it, or for the way it benefits others (see Freidson, 1990). In such circumstances we find a professionalism that is by choice or necessity stripped of the compromising institutions that assure workers a living, a professionalism expressed purely as dedication to the committed practice of a complex craft that is of value to others. To liberate it from material self-interest is the most radical way by which professionalism could be reborn.

NOTES

1　I use the word "profession" to refer to an occupation that controls its own work, organized by a special set of institutions sustained in part by a particular ideology of expertise and service. I use the word "professionalism" to refer to that ideology and special set of institutions. These usages have evolved over time and are not clearly distinguished in all the essays in this volume.

2　For a selection of my essays on medicine and health care, see Eliot Freidson, *Medical Work in America* (New Haven: Yale University Press, 1989).

3　In what follows I try to provide a brief overview of the development of the sociology of the professions. The references I give are not exhaustive, referring either to key writers, or illustrating a body of writing that is not cited in the essays in this volume.

4　The careful reader will note discrepancies between the publication dates of my citations, and my periodization. I assume a considerable lag between conception and publication, estimating a delay of between three and five years for an article in a scholarly journal and between eight and ten years for an academic book.

PART I

CLARIFYING THE ISSUES

1

The Theory of Professions:
State of the Art[1]

While professions have never been among the core topics for sociological theorizing, a surprising number of the most prominent English-language sociologists, from Herbert Spencer (1914, pp. 179–324) to Talcott Parsons (1968), have paid them rather more than glancing attention. Until recently, most sociologists have been inclined to see professions as honored servants of public need, conceiving of them as occupations especially distinguished from others by their orientation to serving the needs of the public through the schooled application of their unusually esoteric knowledge and complex skill. In contrast, representatives of the other social sciences have stressed quite different characteristics of the professions. Economists have been inclined to note the closed, mono-polistic character of the professionalized labor market (Cairnes, 1887, pp. 66–7; Friedman, 1962, pp. 137–60). Political scientists have been inclined to concern about professions as privileged private governments (Gilb, 1966). And policy-makers have been inclined to see professional experts as overnarrow and insular in their vision of what is good for the public (Laski, 1931).

The 1960s marked a watershed in sociological writings on the professions. For one thing, the evaluative flavour of the literature has changed. Whereas most sociologists had earlier emphasized the positive functions and achievements of the professions (though they were not unaware of their deficiencies), recent writers have been consistently more critical. Furthermore, the substantive preoccupation of the literature changed. In the earlier literature, the major scholarly writers focused primarily on the analysis of professional norms and role relations and on interaction in work settings. While they all acknowledged the importance of political and economic factors, they did not analyze them at any length. The more recent scholarly literature, on the other hand, focuses on the political influence of professions (Freidson, 1988), on the relation of professions to political and economic elites and the state (Johnson, 1972), and on the relation of professions to the market and the class system (Larson, 1977).

But while there have been significant changes in the evaluative and substantive emphasis of sociological writings on the professions, they reflect changes in the *content* of theorizing while remaining unchanged in the *nature* of theorizing. This has been the case even though some of the recent criticism of the traditional approach has been metatheoretical in character. Unfortunately, those metatheoretical critiques have addressed either false issues or issues which are essentially insoluble because of the very nature of the concept of profession itself. For this reason, there has not been any significant advance in developing a theory of professions over the past decade or so that does not have as many deficiencies as past theories.

This is the point of the present paper. In it, I shall examine several common metatheoretical issues addressed by recent writings on the professions, and evaluate both their validity and their utility for advancing a theory of professions. In doing so, it will be necessary to address the concept of profession itself. The very nature of that concept, I shall argue, plays a critical role in creating some of the problems addressed by metatheoretical writings and precludes their solution in abstract, theoretical terms. The nature of the concept of profession, I shall argue, provides us with a limited number of options. The option that can lead to a coherent and systematic method of analysis is one that requires forsaking the attempt to treat profession as a generic concept and turning instead to formulating a generic conception of occupation within which we can locate analytically the particular occupations that have been labelled professions. To advance a theory of professions, however, requires a rather different option, which treats the concept as a historical construction in a limited number of societies, and studies its development, use, and consequences in those societies without attempting more than the most modest generalizations.

THE PROBLEM OF DEFINITION

Much debate, going back at least as far as Flexner (1915), has centered around how professions should be defined – which occupations should be called professions, and by what institutional criteria. But while most definitions overlap in the elements, traits, or attributes they include, a number of tallies have demonstrated a persistent lack of consensus about which traits are to be emphasized in theorizing (Millerson, 1964, p. 5).

No small part of the criticism of the traditional literature on the professions has been devoted to pointing out a lack of consensus. Because we seem to be no nearer consensus than we were in 1915, and because usage varies substantively, logically, and conceptually (Freidson, 1977), some analysts have given the impression of condemning the very practice of seeking a definition. But surely such condemnation is inappropriate. In order to think clearly and systematically about anything, one must delimit the subject-matter to be addressed by empirical and intellectual analysis. We cannot develop theory if we are not certain what we are talking about.

One method of attempting to solve the problem of definition has been to deprecate the value of defining the characteristics of professions as "inherently distinct from other occupations" (Klegon, 1978, p. 268) and to urge instead discussing the process by which occupations claim or gain professional status. The outcome of such a position, however, is to avoid entirely any *conscious* definition while in fact covertly advancing an implicit and unsatisfactorily vague definition of a profession as an occupation that has gained professional status. What is professional status? How does one determine when it does and when it does not exist? What are its characteristics?

A closely related suggestion is to shift focus from a "static" conception of profession as a distinct type of occupation to the process by which occupations are professionalized (Vollmer and Mills, 1966). However, as Turner and Hodge (1970, p. 23) and Johnson (1972, p. 31) have correctly noted, an emphasis on process rather than structure, on professionalization rather than on the attributes of professions, does not really solve the problem of definition. To speak about the process of professionalization requires one to define the direction of the process, and the end-state of professionalism toward which an occupation may be moving. Without *some* definition of profession the concept of professionalization is virtually meaningless, as is the intention to study process rather than structure. One cannot study process without a definition guiding one's focus any more fruitfully than one can study structure without a definition.

In all, the issue of definition for a theory of professions cannot be dealt with profitably either by denial or by avoidance. A word with so many connotations and denotations cannot be employed in precise discourse without definition. One can avoid the issue of definition only if one adopts the patently anti-analytical position that all occupations – whether casual day-labor, assembly-line work, teaching, surgery, or systems analysis – are so much alike that there is no point in making distinctions of any kind among them. That there are no differences of any analytic importance must be firmly denied.

Given the necessity of definition, one may note that the character of an adequate definition must be such as to specify a set of referents by which the phenomenon may be discriminated in the empirical world – that is, specifying attributes, traits, or defining characteristics. Unfortunately, there has been a tendency in the recent critical literature to confuse the act of specifying defining characteristics with the particular characteristics specified by earlier writers. One can criticize a definition because of the analytically and empirically ambiguous traits it singles out (Freidson, 1988), or because its traits have no systematic interrelations and no theoretical rationale (Johnson, 1972). But it is not the fact that a definition is composed of traits or attributes that can be justifiably criticized.

In all, then, it would seem that, in the present state of the art of theorizing about professions, recent comments on the issue of definition miss the mark. The definitional problem that has plagued the field for over half a century is not one created by squabbling pedants, to be solved by eschewing definition entirely. Nor is the problem created by the adoption of a static "structural" or "functional" approach, to be solved by a "process" or "conflict" approach. Nor is the problem created by including traits or attributes in a definition. The problem, I suggest, lies much deeper than that. It is created by attempting to treat profession as if it were a generic rather than a changing historic concept, with particular roots in an industrial nation strongly influenced by Anglo-American institutions.

THE PAROCHIALISM OF THE INSTITUTIONAL CONCEPT OF PROFESSION

In order to elaborate my argument about the nature of the concept of profession, it is necessary first of all to emphasize the difference between two very different usages which are sometimes confused. First, there is the concept of profession that refers to a broad stratum of relatively prestigious but quite varied occupations whose members have all had some kind of higher education and who are identified more by their educational status than by their specific occupational skills. Second, there is the concept of profession as a limited number of occupations which have particular institutional and ideological traits more or less in common. It is only this second concept which allows us to think of "professionalism" as, in Johnson's terms, a way of organizing an occupation (Johnson, 1972, p. 45). It represents much more than only a status, for it produces distinctive occupational identities and exclusionary market shelters (cf. Parkin, 1979) which set each occupation apart from (and often in opposition to) the others.

Furthermore, the two differ markedly in their relevance to present-day industrial societies. The concept of profession as a very broad, educated stratum has been applied without much difficulty to all industrial nations (for example, Ben-David, 1977, p. 30). But it refers to a much more general and vague phenomenon than does the institutional concept of profession as a distinctive form of organized occupation. The major theoretical writings on the professions have all addressed themselves to professions in this second sense – as a fairly limited number of occupations which share characteristics of considerably greater specificity than higher education alone, and which are distinctive as separate occupations. Their members conceive of themselves by their occupation first and by their "class," if at all, only second. It is precisely this institutional concept of profession which is very difficult to apply to the entire range of occupations in the "professional stratum" of any industrial nation, or even to those middle-class occupations in Europe which would, in Anglo-American nations, be considered professions in the more narrow sense.

Occupations called professions in English have had a rather special history. As we all know, the medieval universities of Europe spawned the three original learned professions of medicine, law, and the clergy (of which university teaching was part). Elliott (1972, pp. 14, 32) has suggested the term "status professions" for them, pointing out quite accurately their marked difference from the recent "occupational professions."

As the occupational structure of capitalist industrialism developed during the nineteenth century in England, and then later in the United States, terminological consensus became greatly confused by the efforts of newly reorganized or newly formed middle-class occupations to seek the title of "profession" because it was connected with the gentlemanly status of the traditional learned professions (Reader, 1967; Larson, 1977). While there were very important differences between the two nations, they had in common a comparatively passive state apparatus with a strong but by no means unambivalent *laissez-faire* philosophy, and a small civil service.

Occupations seeking a secure and privileged place in the economy of those countries could not do more than seek state support for an exclusionary shelter in the open market where they had to compete with rival occupations. They had to organize their own training and credentialling institutions, since the state played a passive role in such affairs. Unlike in other countries, the title "profession" was used to establish the status of successful occupations; it became part of the official occupational classification scheme in the United States and in England, expanding its coverage slowly by including more occupations in the same

category, with the same title, as the original status professions of the
medieval universities (see Reader, 1967, pp. 146–66, 207–11) Gaining
recognition as a "profession" was important to occupations not only
because it was associated with traditional gentry status, but also because
its traditional connotations of disinterested dedication and learning
legitimated the effort to gain protection from competition in the labor
market. Given *laissez-faire* philosophy, only quite special excuses could
justify the state-sanctioned creation of a market shelter. The ideologies of
special expertise and moral probity provided by the traditional concept
of status profession, sustained by ostensibly supportive occupational institutions, provided just such a basis for legitimating protection from the
winds of occupational competition.

In England and the United States, the tendency was for each occupation to have to mount its own movement for recognition and protection.
Its members' loyalties and identities were attached to their individual occupation and its institutions. The situation was rather different in Europe,
where the state was much more active in organizing both training and
employment. The traditional status professions maintained their occupational distinctions as they reorganized their corporate bodies, but the
new, middle-class occupations did not seek classification as "professions"
to gain status and justify a market shelter: such an umbrella title imputing
special institutional characteristics to them is not employed to distinguish
them (see Hughes, 1971, pp. 387–8). Rather, their status and security are
gained by their attendance at state-controlled, elite institutions of higher
education which assures them of elite positions in the civil service or
other technical-managerial positions. In nineteenth-century Russia and
Poland, merely to be a graduate of a *gymnasium* was what was important,
not one's occupation (Gella, 1976). In Germany, what was important was
to be a university graduate, an *Akademiker* (Rueschemeyer, 1973, pp. 63–
122; Ringer, 1979, p. 411). In France, one's fortunes flowed from attending one of the *grandes écoles* (Ben-David, 1977, pp. 38–46). Primary
identity was not given by occupation, but by the status gained by elite
education no matter what the particular specialty. As Ben-David noted
for France,

> the technically competent . . . whom the [*grandes écoles*] system was
> . . . designed to produce . . . do not primarily identify themselves
> by their professional qualifications, but by their employment. If
> they are in private practice, they tend to consider themselves part
> of the *bourgeois entrepreneur* class, and if they are salaried, they
> consider themselves officials of a certain rank, rather than chemists
> or engineers. (1977, p. 46)

This is a far cry from Anglo-American professions, which gain their distinction and position in the market-place less from the prestige of the institutions in which they were educated than from their training and identity as particular, corporately organized occupations to which specialized knowledge, ethicality, and importance to society are imputed, and for which privilege is claimed.[2]

It is thus not without justice that professionalism has been called "the British disease" (Fores and Glover, 1978, p. 15), though I would prefer to call it an "Anglo-American disease." Nor is it an accident that the theoretical literature on the professions is almost wholly Anglo-American, European reviews and use of the Anglo-American literature notwithstanding (Maurice, 1972, pp. 213–25). All in all, I would argue that, as an institutional concept, the term "profession" is intrinsically bound up with a particular period of history and with only a limited number of nations in that period of history.

THE INEVITABILITY OF APOLOGETICS AND POLEMICS

If we grant the concrete, historically bound character of the term, we can better understand some of the other controversies surrounding definition in the recent literature. Metatheoretical critiques have frequently noted that earlier writings on the professions created definitions which were reflections of what spokesmen for Anglo-American occupations seeking social recognition as professions say about themselves (Freidson, 1988, pp. 77–84; Gyarmati, 1975, pp. 629–54). Roth (1974, p. 17) put this criticism very forcefully: "Sociologists ... have become the dupe of established professions (helping them justify their dominant position and its payoff) and arbiters of occupations on the make." The implication of such criticism is that theorizers should in some sense strive to create a definition which does not reflect the interests of the groups it attempts to delineate, that their definition should be more detached in its perspective. However, because of the very nature of the concept, one cannot avoid its intrinsic connection with the evaluative social processes which create it.

For the professions, the issues for commentary and analysis are determined more or less by the national history of the term itself, and by the usage of that term both by members of particular occupations and by members of other groups in Anglo-American society. Given the historical fact that the term is a socially valued label, with the possibility of social, economic, political, or at the very least symbolic rewards accruing to those so labelled, it seems inevitable both that disagreement about its application to particular persons or occupations will exist, and that disagreement will exist about the propriety of the special rewards accruing to those to whom it is applied. Because of the nature of the concept, *any* enterprise of defining and analysing it is inevitably subject to the possibility of being employed to direct the assignment and justification of rewards to some, and the withholding of rewards from others.

It follows, therefore, that those whom Roth described as "dupes" sustain the positions both of established professions and those attempting to gain their success by emulating them. It also follows, however, that those, including myself and Roth, who undertake highly critical evaluations of others' definitions and analyses, also serve as "dupes," though of different agents – "dupes" both of managerial programs of deskilling and proletarianizing professional work, and of working-class movements aimed at reducing pay differentials and barriers to entry into "professional" jobs. Both sets of writers, while differing in substance, do not differ in intellectual approach to the concept. The watershed of the scholarly literature that I noted as occurring in the 1960s was a watershed in changing social sympathy and substantive interest, but marked no break with the earlier preoccupation of adjudicating the application of the label and its rewards. Perhaps that is why there have not been any coherent advances in theorizing in spite of the marked change in the tone of the literature – because the *basis* for theorizing has not changed.

THE PHENOMENOLOGY OF PROFESSION

A "profession" may be described as a folk concept, then the research strategy appropriate to it is phenomenological in character. One does not attempt to determine what profession is in an absolute sense so much as how people in a society determine who is a professional and who is not, how they "make" or "accomplish" professions by their activities, and what the consequences are for the way in which they see themselves and perform their work. This is not, however, a simple undertaking, for we cannot realistically assume that there is a holistic folk which produces only one folk concept of profession in societies as complex as ours. There must be a number of folk and thus a number of folk concepts. Surely it seems likely that rather different concepts of profession would be advanced by occupations seeking the rewards of a professional label than by other occupations attempting to preserve the rewards they have already won, or by sets of employers or clients seeking to control the terms, conditions, and content of the jobs they wish done, or by government agencies seeking to create a systematic means by which to classify and account for the occupations of the labor force, or by the general public. Indeed, the very fact of such a variety of group interests and perspectives may be seen to be responsible for the variety of conceptions of profession advanced, each to its own appreciative audience, responsible for the dissensus characteristic of the usage and concrete occupational referents of the term. Is there, however, one of those perspectives which can be said to be authoritative? Are there others which can be said to be invalid or unimportant?

Many recent critics of the literature on professions seem to feel that it is somehow inappropriate for sociologists to make their own pronouncements about the essence of the concept of profession, and thus to serve as arbiters or dupes. Some urge that sociologists should instead study how other members of society employ the concept without projecting their own conceptions. In a well-reasoned statement, Dingwall (1976, pp. 331–49) suggested that, rather than define professions by fiat, sociologists would do better to devote themselves to the study and explication of the way ordinary members of particular occupations invoke and employ the term during the course of their everyday activities, to study how such members "accomplish" profession independently of sociologists' definitions. However, unlike most critics, who are content with exhortation alone, Dingwall goes on to present data from an interesting study of his own which took that advice seriously. But my reading of his study indicates that such accomplishment on the part of the members of one occupation cannot fail to include taking into account the conceptions of members of other occupations with whom interaction takes place, and negotiating with them some workable agreement on usage and the activities and relationships it implies. Nonetheless, even that is not enough: among the groups which have to be taken into account are the very sociologists who define profession by fiat, since they, too, are members of the phenomenological world of occupations.

Sociologists are part of social life, and they produce some of the symbolic resources employed by other members of their society, most especially when they play the deliberately accessible role of commenting on and analysing contemporary social issues. In their way, serving in their special role of intellectual, sociologists accomplish profession as much as do the occupations they discuss. Even without efforts at disseminating their analyses widely by popularization, the esoteric, specialized work of sociologists is sought out by others and, if not taken as authoritative, then at least considered worth thinking about. Perhaps most consequentially for the actual process of professionalization, some sociological formations are employed in part as rationale and justification for the creation of the official occupational categories by which modern governmental and corporate agencies sort and classify occupations with an eye to justifying job requirements, perquisites, and wage differentials (Scoville, 1965; Désrosières, n.d.; Davies, 1980). Those official categories, or titles, and the criteria by which they are constituted, pose critical contingencies for the rewards available to an occupation, including the status of "profession."

If they are to succeed in their attempt to gain the official title of profession, it is not enough that occupations accomplish profession interpersonally, negotiating their daily tasks with the others with whom they work. Both the limits and the substance of negotiation are in part given in advance. Only after getting jobs of a given character can the members of an occupation negotiate profession with other workers. In order to obtain the jobs which provide the resources for negotiation, both the institutional characteristics of an occupation and such characteristics of its members as their formal education must conform to official criteria of profession. Cosmetic changes on the institutional face which an occupation presents to the world may not be enough for official recognition. The everyday world of the ordinary members of a striving occupation may also have to change, taking on some of the appearances that sociologists have specified as intrinsically professional, albeit by fiat (Hughes, 1971, p. 339). Thus, how everyday members accomplish profession through their activities may be in part influenced by how sociologists accomplish profession as a concept, and by how official agencies accomplish profession as an administrative category.

What profession is phenomenologically, then, is not determined solely by members of occupations performing work in a way that leads others to respond to them as professionals. There are a number of different perspectives and performances, no one of which may be thought to be better grounded, phenomenologically, than any other. Some, however, are more consequential than others, if only because they are attached to positions in which it is possible to exercise substantial political and economic power of far-ranging significance. While these may not be authoritative in any epistemological sense, they might be taken to be authoritative in a pragmatic sense of setting the political and economic limits within which everyday professional work can go on, and of providing the political and economic resources without which some circumstances and opportunities for work cannot take place.[3] Though such pragmatically authoritative "definitions" are themselves negotiated and changed by the efforts of organized occupational groups and other agencies, and thus are not so rigid and stable as the terms "official" and "formal" imply, they cannot be dismissed as somehow less legitimate than those of the participants in everyday work.

So, too, may the work of sociologists be viewed. As researchers and consultants in everyday work-settings, and as researchers and theorists whose work is examined and consulted by those formulating the legal and economic parameters of the market-place, sociologists also are legitimate participants. They can no more avoid creating definitions, if only implicitly, than can other participants. The fact of advancing definitions cannot be much of an issue in comparison with the choice of particular interests to advance in the social process of definition. But even there, the diversity of emphases and interests in the sociological literature implies a variety of choices. It also implies that the prospects for unanimity in the future are rather poor. How, then, can the state of the art be advanced?

BEYOND THE FOLK CONCEPT

One way of attempting to resolve the problem of defining and theorizing coherently about professions in institutional terms lies in asserting the role of the sociologist as an especially authoritative analyst who is free to forsake ordinary usage in favour of his own more precise and "scientific" abstractions. Even though sociologists in such a role cannot claim to be independent of their time and place, they can nonetheless attempt to create abstract concepts which are applicable to more than what is to be found in their time and place. Such an attempt has in fact been made by some of the more theoretically inclined writers on the professions. Remaining concerned with analyzing historic professions, they have abandoned the effort to delineate all the traits that professions have in common and attempted instead to emphasize a parsimonious set of circumstances which have analytic importance in themselves and with which other institutional characteristics can be connected systematically (Goode, 1969, pp. 266–313; Freidson, 1988, pp. 71–84; Johnson, 1972, pp. 37–47).

Interesting as those efforts may be, however, they have been too compromised to be successful. They are, as Becker (1970, p. 91) noted, no longer faithful to the folk concept insofar as they abstract and select from it. But at the same time they have stopped short of creating fully abstract concepts which go beyond the folk concept. If those efforts were to be really abstract and "scientific," then their conceptualization would have to be tested by examining all occupations known to have the postulated critical traits of trust, autonomy, collegial control, or whatever, but instead, only the occupations called professions are referred to by such writers. Were they to go beyond the folk concept, no longer would they be addressing professions as such so much as occupations in general. That is the crux of the matter.

I do not believe that it is possible to move beyond the folk concept of profession without forsaking one's preoccupation with professions (Turner and Hodge, 1970, p. 33). In order really to move beyond the folk concept one must ask on the grounds of some reasoned theoretical stance what the features are by which one may usefully and consequentially distinguish among occupations in general and the processes through which they develop, maintain themselves, grow, and decline. On the basis of such features one could distinguish theoretically significant groupings or types of occupations and occupational processes by which historically defined occupations, including professions, could be classified and understood. Since theoretical salience is the issue, and not the historic Anglo-American professions as such, no attempt would be made to create a class into which would fit all the occupations that are called professions. By the nature of the enterprise, no attempt *need* be made. The "essence" of profession ceases to be an issue. One's conceptualization would be evaluated for its capacity to order and guide the explanation of the circumstances of a variety of historical occupations, no matter how they happen to be labelled by one audience or another in a particular country and at a particular time.

Liberated from the concept of profession by such an approach, one is also liberated from the grotesque dichotomy, or continuum, by which an ideal type or model of "profession" is used to order *all* occupations. Since virtually all occupations do not come close to conforming to that model, the whole rich variety is reduced to being merely non-professions, defined negatively and emptily as lacking professional characteristics. When one goes beyond the folk concept and attempts to conceptualize the variety of occupations *among* which are to be counted the historic professions, one is in a position to formulate a considerably more flexible set of concepts about occupations that would go far to remedy the present conceptual poverty that stems from the use of such a parochial and simplistic dichotomy or continuum.

PURSUING THE FOLK CONCEPT

The theoretical program which takes us beyond the folk concept deliberately replaces the task of developing a theory of professions with the task of developing a more general and abstract theory of occupations by which one can analyze the historic professions as well as other occupations in the same conceptual terms, but without assuming that those professions necessarily represent a single, generic type of occupation. But this does not mean that there is no future at all for a theory of professions. The future of a theory of professions seems to lie in adopting a different strategy. Whereas a theory of occupations would be concerned with developing a genuinely abstract theory which attempts to be exhaustive in its applicability, a theory of professions, relieved of the task of broad generalization, would attempt instead to develop better means of understanding and interpreting what is conceived of as a concrete, changing, historical, and national phenomenon. The future of profession lies in embracing the concept as an intrinsically ambiguous, multifaceted folk concept, of which no single definition and no attempt at isolating its essence will ever be generally persuasive. Given the nature of the concept, such a theory is developed by recognizing that there is no single, truly explanatory trait or characteristic – including such a recent candidate as "power" – that can join together all occupations called professions beyond the actual fact of coming to be called professions. Thus, profession is treated as an empirical entity about which there is little ground for generalizing as a homogeneous class or a logically exclusive conceptual category. The task for a theory of professions is to document the untidiness and inconsistency of the empirical phenomenon and to explain its character in those countries where it exists. Such a theory would have, I believe, two major tasks.

First, such a theory should be able to trace and explain the development and significance of the use of the title in Anglo-American societies. Such a task is aided, but not accomplished, by the chronology of usage which the invaluable *Oxford Unabridged Dictionary* provides. A chronology, however, does not tell us why usage developed as it did in English-speaking countries, as opposed to those which have the same root in their vocabularies, but which use the noun form to denote occupations in general and require an adjective "liberal," "free," or "learned" to denote a particular type of occupation. Furthermore, a chronology of usage does not tell us how and why particular occupations came to be labelled professions by their members and recognized as such by others; how and why official classifications employing the term developed; why the occupations so classified changed over time; or what the consequences were of membership in such classifications for both the organized occupation and its members. Some small movement toward the development of a theory of occupational nomenclature has begun (Scoville, 1965; Katz, 1972; Désrosières, n.d.; Sharlin, 1979), as has some modest effort to analyze the development of the official title of profession in English-speaking countries (see Reader, 1967; Davies, 1980), but a great deal more must be done before we are in a position to dignify what we know by calling it a theory.

In contrast to investigating the nature of the official title itself, a great deal has already been done to investigate the special privileges of organized occupations which have gained official recognition as professions. In

addition, numerous field studies have investigated the problems that the
members of those occupations have at work in negotiating with administrators, other occupations, and clients for the prerogatives of the title.
The former body of studies tells us about the consequences of official,
legal use of the title, while the latter tells us how the title is negotiated
and accomplished in everyday work life. As a number of critics have
noted correctly, however, a disproportionate number of those studies is
addressed to health-related occupations that claim the title. Advances in
theorizing about the title and its use positively require the close study of
many more occupations in other industries.

While the first task is concerned primarily with analyzing the title "profession" as a socio-political artifact, the second task is concerned primarily with analyzing in some detail the occupations to which the title
has been applied. In the spirit of the distinction between a sociology of
occupations and a sociology of professions, it follows that the thrust of
such a task is to be concerned with the role of the title in the aspirations
and fortunes of those occupations claiming it, and not with some quality
or trait that all occupations claiming the title may share. The strategy of
analysis, therefore, is particular rather than general, studying occupations
as individual empirical cases rather than as specimens of some more
general, fixed concept.

As individual cases, the question becomes how the quest for the
classification in official categories and, on occasion, for legal status as a
profession interacts with the development of the occupation's corporate
organization and influences its position in the polity and the labor
market, its division of labor, and its members' positions in the concrete
settings where they work. But while virtually all occupations called professions (as well as others rarely so called) may be classified as such in
labor-force or census categories, rather few have the legal status of professions. In the selection of individual occupations for study, therefore,
loose recognition as a profession by the general public, and even the
occupation's own claim (so long as it is taken seriously by some consequential audience), may be employed to locate cases. Thus, not only
traditionally accepted doctors, lawyers, and professors, but also engineers, pharmacists, social workers, schoolteachers, librarians, and many
more to which the title is attached by some audiences but not others, can
all be appropriate cases for analysis no matter how they might otherwise
differ or fail to conform to various definitions.

The outcome of such a program would be at the very least to add to
our knowledge about a number of occupations – knowledge which would
be all the richer for its emphasis on the special characteristics of each
rather than on the comparatively little they share that corresponds to some

simplistic model or ideal type. As important would be the consequence of forsaking the equally simplistic but less formally or self-consciously stated assumptions of recent emphases on "professionalization" – that occupational movements for professionalization are necessarily oriented toward change and mobility, for example, rather than toward stability and security. By expanding the universe of occupations on which we have detailed and systematic data, and by analyzing them as individual, historic cases, we could establish the ground for catholic comparisons that we lack at present. Such a foundation would go far toward portraying the variety of contexts and inconsistencies intrinsic to the notion of profession, as well as the varied role of the notion in the fortunes of a number of occupations and their members in English-speaking societies. Such a portrait is certain to be richer and more varied than that abstract essence toward which the traditional literature aimed, but, in being so, it is likely to be more faithful to reality.

THE OBLIGATION OF DEFINITION

In conclusion, it is incumbent on me to address the problem of definition with which this paper began. It should be clear by now that I do not think the problem can be solved by struggling to formulate a single definition which is hoped to win the day. The concrete, historical character of the concept and the many perspectives from which it can legitimately be viewed, and from which sense can be made of it, preclude the hope of any widely accepted definition of general analytic value.

It is precisely because of the lack of any solution to the problem that I feel that serious writers on the topic should be obliged to display to readers what they have in mind when the word is used – that is, to indicate the definition upon which their exposition is predicated and, for even greater clarity, examples of the occupations they mean to include and those they mean to exclude. Provided with such guidance, readers will then be in a position to judge whether X is really talking about the same thing as Y. If X means to refer only to those few occupations recognized by almost everyone as professions, possessing very high prestige and a genuine monopoly over a set of widely demanded tasks, while Y means to refer as well to occupations which try to ameliorate their low prestige and weak economic position by referring to themselves as professions, then each is talking about incomparable categories and both the writers and their readers should be aware of the fact.

The same obligation should be recognized by those who write about "professionalization," though clarity is more difficult because of the processual character of the concept. Even if one defines the traits constituting the end-point toward which the process is assumed to be headed, how many of those traits, and in what degree, must an occupation display before it makes sense to talk of it as involved in a process of professionalization rather than in a process of merely improving its economic or status position? If it does not make sense to talk of the professionalization of labor in general as the terms and conditions of its work improve over time, what characteristics must exist before it *does* make sense to do so? Must one use the term only retrospectively to label the process by which present-day professions have attained their position? Is there a distinctive difference between professionalization in particular and the collective efforts of occupations in general to improve their job security, working conditions, income, and prestige? No doubt on these issues, as on those connected with defining profession, writers will differ, but they are unlikely to be able to debate the relative virtues of those differences if they are not self-conscious about what they are. It is precisely because differences are inevitable that their specification should be an obligation for the writer and a requirement of the writer by the reader. Such an obligation may not increase consensus, but it would certainly increase the clarity and precision of a body of literature whose status has been vague and chaotic for too long.

NOTES

1 The basic substance of this paper was written while I was Fulbright-Hays Senior Research Scholar at the Laboratoire d'Economie et de Sociologie du Travail (CNRS), Aix-en-Provence. I wish to express my deepest thanks for the hospitality and intellectual stimulation of M Guy Roustang, then Directeur, and M Marc Maurice, Maître de Recherche. An earlier version was read at the annual meeting of the American Sociological Association at Boston in August 1979. So many colleagues have commented helpfully on earlier versions of this paper that it is impossible for me to thank them all here by name.

2 The evidence is overwhelming that, *within* any given profession, differential life-chances are strongly influenced by the prestige of the educational institution from which one receives one's credentials. Thus, I do *not* mean to imply that in Anglo-American countries elite institutions of higher education play no part in occupational careers. I am arguing only that, in English-speaking countries, occupational identity and commitment are considerably more developed than identity as an elite educated class or transoccupational technical-managerial stratum. Thus, the institutional concept of profession is more relevant to them than to European nations.

3   In the United States there are considerable advantages attached to being in an
occupation that has been officially recognized as a profession. Needless to
say, when it is employed as a legal and administrative category, "profession"
must be defined in such a way as to allow practical discrimination among
occupations and occupational roles by those administering the law. The legal
status and definition of professions in tax, immigration, labor, and other bodies
of law (including the rules of evidence) simply begs for thorough investigation
and analysis.

2

How Dominant are the Professions?

Over the past ten years, the number of historical studies of professions in both the United States and Europe has been growing at a rapid rate. So, too, have studies of contemporary professions. This is a very welcome development, but it is not without its intellectual dangers. It is true that we can take each study of each profession in each historical period and each nation at its face value. But what can we conclude about each one? Given a series of studies of, say, engineers, in various nations, can we generalize about engineering as a profession or must we restrict our talk instead to English engineers, French engineers, Japanese engineers, and the like, and, even then, only in particular historical periods? If comparative studies are to be fruitful, they must all provide comparable information – each writer cannot be seeking answers to different questions.

In the previous essay I emphasized the value of studying professions phenomenologically, of avoiding the use of some fixed definition and studying instead the varied perspectives on occupations called professions as well as the way the social status of profession was constructed. As I noted, however, that is only one of two strategies. The second strategy is to create an intellectual construct that will allow using a single standard by which the variety of comparative (and phenomenological) studies can be appraised. Without it, we are hostage to a bewildering variety of conflicting assertions about professions. Here I wish to suggest that a fixed conceptual tool is needed both to make sense of comparative studies and to resolve contradictory appraisals of the position of professions in society. In addition, I wish to suggest that most of such appraisals rest on oversimple conceptions of professionalism and its institutions.

CONTRADICTORY VISIONS OF PROFESSIONAL POWER

A great many studies of professions have asked the same general question – namely, the relationship between professional status and power – but they have been led to diametrically opposed conclusions. Consider the large literature that in one way or another claims that "experts" or "the professions" exercise enormous power over both state policy and the personal affairs of individuals. While some concentrate on the monopolization of particular kinds of work, such as doctoring, by licensing, registration, and other exclusionary devices, others emphasize the power to create artificial dependence on professionals both by determining state policy and by controlling the way people perceive their problems and decide how to cope with them. Havighurst and King (1983, pp. 189–97, 267–8, 276–85, 288–9) link the two by claiming that licensing has created an "ideological monopoly" allowing the American medical profession to dominate both policy and lay perception of health problems and their solution. This view of professional dominance finds at least loose fellowship in Gramsci's conception of intellectuals and their "hegemony," in Foucault's work, and in some works on the professional "class" (e.g., Derber et al., 1990).

The opposite view is that the professions are the passive instruments of capital, the state, or their individual clients, and that they exercise little or no influence of their own over the substance and direction of institutional policy and everyday affairs. At most they merely administer those affairs, captive to the requirements of their masters, though, to the extent that their members interact with lay clients of lesser status, some interpersonal power may remain in their hands. Akin to this position is one postulating *trends* toward powerlessness – a steady decline of professional power that is described as deprofessionalization, proletarianization, rationalization, bureaucratization, or corporatization. Some claim that the professions are losing their cultural authority due to increasing public skepticism, consumer activism and sophistication, and decreasing public respect. Others emphasize the professions' loss of exclusive jurisdictions to competitors, the increasing intervention of the state into the financing and administration of professional practice, and the increasing dependence of the professions on concentrated corporate and state economic power.

HEURISTIC MEASURING RODS

The picture of professional powerlessness is a virtual mirror image of the picture of professional powerfulness. Which picture is true? I believe that question is unanswerable, in part because some are saying, "the cup is half empty," and others, "the cup is half full." More important, most talk past one another because they are not attending to the same data. This stems from the most important consideration of all – the absence of common criteria by which systematically to select and analyze the data bearing on professional status and power. This lack has seriously confused past discussions of professions within individual nations and historic periods and, if it continues to be the case, will prevent comparative studies from realizing their full potential.

If the participants in discussions about the status and power of professions employed the same internally consistent and systematic standard to guide their collection of data and used it to organize their analysis of the position held by different professions in different political economies, there would be some hope that we could arrive at greater consensus and more sophisticated understanding than is now the case. Such a standard should not of course be created out of one nation's historic experience, which, after all, is unique and time-bound. It must be sufficiently abstract to be applicable to a variety of national and historical circumstances and it must include a systematically related set of criteria surrounding a central issue. It must be, in short, a logical, ideal typical model. I suggest that the central issue of professional power lies in the control of work by professional workers themselves, rather than control by consumers in an open market or by the functionaries of a centrally planned and administered firm or state.

The character of such a model can be more easily visualized by first thinking of its opposite – the classic Marxist conception of the industrial proletariat composed of absolutely powerless workers. The industrial proletariat possess neither land nor capital but only their labor, so they have no choice but to work for those with capital in return for the wages by which they can gain a living. Their employers create, organize, supervise, and evaluate the work they must do, purposefully reducing it to simple tasks that any ordinary person can perform without special training so that the cost of labor is kept as low as possible. Thus, the proletariat possess only labor power, with no distinctive skill or body of specialized knowledge of their own and no control over the work they do. Furthermore, since their work is so fragmented by virtue of its simplification, they have little sense of its relationship to the productive whole, nor any sense of connection to their fellow workers or to society at large. Individually in the workplace and collectively in the marketplace and the political economy, they are totally without organization and power.

By contrast, professions with total power to control their own work are organized by associations that are independent both of the state and of capital, and that organize and administer the practice of an unambiguously demarcated body of knowledge and skill or jurisdiction which their members monopolize. Those associations determine the qualifications and number of those to be trained for practice, the substance of that training, the requirements for satisfactory completion of training and admission to practice, and the terms, conditions, and goals of practice itself. They also determine the ethical and technical criteria by which their members' practices are evaluated, and have the exclusive right to exercise discipline over their members. Within the limits of the rules and standards laid down by their authoritative associations, individual members are autonomous in their workplaces. And the professions serve as the ultimate authorities on those personal, social, economic, cultural, and political affairs which their body of knowledge and skill addresses. Their modes of formulating and interpreting events permeate both popular consciousness and official policy.

SCOPE AND METHOD OF ANALYSIS

Both these models are "ideal" in the sense that they are logically consistent *extremes* rather than faithful descriptions of any real institution. Furthermore, they specify a number of different phenomena to examine as well as the criteria for analyzing them. A truly comprehensive and authoritative appraisal of the power of any particular "profession" in time or place requires examining all the elements of the model rather than just one or two. In the case of the medical profession, for example, only part of its strength or weakness can be revealed by analyzing the formal administrative devices by which its services are organized and financed, or by which its professional associations are linked with the state. As we shall see, without attention to such things as the status of its specialized body of knowledge and skill and the character of its internal organization, one is likely to gain an incomplete and distorted view of its powers, characterizing the whole by only a few of many equally significant but ignored parts.

Furthermore, it is essential that analysis not stop with gross, formal arrangements, but examine both the full range of institutions that lie behind such global concepts as "the state" and "corporate capital," including the characteristics of their personnel, and the concrete ways they formulate and implement policy. When one looks behind the facade of formal institutions to the way they are realized in practice, one gains a considerably more complex and precise view of the exercise of power or influence than is provided by official charters, tables of organization, and legislation.

Finally, a methodological point. In undertaking analysis, it is essential to avoid the use of a misleading kind of rhetoric that is common in the literature that analyzes contemporary professional power as process – a rhetoric that masquerades anticipation of the future as description of the present. In studies of the historic process by which a profession developed over some period in the past, analysis is of *events that have actually occurred*. However, in studies of present-day professions that adopt a processual approach, the rhetorical emphasis of far too many is on *events that have not yet occurred*. For example, significance is read into newly instituted financial policies and administrative mechanisms designed to exercise more control over professional work largely on the assumption that they will continue and grow in the future. Yet the corridors of history are littered with policies that have been greatly modified, even reversed, in the face of political challenge after their initiation, and others that have been subverted and turned to the advantage of those they were intended to control.

In addition, the significance of new and truly important recent events bearing on professional power is seriously exaggerated by the use of a rhetoric that implies their continuous growth into the future. Thus, in the case of health affairs in the United States, those who stress the significance of the activity of consumers in changing the balance of power in the consulting room use a rhetoric that does not describe the *present* strength of the consumer movement but instead declares it to be "growing." Such relatively new institutional forms as for-profit, lay-investor-owned health-care enterprises are described as "increasing rapidly." Even though they are proportionately few, they are discussed as if they will become the dominant form in the future. Yet we know from history that change is heavily contingent on unpredictable natural, political, and economic circumstances. Many institutions that were developed with high hope (or contemplated with despair) in the past have failed to become the norm, some disappearing entirely and others persisting only in a minor, specialized form. The assumption of steady, linear growth of any institution into the future is often unjustified.

We also know that some critically important circumstances affecting the position of professions occur cyclically rather than grow continuously or persist indefinitely. To take an obvious example, capitalist economies characteristically follow a cycle of boom, bust, and then, eventually, boom again. Thus, it is probably as mistaken to project the economic difficulties of the 1990s into the indefinite future as it was to project the boom (and social movements) of the 1960s into the present. Similarly, it is treacherous to assume that an "oversupply" of practitioners today will continue into the future and permanently affect the market position of professionals. The history of many professions in many nations shows that perceived "oversupply" stimulates efforts to restrict future supply, and that demand itself can expand to create relative scarcity.

In sum, it is essential for fruitful discussion that analyses of the contemporary position of professions make a clear distinction between describing and appraising what actually exists today and prophesying the direction of change in the future. In describing the present, the most informative analysis is one guided by a systematic model, eschewing reliance on global concepts while emphasizing concrete institutions and the processes that underlie them. In the case of prophesying, or projecting trends into the future, due caution requires being aware of the danger of mistaking short-term, ephemeral trends for long-term trends, and cyclical change for linear, progressive change.

THE COMPLEXITY OF PROFESSIONS

The model of professionalism that I sketched contains a number of inter-related and sometimes interdependent parameters, but the literature analyzing the status and power of professions rarely goes beyond discussing the income, prestige, and working conditions of rank-and-file practitioners or the political and economic activities of corporate professional bodies. Those topics are certainly important, but there is much more to a profession than that. Its members do not constitute a homogeneous aggregate but rather are differentiated by substantive specialties and segments, by varying circumstances of practice, by their roles as rank-and-file practitioner, teacher, researcher, and manager, and by their relative pre-eminence as cultural, political, and intellectual leaders within the profession and in the lay world outside. These differences are often mirrored in separate associations, or sections within an association, including both associations devoted to the political and economic interests of their members and those devoted primarily to the advancement and communication of scientific or scholarly knowledge and procedures. In addition, some associations may be formally allied with particular political parties.

It is only when we conceive of the composition and organization of a profession in such broad terms that we can visualize the kind of influence claimed by those who invoke "technocracy" and the power of "technique" in shaping public policy (e.g., Ellul, 1964), as well as those asserting professional "hegemony" and "monopoly of discourse" in shaping public consciousness (e.g., Illich, 1980). The sole generic resource of professions is, like all labor, their capacity to perform particular kinds of work. They distinguish themselves from other occupations by the particular tasks they claim, and by the special character of the knowledge and skill required to perform them. The authority of knowledge is central to professionalism, and is expressed and conveyed by a variety of agents and institutions: it is not solely contingent on practitioner–client relationships or on the official activities of associations.

Furthermore, it is necessary to remember that professions are differentiated by intellectual orientation and substantive emphasis as well as by substantive specialty, work-setting, and role. It must be assumed that any profession will contain more than one orientation toward its body of knowledge and skill, with contending theories and practices advanced by different formal specialties and informal segments or schools. Thus, different members of the same profession can advance markedly different ideas and still remain bona fide members, even if of a minority school of thought that is ignored by the official representatives of the profession and deprecated by the majority. They may also have a separate association of their own that speaks independently of the one taken to represent the profession as a whole. One should not rule minority views within a profession out of bounds, or "unprofessional," because schools of thought and accepted practices shift in prominence and change over time. If one rules out minority views, one often loses the capacity to trace the many informal and unofficial ways by which segments of professional knowledge influence human affairs and professions themselves change. This is nowhere more apparent than in the relation of the professions to the state, for those in power may find a minority school of professional thought more compatible with their political ideology than the majority and initiate a considerable shift in the fortunes of the members of each.

THE ACTIVITIES OF THE STATE AND ITS AGENCIES

Comparativists have rightly noted that nations differ greatly in the degree to which the state and its agencies exercise centralized control over social and economic institutions. At one extreme is "high stateness" (Heidenheimer, 1989, pp. 530–1), exemplified by a nation such as the erstwhile Soviet Union. It had a centrally planned (command) political economy, governed unilaterally by the Communist Party in conjunction with state agencies, and it permitted the existence of few if any independent, "private" associations or enterprises. Somewhat less extreme is a nation such as France, which has a strong central government that engages in centralized control and planning but allows considerable room for independent economic and political activities. Still less centralized is Germany, with a federal structure in which a national government lays down and enforces basic rules within which strong provincial or state (*Land*) governments exercise control over the economic and social activities within their jurisdiction through their well-developed civil service, but allow much organized, private activity. At the other extreme is "low stateness," exemplified by the United States, which has a comparatively passive national government that allows extensive autonomy to federated state governments and to private associations and economic enterprises. National and state governments organize and control few social or economic enterprises of their own, relying instead on private agents to do so and functioning more as referees than as active players in the political economy.

The tendency in the literature is to assume that in "high-stateness" nations professions have little power because they cannot organize themselves as private, autonomous groups. Indeed, largely for that reason Field (1957, p. 45) describes medicine as having lost its professional status under the Bolshevik regime in the Soviet Union, and Jarausch (1990) claims "deprofessionalization" during the Nazi period (though he sees it as a process that began during the Weimar period, and declares "reprofessionalization" after World War II).

The implication is that under conditions of "high stateness," when professions have no formal association that is independent of the state and state agencies are responsible for legitimizing and directing their affairs, they lack power to influence state policy toward the way their members are selected and trained, their position in the division of labor and the labor force, their income and prestige, their working conditions, and their relations with their clients in particular and the public in general. But such a conclusion can be sustained only by ignoring the way states function in large, complex industrial societies. Even under circumstances of "high stateness," at least some professions, medicine among them, can wield important powers.

If one avoids a holistic concept of "the state" and asks how it actually functions, one is likely to find many places where professional knowledge is a critical resource. Björkman (1989, p. 29) suggests a number of major channels through which professionals influence state policy and action, but let me note just a few here. In order to exercise complete control over its political economy, "the state" requires, first of all, concrete agencies – ministries of education, for example, or ministries of health. Furthermore, in order to function effectively, those agencies must be staffed with personnel who know enough about their domains to

be able to formulate relevant directives and understand and evaluate
the information received from the practicing institutions under their
jurisdiction.

In appraising the status of professions in circumstances in which they
have no autonomous associations and are ostensibly creatures of the state,
it is therefore critical to examine the qualifications of those chosen to
direct and staff the agencies that formulate and implement policy in their
domains. If the staff is composed solely of lay people without any professional qualifications, then we can say that the profession whose activities
it directs is indeed powerless on that level. But except in truly revolutionary times, and even then, usually only during a brief period, lay people
have not been appointed to positions involving the formulation and administration of concrete policies governing the organization and operation of
such professional institutions as schools, hospitals, courts, factories, and
research institutes. In the case of health policy in the Soviet Union of
some twenty years ago, Navarro's analysis (1977, pp. 64–5) indicates
domination by a medical elite of academic and clinical professionals. This
hardly supports a characterization of "deprofessionalization."

It is true that, even in "low-stateness" nations such as the United States,
agency heads or ministers are often lay people chosen for their political
acceptability and reliability (Freidson, 1986, pp. 191–9), and that professional credentials must be accompanied by acceptable political credentials. But within those constraints, if they or at least the bulk of their
managerial subordinates are qualified members of the profession, we must
recognize that the profession exercises an important degree of influence
on state affairs. The need for the additional credential of Communist or
Nazi Party membership, or of being a Conservative Republican, does indeed qualify the power of purely professional credentials, but that does
not mean that professional knowledge is actually replaced by lay ideas.

It is often the case that changes in the direction of the state bring
changes in policies connected with professional affairs, changes that can
be quite drastic following a political revolution. However, those changes
need not be, and are usually not in fact, based on substituting lay ideas
for professional expertise. Instead, they usually entail a shift in emphasis
from one cognitive strand or school of thought *within* the legitimate body
of professional ideas to another, as when a regime empowers professionals to advance policies oriented toward preventive care and public health
while displacing those representing academic and clinical medicine. Such
a shift cannot be said necessarily to weaken or deprofessionalize "a"
profession so much as to weaken one of its segments.

Similar considerations should lead to caution in evaluating the imposition by the state of political criteria for admission to the profession and

the distribution of jobs, for, even there, some members of the profession might consider qualification for practice to require more than purely cognitive skills. For example, when the state intervenes to establish affirmative action policies that give priority to the admission of women, blacks, the children of peasants, industrial workers, or other previously deprived members of the population to professional schools and practice positions, it overrules the segment of the profession that prefers other criteria (such as Shils, 1982), but it advances the preferences of another.

It is also implausible to assume that even under a "high-stateness" regime government ministers and their staffs are merely passive instruments of those who are ultimately in command. It is far more reasonable to assume that they have some significant commitment to advancing the fortunes of the domain for which they are responsible – that the minister of health, for example, will struggle for greater recognition and increased resources for health affairs. In general, one must assume that even in an authoritarian and centralized state, where there is a state ministry for a professional domain, there is also someone with considerable influence seeking to advance some version of a profession's, or a segment of a profession's, interests.

Turning from the general formulation of state policy to its implementation, one must ask again what agents are involved. Some analysts have argued that in continental Europe professions have markedly different status and power than those in English-speaking countries because "the state" and its civil servants, rather than private professional associations or their agents, set the standards for entrance to professional training, qualifying for practice, and obtaining positions in which to practice. But formal administrative authority does not tell us enough. In many such nations, state service is a major career option for professionals because state agencies concerned with professional domains need qualified people to do their work. And where does "the state" get its standards? Who creates the curricula of the state professional schools, and the criteria by which competent practice is evaluated? Who creates entrance examinations for professional schools and qualifying examinations for practice, and who grades them? Such agencies routinely rely on the advice of "outside" professional authorities (often the faculty of professional schools) for setting standards in general, and for formulating, approving, and grading examinations in particular.

Examinations represent only a small element of a much larger and more consequential issue – namely, the setting of official standards in general. The affairs of an advanced industrial nation are extremely complex and can avoid chaos only by the institution of common guidelines that allow some predictability and reliability in the production of critical goods and services, and in the procedures by which they are evaluated. In the United States, many such standards are set by private professional and industrial associations (see Freidson, 1986, pp. 199–205) but, as is even more the norm for state-centered nations, others are formulated by state agencies. If, as is likely to be true for even the most totalitarian states, authoritative professional expertise provides the substance of those standards, duly tempered everywhere by political and economic considerations, we find additional evidence of its influence. That official standards are implemented or enforced by lay rather than professional functionaries is of course important, but this does not reduce the importance of the professional source of the standards they are obliged to follow.

I hope it is clear by now that when we avoid addressing "the state" as a formal monolith, look beyond the facade into its internal organization and the characteristics of its personnel, and examine how and by whom policy is implemented, we can see how professionals can exercise important kinds of control over the position of their profession. And we can see more potential for influence by examining the activities of those who have the ears of the powerful. No study worth its salt can afford to assume that state policy is made solely by formal committees and agencies. A leader, elected or unelected, exercises influence out of proportion to being merely one individual, and below the head of state there are other more-than-ordinarily-influential ministers. But none of them, however absolute, tyrannical, or even mad, can function without the advice of others – there are simply too many issues and too many details for one person to command. In matters connected with the domains of the professions,therefore, we must ask who, beyond official representatives of the profession, has the ears of leaders, who are the trusted advisors without portfolio or public recognition? In scientific affairs in the Soviet Union, Lysenko's role as influential advisor was notorious, as were the roles of a handful of physical scientists in the United States during the 1940s and 1950s. Quite apart from the formal advice advanced by professional organizations and their official representatives, individual professionals who are considered to be the source of especially authoritative knowledge must be counted among the sources of influence that contribute to the sum of professional power.

THE CONCENTRATION, ORGANIZATION, AND DISPOSITION
OF CAPITAL

I have already noted that professions have no intrinsic resources other than their command over a body of knowledge and skill that has not been appropriated by others. However, cultural or human capital has no intrinsic material resources, so professions are dependent on economic capital as well as political power for their very survival, let alone their level of material and social comfort. How economic capital is concentrated and organized, therefore, cannot fail to influence the power professions have as corporate organizations and the autonomy that individual practitioners have in their workplaces. Nonetheless, its particular body of specialized knowledge and skill also plays a role in shaping a profession's position in the political economy.

When a profession's body of knowledge and skill is such that it can characteristically provide a personal service to individual clients, its members have more leeway to find work than would otherwise be the case. Members of professions such as medicine and law have the option of practicing independently of organizations, of being "self-employed." But such professionals as engineers, professors, clergymen, and scientists must work in and for organizations.

Some analysts have taken the formal status of self-employment to be a major index of the capacity of professions to dominate the terms, conditions, and goals of work, but in fact this cannot be the case except under very favorable circumstances (see Freidson, 1986, pp. 123–30). When economic resources are profusely distributed among a large population of individuals eagerly seeking a professional service, and when the number of practitioners is relatively small, self-employment does indeed provide considerable freedom for professionals to control the content, terms, conditions, and goals of their work. The growth of such a favorable market-place for medicine in the nineteenth century shifted dependence on a few very wealthy patrons who did not hesitate to impose their prejudices on those they consulted to dependence on a multitude of individuals able to pay fees out of pocket and willing to accept professional authority. Jewson (1974) suggests that the change from patronage by the few to patronage by the many (Johnson, 1972, pp. 41–7) also changed the very content of medicine itself.

The twentieth century has seen yet another major shift in the organization of the medical market-place from patronage by many to mediation between practitioner and consumer by concentrations of state or private capital. This, too, is likely to change some of the content of medicine and the strategy of its practice. Yet throughout the two centuries during which these two major changes have occurred in medicine, its practitioners in most capitalist nations have been nominally self-employed. This suggests that self-employment is too crude a measure of the degree to which professions are free to control their own work.

Neither is the formal status of being employed a useful measure of professional power. Both the structure of the market-place and the organization of firms or agencies vary in ways that can make an enormous difference in the power of professionals to determine the content, terms, conditions and goals of their work. The fact that professional skills are both discretionary in character and transferable from one worksetting to another rather than being "firm-specific" in itself reduces dependence on any single institution for employment, particularly when both credentialism and conscious efforts to limit the supply of qualified professionals sustain high demand, and when resources are plentiful.

Furthermore, considerable variation in the concrete ways organizations are administered and staffed cannot fail to have differential impact on practitioners. Organizations in which professionals work may be owned by the state, by a for-profit or non-profit organization, or by some, if not all, of the professional workers themselves. They may be free-standing, such as an engineering, architectural, or law firm, or a subordinate unit of a larger enterprise, such as a research and development, architectural design, or law department in a firm or agency. Direction may be by either a lay or a professionally credentialed executive officer who may be selected by and responsible to either lay outsiders who exercise ultimate political or economic control or the professional members of the organization itself. Such variation in the concrete arrangements of employment seems far more consequential than the gross fact of being employed.

In no case that I know of has genuine "proletarianization" or literal deskilling of professionals been documented: a significant measure of discretion seems to be an intrinsic social requirement for the work professionals claim. This zone of discretion may create in turn the capacity to resist efforts at control by others. Fortescue (1987) described how in the Soviet Union, where the attempt was made to extend political control down into the workplace through "Party cells," or Primary Party Organizations, shared professional norms in scientific institutes seemed to subvert the effort. Analyzing scientific research, he rejected both "totalitarian" and "vanguard party" theories of control after documenting the influence of prominent scientists on policy-makers and the zones of autonomy carved out by the working staff and their supervisors in research institutes. Unfortunately, no analogous studies seem to exist for the other major professions in the Soviet Union, but since countless empirical surveys elsewhere have shown how those in concrete settings can transform, if not entirely subvert, formal rules established by higher, remote policy-makers, it is essential for analysts to study not only how policies are established on the level of the corporate board or the state ministry but also how they are *actually* carried out in the workplace.

A final element of importance lies in the absolute amount of capital – the resources – that are available in an economy at large and in individual work-settings in particular. Both depend on the state of the economy itself, which is beyond the control of professions but which may seriously affect the position of their members in the market-place. Where the market-place is relatively free, those professions whose services are considered essential rather than a luxury are of course likely to suffer less from a depressed or weak economy than others. Furthermore, both the state and investment capital may choose to invest more resources in one sector of the economy than in another, as the Soviet Union chose to invest more resources in industrial defense production than in health care.

Investment decisions, of course, change, so what they are in one time cannot predict what they will be in another. Nor are they made unilaterally, in a political and economic vacuum. Both influential individual professionals and professional associations are likely to participate in influencing decisions involving the allocation of resources to their domain. When an association is unified, well financed, and able to mobilize its membership for collective action, it is likely to have more influence on decisions allocating resources, as Wilsford (1991) argues in his comparison of France with the United States. Within their own domain or sector of the economy, of course, segments of professions struggle with each other over how the resources made available to them are to be divided up.

KNOWLEDGE, CULTURE, AND THE PUBLIC

My discussion thus far has been seriously incomplete in that it takes no account of three critical elements – the particular bodies of knowledge and skill claimed by professions, the public itself, and the institutions that convey to the public the information and ideas which shape its members' conceptions of themselves and their world. These three elements are essential for explaining some of the variation in allocation of resources to sectors of the economy and to different institutions within any single sector. They are also essential for understanding the demand for different professional services and the value assigned to them, the support the public may provide to efforts by the state or capital to enlarge, restrict, or control professional enterprises, and the prestige and authority of professions themselves.

The most pressing need confronting the study of professions is for an adequate method of conceptualizing knowledge itself. While the literature does provide some useful distinctions (e.g., Halliday, 1985; Abbott, 1988, pp. 33–58, 177–211; Larson, 1990), modes of analysis are not well developed, and there has not been much examination of the different ways bodies of knowledge influence policy-making, culture, and consciousness. I have already mentioned the importance of the process by which official standards are developed to guide both the production of the material goods we consume and the staffing of the institutions we rely on for critical services. Underlying it is an even more important process – the role of professional knowledge in creating and explaining the officially accepted "facts" about the social and physical world that form our consciousness.

Those who produce and convey professional knowledge are in interaction with the institutions that distribute knowledge to the public. Much of what the average person "knows" stems from the approved texts used to socialize children in the elementary and secondary grades. Much of what *we* "know" stems from the texts used to provide "higher" education and "cultivation" to the children of the more privileged classes attending post-secondary technical schools and universities. One may presume that those texts draw heavily on professionally approved knowledge, though politics everywhere qualifies and sometimes circumvents professional influence to a greater or lesser degree. In addition to official texts, of course, and perhaps even more important for shaping common knowledge and consciousness, are the mass media. While, in democratic nations, at least, they are sufficiently independent to be able to advance a considerable number of ideas that run against professionally approved knowledge, I would guess nonetheless that they rely upon professionals as their authoritative sources of knowledge and interpretation.

HOW DOMINANT ARE THE PROFESSIONS?

Well then, how dominant are the professions? Given the issues and the varied actors and institutions I have touched upon, it is clear that the question can be answered only arbitrarily and stereotypically. When one focuses on practitioners interacting with demanding consumers, one is likely to draw a markedly different conclusion than when one focuses on prominent professionals advising policy-makers or being interviewed on television. Contradictory as they may seem, both are true, but both are equally partial. The larger reality of which both are but part is too complex to be reduced to such simple and sweeping characterizations as "dominant," "hegemonic," "proletarianized," "corporatized," "bureaucratized," "rationalized," or "deprofessionalized." To which segment of the profession is one referring, at what level of analysis, and in what arenas? In no case in any industrial country today including those with command political economies, can one use any one of those words accurately to characterize all segments, at every level, and in every arena. They are too gross to characterize such a complex whole as a profession.

It is true that over the past forty years the rank-and-file practitioners of some professions have lost some of their privileges in many industrial nations, so one can rightly argue a relative decline in their position. On the other hand, when one looks at some of the other members of their professions in other arenas in those same nations, where both the state and capital depend on professional knowledge for formulating, directing, and legitimizing policy, one can argue for an increase in professional power over the same period.

But note my use of the word "argue." It rightly implies rhetoric, the deliberate use of language to persuade. This, I believe, is at the bottom of the character of much of the discussion about the power of professions. One needs some large, simple, but intrinsically vague idea to characterize a position in a striking manner. Such rhetoric is especially useful for teaching undergraduates, which, because it is what many of us do for a living, cannot fail to affect how we present our ideas. It creates simple oppositions that provide convenient pigeon-holes into which students can sort varied data that can otherwise be overwhelming. And it is convenient for multiple-choice examinations. It is also a useful tool for our scholarly activities, for we too need ways of labeling data in a simple and striking fashion, and ways of attracting the attention of our colleagues by presenting a stereotyped intellectual position against which we can advance its opposite.

Simple opposites, however, are a poor guide for understanding. Because the value and integrity of our knowledge depend on maintaining a comprehensive and sophisticated view of what we analyze, we ought to avoid such simplification wherever we can. This means that before we even pretend to be able to determine whether professions are powerful or powerless, we examine the entire range of professional institutions and their connections with the ultimate sources of power – the state and capital. Should we do that scrupulously, and examine the *workings* of the state and of corporate capital rather than merely their formal structure, and the actual professional labor-process rather than the formal administrative procedures said to control it, I think we would avoid much of the sterile debate that has exercised us for so long, and instead collect and exchange new, richer information that would be considerably more enlightening even if not so striking or entertaining.

PART II

ELEMENTS OF A THEORY OF PROFESSIONALISM

3

The Division of Labor as Social Interaction[1]

It is now the two hundredth anniversary of the publication of Adam Smith's *The Wealth of Nations,* a book noteworthy for its emphasis on the division of labor as the source of increased productivity. But for all the extensive reference to and use made of the concept by a host of writers in the interim, one hundred seventeen years after its date of publication Emile Durkheim could state that "the theory of the division of labor has made . . . little progress since Adam Smith" (Durkheim, 1947, p. 46). And into the present decade writers are still claiming that the concept is "one of the most neglected," that "it has received far less attention than it merits" (Clemente, 1972, p. 31).

ADAM SMITH

If it were some other writer than Adam Smith who was responsible for emphasizing the concept, with some other purpose than his, the received notion of the division of labor would no doubt have had a different content. Smith, after all, was concerned both with the analysis of the growth of productivity and capital and with developing an argument for a particular national economic policy he believed would lead to "universal opulence." Given his purpose, the concept warranted little attention in and of itself; it figured as a source of productivity and exchange, and little more.

In visualizing the division of labor through the lens of his prescriptive conception of a state of perfect liberty, Smith was inclined to see it as composed of shifting tasks rather than stable social roles, tasks essentially unorganized by those who performed them, and arrayed into a functionally interdependent and efficient productive system by the operation of free and unfettered individual competition in the market. His conceptual scheme could not tolerate any deliberate social organization independent of that created by the market. Indeed, the system could be seen as automatic, self-adjusting and efficient only *because* there was no organized interference with it. Thus, in Smith's usage, a comparatively unproductive division of labor was constituted by a set of tasks stabilized into social roles and organized by worker or employer combinations, while a productive division of labor was constituted by tasks responsive to market demand, performed by individual workers who were not organized into social groups which interfere with responsiveness to market demand.

DURKHEIM'S USAGES

While Adam Smith did his best to interpret the social organization of the division of labor as something artificial, Durkheim may be said to have argued precisely the reverse. "The division of labor can be effectuated only among members of an already constituted society," he wrote (Durkheim, 1947, p. 275). Smith's combinations, as well as what Durkheim called the "restitutive law" – that is, the civil and administrative law governing the rights and obligations of participants in the division of labor – composed a part of that "already constituted society" which, as "the policies of Europe," was attacked by Smith. Durkheim insisted that the division of labor was socially regulated, and was not a mere aggregate of individually contracted exchanges.

But Durkheim did not really develop his position well. As Kemper (1972) correctly noted, in *The Division of Labor in Society* Durkheim was preoccupied with refuting the Utilitarians, and most especially Herbert Spencer who, compatibly with Smith, saw the division of labor as a precondition for the possibility of exchange and contractual relations and thus in some sense prior to and independent of established, organized social usages and norms (cf. LaCapra, 1972). Durkheim was concerned with arguing precisely the reverse, and was not so much concerned with a close examination and articulation of the concept of the division of labor itself as with considering the kinds of social regulation and cohesion it presupposed. While, as I shall note, he did here and there deal with the empirical referent of the concept, and the extent to which it is socially ordered, he never really addressed the division of labor directly. Like Smith, he used the concept as a medium for dealing with another, more central preoccupation.

THE DIVISION OF LABOR AS SPECIALIZATION

In order to elaborate Durkheim's basic approach to the division of labor as a sociological rather than ecological or economic order, it is useful to ask, "What is it people are talking about when they refer to the division of labor?" What, in other words, is its empirical referent? Curiously enough, the literature provides little direct and extended discussion of the empirical referents of the term. This is not to say that there have not been definitions. Commonly, from Smith to the present, the division of labor has been defined as "specialization" of productive labor, or, as Durkheim put it, the "apportionment of functions" (Durkheim, 1947, p. 56).

Such a definition, however, only substitutes one abstraction for another without providing any guide as to how one may move from it to empirical reality. Indeed, "specialization" is an especially ambiguous abstraction, for it is intrinsically relative. Short of a mythical isolate such as Robinson Crusoe before the arrival of Friday, it is impossible to imagine the absence of specialized or divided labor. The very notion of some "whole task" which, when broken down into separate tasks, is transformed into "specialization" is entirely arbitrary. In Smith's famous example of the production of pins, the "whole task" was the making of a pin all by oneself, specialization occurring when the process was broken down into separate tasks such as drawing the wire, pointing it, making the head, fastening the head, and the like. But the making of a pin all by oneself as one's exclusive task is itself a specialization in that one cannot subsist on the pins made without entering into an exchange relationship with others to obtain the "necessaries" of life, such as food, clothing, and shelter. Even the ultimate "whole task" of directly creating one's own subsistence tends to involve specialization by members of the self-sufficient household (cf. Bücher, 1907), though the specialized workers may not participate in a market economy and so may not be considered productive workers.

Thus specialization cannot be defined empirically without reference to a concrete, historical process, bounded in time and space, by which a task once performed by one person or class of persons becomes replaced by more than one task performed by more than one worker or class of workers. As Bücher pointed out, it involves the transfer of "an economic task . . . from the one person hitherto performing it to several persons . . . so that each of these performs but a separate part of the previous total labour" (Bücher, 1907, p. 289). The reality is a *prior* task, not a logically whole or complete task.

Furthermore, it is neither logical nor functional task differentiation that constitutes the historical reality of specialization but rather the *social* differentiation of productive labor which is *interpreted* as task differentiation.

Where there was once a worker who made pins, there came to be a number of different types of workers whose separate activities, taken together, resulted in the production of pins. The empirical referent of specialization, like the referent of the division of labor itself, thus lies in socially created, historically defined work roles. "Whole tasks" and "specialized tasks" are either inferred from or imputed to those work roles and do not exist apart from them.

THE DIVISION OF LABOR AS AN ADMINISTRATIVE ARTIFACT

It is ironic that Durkheim's analysis of the division of labor is more often than not invoked today by scholars whose thinking is more compatible with that of Herbert Spencer than of Durkheim himself. Human ecologists have seized upon a comparatively small and unimportant facet of Durkheim's essay, in which he emphasized the importance of social or moral density and "social volume," or number, in necessitating a "greater" division of labor (Durkheim, 1947, p. 262, and see Schnore, 1958). In spite of Durkheim's insistence on the priority of social regulation, human ecologists have used Durkheim's comments to develop a conception of an essentially automatic relationship between the size of a population and its division of labor, a relationship where culture or social norms play no part (cf. Gibbs and Martin, 1962, p. 677).

In the paper which seems to have initiated this ecological approach to the division of labor in our own day, Gibbs and Martin made an important distinction between two general ideas associated with the concept – first, occupational differentiation as such, designated as the *degree* of the division of labor; second, the *basis* on which a person's occupation in the division of labor is determined (Gibbs and Martin, 1962, p. 669). In a subsequent paper, Labovitz and Gibbs defined the degree of the division of labor as the number of occupations in a population, and the evenness of distribution of the population through those occupations. "The maximum degree of division of labor occurs when no two persons have a common occupation" (Labovitz and Gibbs, 1964, p. 5). Rushing, using those distinctions in a study of formal organizations, called them "*structural differentiation* and structurally determined *individual differentiation* (or extent of dispersion)" (Rushing, 1968, p. 235). Attention to the distinction between the *degree* and the *basis* of the division of labor had disappeared, and, ten years after the publication of the Gibbs and Martin paper, simply the number of occupational roles and the distribution of the work force through them became the accepted best representation of the division of labor as such (cf. Clemente, 1972). The division of labor was treated as an aggregate of individuals assumed to be performing different tasks by virtue of the occupational titles and classifications assigned them by official statistics.

The difficulty of this approach, however, lies in its helpless dependence on the social forces which constitute the *basis* of the division of labor. Tasks are embodied in occupational roles, and occupational roles, as roles, are organized, full-time work enterprises defined and enumerated by the functionaries of both industrial organizations and the state. Their very existence as differentiated or classified roles presupposes social organization in which culture and social norms, not to speak of power, play a major part. "Occupational classifications are made to fit administrative needs" (Form, 1968, p. 24). The notion of occupational role, along with a methodology which relies on official statistics for its data, presupposes selective, organizing forces which establish the *basis* for both delineating a role and assigning individuals to it. The degree of the division of labor is thus inseparable from the bases for the division of labor. The division of labor cannot be represented adequately as a simple aggregate of tasks evolved without normative intervention, if only because, in order to determine empirically what those tasks are and how many there are, one must rely on some organized force with the social authority to constitute, represent, and enumerate them for the purposes it has chosen. That authority must be seen as a critical variable intervening between the putatively causal variable of size and its presumed outcome – the officially represented number of officially differentiated tasks.

Analogous problems connected with this rather mechanical and asocial conception of the division of labor are found in the work of scholars who do not clearly identify themselves as ecologists but who in fact employ the same kind of assumptions. And their work demonstrates the same limited character. I refer to those organizational theorists preoccupied with exploring the relation between organizational size and a number of other variables, most particularly the number of organizational positions – that is, the degree of the division of labor, sometimes called instead "structural differentiation."

Even more obviously than in the ecological literature, organizational studies have been fatally dependent upon administrative authority for their "empirical" representations of the division of labor. Little attention has been paid, however, to the role of that administrative authority itself in how the organization is constituted and represented. Only in instances in which theoretical expectations are not met – as was the case, for example, in a study of military organizations (Childers et al., 1971) – is the power and self-conceived purpose of that authority invoked to explain the "anomolous" findings. As Argyris (1972, p. 16) shrewdly noted, "theory" is often "confirmed" by the study of organizations set up and run in conscious conformity to that very same "theory."

THE DIVISION OF LABOR AS SOCIAL ORGANIZATION

That social organization strongly influences the real rather than his ideal division of labor was directly asserted by Adam Smith in his discussion of the "policies of Europe" which have interfered with the free market. It was also asserted in a rather different context by Durkheim during the course of his discussion of how "restitutive law" orders and limits the contractual relations of the division of labor. And Marx, of course, asserted over and over again that it was the capitalist who determined the concrete, historical form of the division of labor and not technological necessity or nature as such (e.g., Marx, 1963, pp. 127–44).

Indeed, it does not require the invocation of classical authority to see that the forces of social organization are inseparable from the empirical division of labor, that they influence the number of occupational roles, the selection and distribution of individuals through them, and even the content of those roles. Where work is organized by the occupational principle of control (Freidson, 1973) – where, for example, guilds, crafts or professions are strong – the number and mode of selection of workers in an occupation, and the number of occupations, is limited and the external labor market "balkanized" (Kerr, 1954). Proliferation and differentiation of occupational roles is resisted, and their substance or content is stabilized and becomes highly resistant to change.

Occupational combinations are not the only source of influence on the degree, basis, and substance of the division of labor, however. Most of the division of labor developed in industry since Adam Smith, after all, was either created by the authority of capitalist management, protected by the laws of the state, or, in non-capitalist nations, created by managerial agents of the state. Under such circumstances we find administrative authority possessing the power freely to establish most components of the division of labor according to its own goals and preconceptions about the best way to attain those goals efficiently. However, its preconceptions or theories about the best means of attaining its goals, as well as the goals themselves, are not constants. Bendix (1956) has shown us how managerial conceptions have changed historically, and how they have varied from nation to nation, and Woodward (1958) has noted in her comparative study of British firms how fashion in business administration theory has determined important elements of how the division of labor of industrial organizations varies.

There is no need to present many examples of how the number and type of occupational roles, as well as of how the basis for selecting and distributing workers through those roles is influenced by combinations of both workers and managers. It does seem useful, however, to note that the classic writers were preoccupied with delineating various "pure" ways by which the division of labor could or should be organized in modern, industrial society. The principles of organization they stress may be seen to shape the structure of the division of labor, of the labor market, of work careers, and of the jurisdictional boundaries and so content of the occupational roles involved. It is possible to suggest at least three distinct ways of organizing a division of labor in both societies and work enterprises (cf. Johnson, 1972, p. 45ff).

Adam Smith clearly suggests one way of organizing the division of labor. His state of perfect liberty asserted the principle of organizing labor solely by a free market, without interference by any other kind of social organization. Such a principle implies that the division of labor would be very fluid, occupational roles and commercial and productive enterprises emerging, flourishing, and disappearing as market demand and competition by others change. Manufacturers would freely shift from one product to another as market demand and competition dictate. Workers would flow into one role in one community and as freely flow out into another as fluctuating wage levels dictate. Jurisdictional boundaries for work would thus be so unstable and shifting that it may even be difficult to conceive of work as something stable and organized – that is, as involving occupational roles. Work is likely to be a succession of diverse and temporary jobs. The labor market would be entirely fluid in its constitution, and the worker's career a job career rather than an occupational career. The organization or shape of the division of labor is likely to be diffuse.

In contrast to the free market principle of organizing labor, Max Weber's analysis of the rationalization of work in rational-legal bureaucracy implies a different perspective. In such an institution, or in a planned society, a monocratic intelligence plans in formal and rational detail what each task shall be and who shall be qualified to perform it. Workers are assured positions, but not necessarily any one particular occupational role, for the administration is free to wipe out one occupational role and create others, to replace it in the interest of what it regards as efficiency. The worker is expected to move from one to another as the plan requires, and is likely to receive retraining while retaining his tenure through the principle of seniority. The jurisdictional boundaries between occupational roles are likely to be specified in formal detail (as in job descriptions and tables of organization) and the labor market likely to be organized and planned rather than "free." The mobility of the worker is likely to be less than in a free market, if only because the number of occupational roles is likely to be fewer and more clearly defined as part of a rational plan. Under such circumstances the organization of the division of labor may be comparatively hierarchical and formal, and the career of the worker may be regular and orderly, an organizational career.

In addition to those two types of organization described by classic writers, there is another substantive possibility which was perhaps more prominent before the Industrial Revolution, but which has continued to show vitality. I refer to circumstances in which the worker himself exercises control over his work and sets the organization of the division of labour. Historically, guilds, crafts, and professions have exercised such control in at least some segments of the economy. Committed to both their security and their work, they have stabilized their work for their lifetime by negotiating power from the state to set comparatively stable boundaries between occupational roles, and to control recruitment, training, and access to jobs (Gilb, 1966). As Stinchcombe (1959, p. 186) put it, "continuity in status in a labor market instead of an organization, we take to be the defining characteristic of professional institutions." Thus, the number of occupational roles is likely to be comparatively small, and movement between them comparatively slight. Under such circumstances, the organization of the division of labor, like that of the labor market, may be divided among various parallel industrial groupings of cooperating and interdependent occupational firms similar to that posed by Machlup (1962, pp. 45–6) as an alternative mode of analyzing the production and distribution of knowledge. The groupings of occupations may themselves have a hierarchical shape due to the imputation of superior skill and responsibility to some occupations, which thereby gain the right to order or coordinate others (Freidson, 1988, pp. 127–64), but it is likely to be more flat and less complex and formal than a bureaucratically organized administration of the division of labor.

THE ULTIMATE CHARACTER OF THE DIVISION OF LABOR

In my discussion of the division of labor as social organization, I have tried to make it obvious how variations in power on the part of its participants influence the basis, degree, and content of the division of labor. More particularly, by pointing to three distinct *bases* for the division of labor, I have tried to suggest how systematic effect on the *degree* of the division of labor is produced. Each type is of course only a logical construct. The empirical reality of the division of labor at any point in history is always more complex than each basis for organization, taken singly, implies. Indeed, strands of all three foci for organization are probably always present, though with varying degrees of importance in any historical moment.

Perhaps it is because all three are always present in one degree or another that different modes of analysis – classical economic, ecological, organizational, and occupational – can be practiced with enough success to encourage continued espousal to each by various academicians, explaining some of the variance but never all or even most. But since each type of organization is logically hostile to and incompatible with the other, how can they possibly co-exist in "reality"? They can co-exist because, as formal models, they are principles and plans for human activities and as such are in a sense separate from the work activities they purport to order. They are diffused when translated into work. In and of themselves, the concrete work activities of the division of labor are interactive and emergent in character. Individuals and groups are engaged in a continuous process of conspiracy, evasion, negotiation, and conflict in the course of coping with the varying circumstances and situations of their work, in some sense shaping the terms, conditions, and content of their work no matter what the formal mode of organization being used to justify, control, or conceptualize their activities. It is that ultimate reality which is responsible for blurring the edges and unbalancing the symmetry of both formal plans and concepts.

Evidence to support this view is available in great abundance for each of the conventional models of organization I have discussed. In the case of the free market, the development of combinations and other monopolies by workers, employers, and investors seeking to gain stability and advantage has occurred continuously no matter what the efforts of the state to prevent it. The genuinely free market has, for that reason, never been anything more than an ideological reality. In the case of formal bureaucratic organization in private or state enterprise, sociologists have long recognized that, underneath the formal legislation, the Plan, the table of organization, the official record and report, and even the knowledge of those in positions of formal authority, there is an "informal organization" constructed and maintained by those actually engaged in doing the work of management and production.

The concept of informal organization is the analyst's abstraction of what is a process of negotiative interaction. It is much more extensive than the mere restriction of production by semi-skilled factory workers that has received so much attention. Interaction among workers and between workers and supervisors also determines how tasks shall be conceived, who shall perform them, and how they shall be performed –

how, in short, at least some of the dimensions of "job," "task," "technology," and "differentiation" shall be put into practice. (The basic work for analysis of interaction among occupations is Hughes (1971). For a recent study of how specialized roles emerge in a productive organization, see Pettigrew (1973). The same may be said for circumstances in which work is ostensibly organized by formal occupational authority. The formal boundaries of jurisdictions are often established by legislation, produced and reproduced in the course of a process of political struggle and negotiation during which occupational spokesmen seek to sustain or improve their relative position in the interoccupational organization we call the division of labor (Bucher and Strauss, 1961; for a case study, see Akers, 1968). This is not to say that such legal regulation is rigidly constraining on interaction at work, however, for we have good evidence of the permeability of many formal jurisdictional boundaries in concrete situations of work (Bucher and Stelling, 1969). And within occupations may be seen processes whereby specialty groups infringe upon each other and engage in renegotiating boundaries; within specialties "segments" struggle for the power to change the definition of the characteristic tasks of the specialty, and even its identity (Bucher, 1962).

At bottom, then, in the everyday world of work from which we abstract conceptions of the division of labor, it seems accurate to see the division of labor as a process of social interaction in the course of which the participants are continuously engaged in attempting to define, establish, maintain, and renew the tasks they perform and the relationships with others which their tasks presuppose. However, it would be a great mistake to assume that such interaction is entirely free and thus, unwittingly, to return to Adam Smith's labor market composed of entirely individualistic competition. In reality, individuals are always involved in collective attempts to control their work, and those collective attempts may be represented as social organization. As Herbert Blumer (1969, pp. 87–8) put it, "Social organization is a framework inside of which acting units develop their actions... It sets conditions for their action but does not determine their actions... It shapes situations in which people act, and... it supplies fixed sets of symbols which people use in interpreting their situations." Social interaction takes place within social organization and not independently of it; and it is social rather than purely and spontaneously individual.

Thus, the interaction that takes place in the division of labor must be seen to operate within certain broad and permissive limits such as those addressed by ecologists, organizational theorists, and others. Among the individuals on the factory shop floor or on the hospital ward, and among the groups engaged in negotiating legislation and formal plans for controlling work, there are boundaries set on what will be considered legitimate to negotiate, how the negotiation will take place, and what bargains can be struck. Some are unselfconscious and taken for granted, some are specifically understood as scientifically incontrovertible necessity, and others as legitimate laws, rules and regulations, and practices. Most of the time the limits to interaction posed by consensual conceptions of "scientific" necessity and legal propriety are sufficiently broad and permissive that a variety of bargains is possible for the participants. It is in that practical variety where we see the division of labor as, ultimately, a process of social interaction whereby the participants create their own specialized jobs and work relationships.

THE PROBLEM OF THE DIVISION OF LABOR

My conclusion may make it seem that the division of labor can be analyzed satisfactorily on a wholly social level, independently of the material world of technology and production. This is so, but only on the basis of understanding that the material world is known and assessed through the social world. One may not doubt that the material world exercises its own constraints on work quite apart from human conceptions. It must be taken into account by any realistic conception of the organization of work. Thus, the "efficiency" and "productivity" of any particular method of organizing work constitute elements independent of social interaction and the arbitrary exercise of social and economic power to select and define work roles and assign people to them. But since we cannot know that material world except through the social world which has already made its choices, the "objectively necessary" division of labor for gaining a particular end will always be problematic.

What division of labor is "objectively necessary" for a given productive outcome constitutes the focus for one of the most critical social problems – the organization of work. Most observers agree that hierarchical control of an elaborately planned system of carefully defined and supervised tasks which have been simplified and standardized has become the dominant principle for organizing the division of labor in all industrial societies. Many also agree that such a principle has led to the objective and subjective alienation of the worker from his work, though opinions vary about the magnitude and significance of such alienation.

Even conceding such alienation, however, the continued use of that principle of organization is justified by claiming its superior efficiency and productivity. Hierarchy and managerial task differentiation are held to be functional necessities. Critics, on the other hand, argue that neither technological necessity nor superior productivity are proven, and that the real issue is one of control – whether human work and its products are to be controlled by the worker himself, or by the authority of capitalist or state socialist management (e.g., Marglin, 1974). How can work be organized so as to be sufficiently productive to make available to all a variety of goods and services and at the same time be rewarding to those who must perform it in order to make a living? Better answers to that question than now exist may stem from recognition of the different conceptual levels embodied in various usages of the concept of the division of labor. And above all, better assessments of answers may stem from recognition that the ultimate test of the theory and ideology embodied in schemes for organizing the division of labor lies in the social interaction of participants in their everyday work settings.

NOTES

1   This is the revision of a paper read at the annual meetings of the American Sociological Association, Montreal, in 1974. Support from the Russell Sage Foundation for work which allowed its preparation is gratefully acknowledged.

4

Professions and the Occupational Principle

For countries presently in an advanced stage of industrialization, the professions have come to assume an importance which has been of increasing interest to scholars and practical men alike. While the usage of the word is highly confused, and its definition for purposes both of scholarship and social accounting a matter of wearisome debate, the phenomena addressed are of very special theoretical and practical importance (cf. Parsons, 1968). The growth of the professions in the twentieth century represents the rebirth of a principle for organizing work which has been virtually dormant since the Industrial Revolution. It might be called the occupational principle, one which is implied, though almost completely undeveloped, in Durkheim's vision of society as a division of labor. It is logically and substantively in contrast to what might be called the administrative principle, which figures prominently in Max Weber's view of the rationalization of society. Let us examine the two.

THE EMPIRICAL WEAKENING OF THE ADMINISTRATIVE
PRINCIPLE

The administrative principle of organizing and controlling work is of course a conceptual construct designed to point to important elements of the world of empirical experience. Like any concept, it does not describe the world completely and faithfully so much as highlight particular elements in it. Its usefulness is evaluated partly by its "fit" with that world. Up until this century, it has been quite faithful to the essential facts of the organization of work in manufacturing enterprises. But when governmental regulation imposed standards of employment, safety, and hygiene on management, and when the workers themselves organized into stable collective bargaining units, the character of the authority of management over the organization of work became considerably less direct and straightforward. From that point in history on, models of work organizations which presuppose a truly monocratic administration or management could only be literally inaccurate even if still analytically useful.

Apart from governmental regulation of work organizations, which may be seen as a higher level of rationalization and application of the administrative principle than the actions of management, the rise of industrial trade unionism represents a weakening of management's capacity to control and organize work and as an assertion of worker control. But it is a rather incomplete form of control over work, an important but nonetheless highly "impure" empirical instance of the occupational principle. The industrial union represents a source of the organization of work which largely influences economic and other terms and conditions of work, but generally it does not influence the content of work itself. What the job should be, how it should be performed, and who should perform it pretty much remain matters to be determined by management, and management remains fairly, even if not entirely, free to continue to fragment, mechanize and rationalize tasks in the same way it did at the outset of the Industrial Revolution. However, yet another source of control over work has developed in the twentieth century which, unlike unionization, removes or withholds from the hands of management the authority to create and direct the substance, the performance, and even the goals of the work itself. That source of organization stems from the professionalization of occupations.

PROFESSIONALIZATION AND ADMINISTRATION

Professionalization might be defined as a process by which an organized occupation, usually but not always by virtue of making a claim to special esoteric competence and to concern for the quality of its work and its benefits to society, obtains the exclusive right to perform a particular kind of work, control training for and access to it, and control the right of determining and evaluating the way the work is performed (cf. Vollmer and Mills, 1966). It represents a basis for organizing jobs and work in a division of labor which is entirely different from the administrative principle. It is not a historically new form of organization, since it was manifested in earlier days primarily in the guilds and the crafts. But by the middle of the twentieth century its renewed vigor established it as a source of control which may well rival that of management.

Part of its recent vigor might stem from the strength it gains from the growing number of workers obtaining or aspiring to professional status, and from the class position of their leaders – educated members of the upper-middle class who have become committed to careers of performing productive or substantive rather than entrepreneurial or managerial labor. The contemporary professions might be regarded as an educated, middle-class variant of the occupational principle of organization already represented by the working-class crafts, the difference between the two being that the claim for autonomy and self-control among professions is usually based on formal "higher" education rather than on trade school or long apprenticeship in practicing some manual skill said to require complex judgment.

In any case, when an occupation has become fully professionalized, even if its work characteristically goes on in an organization, management can control the resources connected with work, but cannot control most of what the workers do and how they do it. Indeed, the position of management in such a situation is so far removed from the kind of administrative authority sketched out by Max Weber that it could be argued that the use of a model predicated on the administrative principle obscures more than it illuminates. This is not to say that one must deny the empirical fact that there is an administration; rather, one questions only its capacity for imperative coordination. If one were to use instead an occupational model, one could conceive of the work organization as being composed of an administrative framework organized monocratically, but without authority over work, and a set of jobs whose performance is determined and organized by the external occupational groups to which the workers belong, with workers possessing the basic authority over work. Jobs become opportunity points in occupational careers extending across organizations and created and organized by occupations; they are not, as they are in conventional industrial organizations, mere isolated task positions in individual plants created by management for its own purposes, and having no independent existence.

It would be one thing if professionals constituted only one isolated set of workers in a plant, all others subject to administrative and industrial union control. This is largely the case with contemporary manufacturing organizations where, while we do read of the problems posed to and by management in the research and development departments manned by scientists and engineers within the organization, the issues raised do not pervade the entire organization (see Marcson, 1960; Kornhauser, 1962). In such cases, the central tasks of production remain the duty of line workers whose jobs, as I have already noted, remain formulated, evaluated, and controlled by management. It is quite another thing in professionalized service organizations such as law firms, hospitals, correctional agencies, social agencies, schools, accounting firms, and research organizations. There, the central task around which all others swing is performed or controlled by professional or would-be professional workers, not by semi-skilled workers without singular occupational identity or aspiration. And it escapes or at least strongly resists the exercise of administrative authority over the work.

When the central, strategic task of an organization is formulated, controlled, and evaluated primarily by the workers, as it is in the case of the established professions, management does perform logistic functions, but is essentially stripped of what Weber considered to be the prime characteristic of administrative authority – the legitimate right to exercise imperative coordination. Management may control the terms and conditions of work by virtue of a buyer's labor market, but the professional worker controls the work itself, and the work itself is the key to production. In unionized industrial settings, the situation is usually precisely reversed: the organized worker controls many of the terms and conditions of his work through his union, and can stop the work by walking out, but management controls the work that is done.

THE ORGANIZATION OF THE DIVISION OF LABOR

In discussing the control of work, it is important to differentiate the work of a particular job, and the relationship of one job to others. The latter, of course, is addressed by the concept of the division of labor, a concept which presupposes some kind of mechanism or set of mechanisms ordering and coordinating the interrelationships of jobs. While he emphasized the division of labor, Durkheim did not really discuss its mechanisms, more or less assuming an automatic, functional interdependence of various kinds of tasks and workers. Weber, on the other hand, did not dwell on the idea of the division of labor, but he specified administrative authority, or the authority of office, as the major mechanism of "imperative coordination." Administrative authority is not, however, the only possible coordinating mechanism. There is also the authority implied by the occupational principle – the authority of imputed expertise. A worker can get to control his own work because he has managed to persuade others that he and only he is competent to do so. A worker can get to control the work of others when belief in their functional interdependence exists to link their work with his, and when there is belief in the greater salience of his work as well as the superiority of his knowledge and skill compared with the others in the division of labor. "Objective" functional interdependence independent of historically established social meanings need not be assumed, and in fact is not assumed here. Nor need it be assumed that there are objective rather than historical and social criteria by which differential salience and superior knowledge and skill are determined. Indeed, it seems most wise to assume that the authority of expertise is as much established by a social and political process as is the authority of administrative office. There is very great intellectual danger in falsely objectifying social variables as "hard" technology, "scientific" knowledge, and "complex" skill.

Predicated on the authority of expertise, professionalization includes the establishment of authority to coordinate a division of labor. Its growth has thus radically changed the position of management in yet another way: management loses much of the authority to control and coordinate the functioning of the division of labor. Unlike research and development in manufacturing organizations, which is but one of many departments, each of which operates more or less separately from the other but which is coordinated around production by upper-level management, professional services in organizations such as schools and hospitals are the most salient activities in the organization-wide division of labor. This means that the work of many other occupations in the organization is coordinated around the professionalized service. Coordination, however, does not take place by orders of management so much as by orders from the professional worker who is dominant in the division of labor. Insofar as it both performs and controls the focal service, the profession must also control the supportive tasks around that service. Thus, not management but the profession coordinates the division of labor in the organization. A hierarchical structure of authority is often found, but it is professional and not administrative, based on the authority of imputed expertise rather than on the authority of administrative office (cf. Freidson, 1988). An administrative structure does exist, but it is restricted largely to authority over supportive economic, clerical, and maintenance services.

Furthermore, in such a highly professionalized domain as health, the interrelations of many of the workers are specified by licensing legislation that exists outside and independently of the organizations in which work takes place. The labor force in the health services, for example, is not only an aggregation of unskilled, semi-skilled, semi-professional and professional workers as labor force and occupational mobility analysis are prone to treat it, but also an imperatively coordinated social organization of occupations. The structural relations among occupations, and what they do, are not established by the management of work organizations, but by the occupational principle – exercise of authority over work by occupations themselves, often with the support of the state which approves exclusive licensing and jurisdiction.

Workers entering the organization enter with their work defined in advance by their training outside, and as part of that work there is the obligation to take orders from some, cooperate with others, and order members of still other occupations. Management does not usually create or control either the work or the jobs, as it does in industry. It merely sets up the organization of occupationally ordained positions and tasks and administers the financial, clerical, and other supportive resources necessary to maintain it. In industry a job title is a creation of management and need not imply an occupation: such is not the case in a professionalized work setting. What work is done, and how, becomes a function of a socially organized division of labor which is largely independent of any particular organization, established by occupational associations and legislatures which form the environment of the organization. This is a radically different mode of organizing work than that which followed the Industrial Revolution in manufacturing. It is in fact a central manifestation of what is being called the post-Industrial Revolution, where services take precedence over goods, where factory hands are replaced by machines, and where much of what human work is left must be performed by highly trained occupations. That the worker may be employed in a bureaucratically organized institution rather than be a free professional or craftsman is considerably less important to the occupational principle than his position in the labor market. Self-employment in a glutted labor market allows little self-determination of task, while a scarce labor market strengthens enormously the position of the employee. What is of direct analytical importance to the occupational principle is the fact of autonomy from direction at work, autonomy which can be lost when one is an employee but equally when one is self-employed. Under some circumstances, including that of a well-controlled labor market, one may work in the service of management, but how he works may remain his own right to determine.

KNOWLEDGE AND THE OCCUPATIONAL PRINCIPLE

Thus far I have emphasized history and change, and in that light the strategic value of attending to a comparatively neglected dimension of human affairs rather than to remain fixed on what may very well be at the present time an overused dimension. I emphasize this not only in light of the past, but also in the light of what seems to be coming in our future. Virtually all prophets – or, as they are now called, futurologists – seem agreed that the future will see ever-increasing reliance on specialized knowledge and skill, and on applying that knowledge to the solution of practical problems by specially trained men (e.g., Bell, 1968). Political leaders need their staffs of experts to provide them with briefings before they can make intelligent decisions (Wilensky, 1967). And once political decisions are made, the programs by which they are put into effect need to be formulated and carried out by a growing army of trained personnel thought to have the knowledge and skill required for practical success. Writers fearful of the consequences of this growing dependence on experts use the word "technocracy." Writers more neutral or positive have used words such as "the knowledgeable society" (Lane, 1966) and "the active society" (Etzioni, 1968).

However, while many of these writers have stressed the increased importance of specialized knowledge in the emerging society of the future, none has addressed himself seriously to the question of where the knowledge comes from, how it gets established as recognized knowledge, and how its development and utilization become organized, evaluated, and controlled. Knowledge, after all, is not disembodied spirit. It is expressed in the activities of men. And knowledgeable men are not mere individuals. Those engaged in the process of creating, communicating, and applying knowledge are identified and identify themselves with recognizable, increasingly organized occupational groups. Scholars, scientists, and engineers are all members of occupations. The production, dissemination, and application of knowledge must be seen as a set of industries (Machlup, 1962) and many of the men working in those industries must be seen as performing definite social roles embedded in particular social circles (Znaniecki, 1968). The occupational organization of the workers in those industries is obviously important to understanding the way knowledge is produced and used in the post-industrial society. Such occupational organization has consequences which the class position of the professional (Ben-David, 1964) by itself does not allow us to predict.

Once we turn to examine how knowledge is related to human activities, we are drawn into the traditional but newly revived field of the sociology of knowledge (especially Holzner, 1968). And in that field, we cannot avoid examining special occupations, and particularly professions, for their role in organizing the activities surrounding knowledge. It is the concept of occupation, and particularly profession, which provides us with the sociological link between knowledge as such and its organized role in present-day society. It is not, after all, the fact of specialized knowledge which has the practical potential for developing a technocracy, but rather the fact of organized occupations and/or agencies, leaders, and classes which have exclusive access to such knowledge. Knowledge itself does not give special power: only *exclusive* knowledge gives power to its possessors. And it is precisely in the occupational principle of organization, by which recruitment, training, and the performance of the work of creating, disseminating, and applying knowledge are controlled by the "knowledge occupations" that such power is obtained.

PROFESSIONS AND POLITICS

I noted earlier in this essay that both the crafts and the established professions are the purest empirical matches of the concept of the occupational principle. They are differentiated largely by the locus of their training and the substance of their claims to exclusive knowledge and skill. But the professions are especially important because they have much more control over the full range of their work than the crafts, and they exercise much greater, wide-ranging control over human affairs. Furthermore, the knowledge of the professions, learned in formal institutions of higher education and phrased in abstract terms, is far more likely to be able successfully to claim privilege on the basis of its esoteric character.

Insofar as privilege is deliberately organized on a legal basis, it has a political foundation. It is the power of government which grants the profession the exclusive right to use or evaluate a certain body of knowledge and skill. Granted the exclusive right to use knowledge, the profession gains power. It is in this sense that the professions are intimately connected with formal political processes. Such connection has generally been implied in many of the sketches of the process of professionalization, in the course of which occupations organize into associations (Millerson, 1964), sometimes change their names, and press both for public recognition and formal political recognition in the form of exclusive registration, licensing, and the like. Quite apart from the *development* of a profession, however, the *maintenance* and *improvement* of the profession's position in the market–place, and in the division of labor surrounding it, requires continuous political activity. No matter how disinterested its concern for knowledge, humanity, art, or whatever, the profession must become an interest group to at once advance its aims and to protect itself from those with competing aims. On the formal associational level, professions are inextricably and deeply involved in politics. The general analysis of Gilb (1966) and the particular studies of such analysts as Jamous and Peloille (1970) are examples of work which is needed to illuminate this almost ignored area of the sociology of professions.

PROFESSIONS AND IDEOLOGY

Perhaps the political context in which professions operate has been underexamined by sociologists because, like most scholars, scientists, and intellectuals, they are not prone to question the status of the knowledge and skill involved. Indeed, special knowledge and skill is used to *define* professions (Goode, 1969) and aspiring occupations have been excluded from consideration as professions on the basis of the sociologist's judgment that they do not possess "basic" knowledge and skill. Once an occupation is accepted as a profession, then by definition it is knowledgeable. When seen as part of a political process, however, knowledge and skill are claimed by a group to advance its interests. True or false the knowledge, disinterested or interested the motive, claims of knowledge function as ideologies, and can be evaluated independently of their validity for their part in gaining public and legislative support for an organized occupation. Indeed, it seems likely that insofar as claims to knowledge and skill are essential elements in a political process which takes place in an arena of conflicting or competing claims from other interest groups, occupational or otherwise, it is highly unlikely that they can remain neutrally descriptive. Patently, they require close attention.

There has been little study of the substance of professional ideology, and even less of the substance of professional "knowledge" as ideology. Dibble's brief but provocative paper (1962) is one of the few to address the question of the analytical differentiation of occupational ideology. In a concrete way, Mills (1942) has shown how an ideology in one professional area can be analyzed, as has Layton (1971) for turn-of-the-century engineering, and Halmos (1966, 1970) for those engaged in personal counseling. My own (Freidson, 1988) analysis of the "clinical mentality" argues that a special way of looking at self and others arises out of the work of consultants who must intervene in everyday practical affairs. And in another context (Freidson, 1970) I have argued that professional ideologies are intrinsically imperialistic, claiming more for the profession's knowledge and skill, and a broader jurisdiction, than can in fact be justified by demonstrable effectiveness. Such imperialism can of course be a function of crude self-interest, but it can as well be seen as a natural outcome of the deep commitment to the value of his work developed by the thoroughly socialized professional who has devoted his entire adult life to it.

Embedded in the claims of each of the professions is what Thomas Kuhn (1962) called a "paradigm," a taken-for-granted conception of what the issue is, and how it is solvable. Each tends to see the world in terms of its own characteristic conception of problems and solutions, and in the political arena each tries to argue for more resources as a way of advancing the general good. Each has its own eloquent spokesmen testifying for more support of pure science, for the capacity of engineering to solve contemporary problems, on the huge cost to the nation of working days lost due to illness, on the essential role of education in training informed citizenry and capable labor force, and so on. Much of the political activity of the professions may be characterized by appeals to the superior importance and relevance of one paradigm over another. Thus the competition between professions for jurisdiction over a particular area may be analyzed as conflicting definitions of the nature of the problem or activity each is seeking to control, and claims about the way they can best be solved or carried out. In a technocracy, the outcome of such competition establishes who is to be the technocrat and who not.

PROFESSIONALS AT WORK

Thus far, I have devoted myself to a discussion of professions as complex organizations, consonant with my concern with professions as manifestations of the occupational principle of organizing work. In particular, I have addressed myself to the issue of the way professions gain the political power in fact to control and organize their work. Such power provides the framework for formal organization and control, the character for what, in his seminal work, Hughes (1958) called "license and mandate." It sets up the legal authority for the profession to recruit, train, examine, license, and review performance, and establishes the formal limits of its exclusive jurisdiction.

It has largely been within a given framework of formal occupational organization that sociologists have studied professionals. (For a recent review by a well-known analyst, along with an extensive bibliography of the American literature, see Moore, 1970. For a recent collection of original papers, primarily British, see Jackson, 1970. For three recent American textbooks, see Hall, 1969, Krause, 1971, and Pavalko, 1971.) Indeed, it seems that most studies have paid rather little attention to the larger political and economic characteristics of the profession which place formal limits on the performance of work by professionals, and on their interaction with colleagues, clients, and members of other occupations.

Nonetheless, studies of individual professionals in particular settings do perform the essential function of building up a comprehensive picture of the way concrete institutions contribute to the development and maintenance of commitments to a particular profession both as a lifelong career and as a special perspective on self and others. Studies of the process of professional education try to show how one's conception of self-as-professional develops, as well as how one learns the knowledge, skill, and perspective which teachers in professional schools expect of their students. Both the substance of the process of choice of profession and of the process of formal socialization in professional school obviously play a great part in explaining the behavior of individuals in work settings.

But while formal education establishes qualifications for work, it does not explain enough of the actual behavior of individuals at work to be satisfactory by itself. Every work setting contains its own special source of influence over the work of individual professionals. For obvious reasons of accessibility and convenience, bureaucratically organized elite settings such as large law firms, teaching hospitals, and universities have been studied considerably more often than the more modest and ubiquitous settings of individual or small practices in community or otherwise ordinary locales. More and more professionals are coming to work in bureaucratically organized settings but, as long as study goes on without comparative examination of work in other settings, it will be difficult if not impossible to tell how significant is its influence on the professional worker's work, or on the character of his relationships with other workers. In the latter case, as I have already noted, where a number of occupations in a particular institution's division of labor are registered or more particularly licensed, their interrelationships at work are in part limited and defined irrespective of administrative authority or their members' negotiative relationships.

PROFESSIONAL CONTROL OVER WORK

The crucial issue for the evaluation of any kind of work is its outcome in quantity and quality. For professional workers the issue is whether they are able to exercise control over their work and its outcome, and what methods of control they use. Control over work performance is of course the basic prize over which occupation and administration contend in particular work settings. The strongest professions have thus far managed to preserve much of the right to be the arbiters of their own work performance, justified by the claim that they are the only ones who know enough to be able to evaluate it properly, and that they are also actively committed to ensuring that performance lives up to basic standards. How responsibly that control is exercised constitutes an essential problem for both theoretical and practical analysis.

It is probably impossible to say whether or not professions in general are any more or less conscientious in maintaining their own work performance standards than, say, a similarly organized set of occupations, the crafts. But it is possible to suggest the *vice d'estime* of professions, which is to say, the typical form taken by their failure to maintain formal standards of work performance, when the failure does occur. When professionals fail to control work so as to have it conform to their own academic standards, they seem to do so because they have chosen to avoid the institution and enforcement of any formal rules or standards. They seem to do so because their members tend to believe that their work is of such a complex character, requiring so much judgment, that formal standards or rules are too arbitrary to be applicable. Typically, they insist on individual discretion, denying the possibility and propriety of formal rules. It is quite the opposite for the typical form failure takes in bureaucracy, for there the administrative organization of work characteristically cripples its capacity for controlling the standards of work performance by proliferating so many formal rules designed to minimize discretion that none can be enforced. Professional failure is marked by dissolution into pure discretion, while administrative failure is marked by petrification of forms.

THE PROSPECTS FOR PROFESSIONS

Clearly, the logics of the occupational principle and the administrative principle are distinctly different, and are in a sense opposed to each other. What, then, is the fate of each to be in the developing post-industrial society of our future? There is evidence for the strengthening of both principles. On the one hand, work organizations have gotten larger and larger, absorbing once small and independently organized units of production into rationalized national corporations. Even the personal services, many of which are new to this century, are being organized on a large scale by both private and public management, and traditionally independent professions such as physicians have more and more been drawn into bureaucratically administered practices. Bureaucratization seems never stronger. But on the other hand, the established professions have reached a position of wealth, prestige, and influence in the twentieth century higher than ever before in past history. And many other occupations have begun to struggle for the same position to such a degree and with such energy that it may not be inappropriate to consider professionalization to be a major social movement of the twentieth century. While there are distinct limits to the occupations likely to become professions (Goode, 1969), the occupations composing a division of labor can be organized around professional authority.

Obviously, predicting outcomes is treacherous. Much has been made of the fact that by coming to work as employees in bureaucratic organizations professions become vulnerable to administrative direction and the loss of autonomy, and that the new, aspiring occupations which developed in administratively organized work settings may be incapable of attaining true professional autonomy simply because they are employees. It may very well be that professions reached the peak of their autonomy in the first half of this century and will, in the second half, lose control over their work and become mere "technical workers," merely a special category of skilled labor in the organizational charts of management.

To evaluate this possibility, however, seems to require taking two factors into careful account. First, it would seem that the likelihood of the further extension of the administrative principle of organization hinges in no small part on the likelihood that management can do for professional work what it did earlier for manual work – break it down into a series of discrete, simple operations which those with minimal training can perform and which, when coordinated and reconstituted by management, together produce the same whole outcome or product as was previously produced by the professional worker. If the work of scientists, professors, lawyers, and doctors can be so rationalized, then the post-Industrial Revolution need not be seen as something very new so much as a natural continuation of the Industrial Revolution, an extension of the rationalization of work from manufacturing to services. Only such administrative rationalization can support the exercise of managerial authority.

But since more and more formal education is being required for work in our time, it is hard to see any trend in the direction of weakening the occupational principle. Quite the contrary, we could see the twentieth century as a point when a particular principle of authority rose and flourished as a challenging alternative to the authority of office, a principle inherent in a truly "knowledgeable" society. I refer to the authority of expertise or skill, institutionalized as the special ground for particular kinds of occupational organization. Such authority, in theory if not in practice once institutionalized, rests upon special knowledge and ability rather than incumbency in office, rests upon productive, even creative craftsmanship rather than upon the management of working men. And its assertion is motivated by the worker's commitment to what he sees as his work and his special capacity to evaluate it because he is the one who does it.

The autonomy connected with skill should not be confused, as it often is in the literature, with the economic autonomy of the traditional self-employed professional. It is something quite different. It is related more to the informal attempts of all workers, even those on assembly lines, to do their work as they see fit on the basis of their own sense of knowing how to do it. That he has been an employee for centuries has not left the professor without important freedom. Control over the terms and conditions of work is certainly weakened by being an employee rather than an entrepreneur in a favorable market-place. Nonetheless, control over the *content* of work is not at all necessarily so weakened. If esoteric knowledge and skill are really necessary to perform most of the work of the future, the grounds for administrative rationalization of work seem likely to become increasingly tenuous and, employee or not, the possibility for the occupational principle to take precedence over the administrative principle becomes greater.

Finally, it must be noted that, in assessing the prospects for increasing the strength of the professions, one must assess not only the status of their knowledge and skill but also the status of their occupational organization, which is an independent and necessary, though perhaps not sufficient, variable. After all, the crafts have managed to resist industrialization far more than our evaluation of their knowledge and skill could lead us to predict. It is by their organization that this has been accomplished. There is no reason to assume that present-day professional associations will continue their present tactics and strategies without change, particularly when their members have become employees, or otherwise economically dependent on some central administrative body. What may happen?

No doubt professional associations will continue to be devoted to influencing legislation which preserves a favorable market for their members, but in order to survive they will also have to develop techniques for collective bargaining. From what has already occurred in Western Europe and North America, the strike seems likely to be such a technique. And the strike is likely to revolve around issues of autonomy at work as much as it will revolve around compensation. In the course of such collective actions, there is no doubt that the rhetoric will justify demands by reference to special knowledge and skill and to the terms and conditions (i.e., professional or academic freedom) which are required for their proper exercise, but the action of the strike itself must be a function of occupational organization. Thus, while the future forms of occupational organization and action among the professional workers of tomorrow are only developing now, and so are inconspicuous, they cannot be assigned less weight than knowledge and skill in assessing how far it is reasonable to assume that managerial control of work will continue to grow. At the least, they will constitute a counterforce to the extension of the administrative principle to the control of professional work. Possibly they will so far sustain the continued growth of the occupational principle that the post-industrial society will be the professional society.

5

Occupational Autonomy and Labor Market Shelters

The concept of occupation has been curiously neglected in sociological theory. In empirical studies of members of occupations, attention is devoted to issues of career, contingencies of work, interaction with clients, colleagues, employers, and the like, while taking the idea of occupation for granted. And in the large body of macrosociological work on inequality and status attainment, where occupation plays a critical role in identifying people's positions in the social structure, occupations are typically lumped together by the use of broad governmental classifications which are not remarkable for their consistency or their theoretical import. Occupation represents much too critical a concept in sociology to be taken for granted, for it represents the productive activities upon which societies are based. Furthermore, it has the special potential for linking the microsociological world of everyday experience and activity, which is explored by most studies in the tradition of Everett Hughes, with the macrosociological world of social structure, which is explored by most studies of class, stratification, and social mobility. It is unlikely to be able to serve that function, however, until its theoretical status is clarified and a systematic strategy for its analysis created.

In this chapter I hope to contribute to a clarification of the theoretical status of occupation. I shall argue, first, that the two major bodies of theory most closely connected with the concept of occupation – organizational theory and class and stratification theory – cannot explain parsimoniously in their own terms certain features that occupations may display. Thus, I shall argue that a theory of occupations must be developed separately, and not as a mere derivative of other bodies of theory. I will then argue that a useful focus for such a theory lies in the capacity of occupations to become organized groups independently of firms and of other occupations in the same class or stratum. It is by becoming an effectively organized group that an occupation can gain for its members a modicum of autonomy from control by others. Finally, I will argue that both as a mechanism by which one can explain how relative autonomy can be established for an occupation, and as a concept which can provide the resources for connecting the microsociological experience and activities of individuals with the macrosociological realities of political economy, the notion of a special kind of labor market segment – the shelter – may be a fruitful point of departure for theorizing about occupational organization and experience. I shall conclude with a sketch of the interrelations of major variables to illustrate how it is possible to reason systematically from the shelter in the political economy to occupational organization, training, career, identity, and the like.

OCCUPATION AND ORGANIZATIONAL AND CLASS THEORY

In principle, it is possible to argue that a theory of occupations is not necessary because, between them, organizational and class theory can both explain how occupations are created and sustained, as well as make sense of occupations as part of an organizational division of labor which is itself linked into the broader political and economic environment that provides the resources for and otherwise surrounds and conditions organizations and their policies. And indeed, it is true that, in all developed industrial societies, many "occupations" are simply formal work roles or positions in complex organizations created and controlled by managerial power being exercised on behalf of either private or state capital, or a mixture of the two.

But not all work roles have such characteristics, either here and now or in other times and places. Many have characteristics which cannot be explained or analyzed adequately by reference to the organizations in which they may be found. Some occupations exist and thrive in the external labor market outside of administratively constituted firms. Other occupations, even when carried on inside firms, are noted as "exceptions" (e.g., Piore, 1975) because they can establish, as Stinchcombe put it (1959, p. 186), "continuity of status in a labor market" in such a fashion that, while their members may hold positions in firms and depend for their livelihood on employment in them, they control the supply of specialized labor and even contribute to increasing the demand for their services. They become the source of defining, controlling, and evaluating the work roles in the organizational positions they fill, a source that is exogenous to the firm. Since, as Moore (1970, p. 9) has noted, "it is extremely unlikely that an occupation will be able to set itself apart from, and above, mere tasks set by the administrative wisdom of superiors without making common cause in a formal organization," such occupations can be conceived of as groups organized independently of firms, and must be conceptualized as something other than a mere derivative of the firm or the formal organization.

The same conclusion may be drawn for both stratification and class theory, though for different reasons. As in the case of the firm, occupation is an essential empirical component of both stratification and class theory. However, what is generic to occupation – its existence as an organized form of differentiated productive activity – is at worst ignored and at best blurred and obscured by the analytic focus of both class and stratification theory. The latter are concerned with the unequal distribution of the goods of life, including as some of the goods of life both the jobs that people have and the economic, political, and symbolic rewards that are attached to them. The distribution of people into various occupations which are rewarded in various ways thus constitutes a central issue of class and stratification theory. But apart from having the potential for explaining who has what jobs and their attendant rewards, class and stratification theory is poorly equipped for explaining how the work of those jobs is performed – how the process of production takes place. Production takes place through the medium of *individual* occupations. To see production, one must see occupations, and not merely broad classes or strata. The intrinsic rationale for class or stratification analysis lies in the *aggregation* of different occupations by some criterion of inequality. The intrinsic rationale required for the analysis of how concrete empirical instances of productive work take place lies in the *differentiation* of occupations in a specialized division of labor. While for class or stratification analysis a file clerk and a typist are the same, they do not do the same things in a productive process which, if we are to understand it, must be conceptualized in terms of those occupational differences.

Finally, I may point out that it has been a persistent problem of class theory to explain the absence of consciousness and organized action in what is defined as a class by theorists (see Mann, 1973). Considerably less of a problem exists for the concept of occupation, for that is the way by which individuals today readily and consciously identify themselves and act in their roles as productive workers. An even more intense collective consciousness and action may be found in empirical circumstances in which occupations have organized as groups independently of productive organizations of firms, and independently of other occupations ostensibly of the same stratum or class (see Krause, 1971, p. 85). While not all or even most occupations of the entire working population today have these characteristics, it is the demonstrable potential of occupations to become conscious, acting, organized groups that poses a serious problem of explanation for both organizational and class theory. That potential might be addressed more satisfactorily by developing a mode of analysis based on the notion of occupation itself rather than by attempting to derive concepts from theories designed to address and explain different issues. The problem is how the concept can be developed, what criteria of salience should form the focus for empirical analysis, and how the elaboration of theory can be accomplished.

THE PROBLEM OF FOCUS

At present, occupations tend to be conceptualized in terms of two criteria, neither of which is theoretically appropriate to them. First, there is the conception of occupations as tasks or functions. In the simplest and most obvious way, we distinguish those people who do welding from those who diagnose diseases, blow glass, or whatever. Superficially, this does make sense. After all, is not that what occupation is all about? However, looked at closely, one cannot usefully conceive of occupation by its technical tasks. Machines also weld and blow glass; computers diagnose disease. Should we really conceive of occupations strictly by the tasks or functions associated with them, without covertly smuggling in unacknowledged assumptions, then we would not be able to make any distinction between occupation and technology.

The second major conception of occupation avoids that difficulty by emphasizing the differential positions of occupations in a class or stratification system. Thus, in conventional stratification and social mobility studies, and in official labor statistics, occupations are distinguished by their location in a hierarchy of prestige, income, power, or control over production. Those with the same broad *quantity* of imputed skill, income, prestige, or education are considered the same, irrespective of the different tasks they may perform. So also does Marx-inspired class analysis group all occupations together that share the same very general social relations of production, irrespective of differences in task (see Wright, 1978, p. 1370).

But while self-employed physicians and self-employed lawyers, for example, share the same very general social relations of production implied by self-employment in a capitalist political economy, and while they belong to the same social stratum, each has a distinctly different social identity and each does different work. The work they do is not subject solely to organization by broad social relations of production, nor can it be understood solely as a function of a given level of skill, responsibility, prestige, or whatever. The particular contingencies of being a doctor rather than a lawyer have consequences of their own for the character of the work setting and the performance of work that cannot be ignored if one wishes to understand and explain the labor processes of doctoring and lawyering. Class theory, with its emphasis on relations of production, cannot tell us much about how and why those productive tasks are performed in the particular way they are, and what the relations of the workers are each to the other, and to other workers. Indeed, what Turner and Hodge (1970, p. 34) called the "macro-statification assumptions" underlying the class approach to the analysis of occupations dissolve what is distinctive about occupations and the work they entail. On the contrary, work is predicated on task differentiation into particular occupations: the socially organized performance of differentiated tasks has specific implications for the social organization and the social psychology of work which cannot be explained in broad class terms.

But if we cannot satisfactorily conceptualize occupations solely by their different tasks, or solely by their place in a class or stratification system, how *can* we do so? I suggest that a fruitful focus lies in analyzing the circumstances in which occupations become organized as social groups, in classifying them by the source, type, and degree of their organization, and in analyzing them in such a way as to explain both how and why their form of organization came to be and could be maintained, and what the consequences of that organization are for the productive division of labor of which they are part. Such an approach has manifest ancestry in Durkheim's discussion of occupational groups in *The Division of Labor in Society* (1947, pp. 1–31) and *Professional Ethics and Civic Morals* (1957, pp. 4–41), although Durkheim was neither concerned with nor in fact developed a systematic method for analyzing occupations as groups.

It is of course impossible to pursue such a focus fruitfully if we deal only with occupations that are exclusively organized groups, for that would exclude the vast majority of all occupations today. Lack of organization must be included among the varieties of organization. Many occupations have no organization beyond that imposed by the market and its consumers of labor (e.g., Morse, 1969; Olesen and Katsuranis, 1978). Others are not exclusively organized as individual occupations, but rather are organized into a transoccupational association like a trade union. Other occupations may be exclusively organized groups whose members share a common occupational identity as well as broad solidarity and commitment, the most obvious being some of those often called professions and crafts.

Clearly, in our ordinary discussions of labor we always pay some attention to occupational organization, for organization is one major connotation of such conventional terms as casual labor, trade unions, professions, and crafts. But those words are unfortunately so vague and imprecise, overlain with so many other connotations that they have collected over their linguistic histories, that they are unlikely to be useful as conceptual tools. What is needed are more precise, logical concepts of occupational organization, rather than fruitless attempts to use those "folk concepts" more precisely or to abstract some essence out of them. Logical notions of differentiation in occupational organization can be created by developing a coherent theoretical conception of the critical parameters underlying the *possibility* for occupational organization and autonomy, influencing both the form they take and their consequences for work and the worker.

As the direct link between individual and economy, a link which can be seen to be mediated by productive firms and by class but which can on occasion stand by itself, occupation must be conceptualized in such a way as to allow us to understand how it can stand by itself, autonomous of class or firm. What may be an anomaly to organizational theory and a contradiction in class theory must be the focal issue for direct explanation by occupational theory. Taking as the central issue how occupation can stand autonomously by itself, linking individuals to economy without firm, and standing separate from other members of their ostensible class, how can that link be made? What mechanism can represent it?

The notion of an occupational group, and particularly that of an occupational community, is quite useful for organizing the data one gains from traditional studies of members of relatively distinct occupations, or segments of occupations (see Salaman, 1974). It allows one to deal with important issues of personal identity, of social relations outside the workplace, and the like. In and of itself, however, it cannot link occupation to political economy because it does not contain the conceptual resources by which one can understand how it can come to be within a particular political economy. Essentially, it takes occupational organization more as a given than as something to be itself explained. If an attempt is made to explain it, it is done by reference to the characteristics of the members of the occupation and their relations to each other (e.g., Lipset et al., 1962), which does not establish effective links to the political economy.

MARKETS AND SHELTERS

A fruitful way of establishing such links has been explored by M. S. Larson in her study of the rise of the professions in the United Kingdom and the United States as a "market project," most particularly a project which "constitute(s) and control(s) a market for their expertise" (Larson, 1977, p. xvi). Such a project involves, as Larson notes, a number of activities, including the delineation and standardization of a distinctive commodity, the formation of a training program and inducing recruits to accept the sacrifices of going through it, the establishment of supportive relations with the dominant class, and the like (Larson, 1977, pp. 9–18, 47–8). In a rather different analysis, Kreckel casts a wider net and delineates five social mechanisms "affecting bargaining strength" between employers and employees in their dealings in the labor market (Kreckel, 1980, pp. 540–1). Occupational success in such a project may be seen, structurally, as the effective monopolization of opportunities to perform a particular bundle of tasks and, furthermore, to perform them under desirable conditions and on favorable terms. In essence, the successful occupation establishes an "exclusionary social closure" in the labor market (Parkin, 1979, pp. 44–73), or a "sinecure" (Collins, 1979, pp. 55–7).

The pejorative connotations of those terms, however, attest to their origin in class theory and to their concern with inequality. Such concern, I have already argued, diverts attention from the analysis of differentiation that is intrinsic to the concept of occupation. Indeed, both major sources of class theory – classical (or capitalist) theory stemming from Adam Smith, and critical (or socialist) theory stemming from Karl Marx – are at bottom hostile to the very idea of a stable, organized occupation. Their notions of inequality are predicated upon implicit conceptions which allow no room for the social organization by which an occupation can be stable enough to allow long-term careers for those who practice it, or to allow the possibility for an occupational community. The utopian model underlying the critique of mercantilism by classical theory is a labor market unconstrained by "combinations," a fluid market in constant motion as individuals freely compete in seeking better paying positions or opportunities. The utopian model underlying Marxist theory, while not as clearly specified, also envisages free movement among various tasks without long-term specialization in any single set of tasks. Both bodies of theory seem to share a vision of a system of perfect mobility, with a very fluid division of labor. Occupational groups are seen as conspiracies, or in any case as undesirable constraints on such fluidity. In both, it is difficult to see how complex work requiring long periods of training and practice for effective performance can be socially viable.

There is no doubt that a social closure is a conspiracy against some would-be workers. But it is also protection for those already at work and for those limited numbers they recruit into their ranks. If our emphasis is on how workers gain control over their work, however, we must consider self-protection as something more than mere conspiracy. To avoid the pejorative connotations of terms drawn from class theory to characterize the segmentation of the labor market as "sinecure" or "social closure," I would suggest the term of Marcia Freedman (1976) – "labor market shelter." Its connotation is one appropriate to the perspective of workers who not unnaturally wish to increase their economic security while continuing to practice the same work rather than having to move from one kind of work to another as externally dictated opportunity and demand dictate.

In essence, I suggest that the arena which can link the macrostructure to the microstructure is the *external* labor market that lies outside the employment and personnel policies of firms which are conceptualized in dual labor market theory as the internal labor market (see Doeringer and Piore, 1971). Furthermore and more particularly, I suggest that the mechanism which can be relatively distinct and separate from the broad stratification or class division of the external labor market, which can constrain the influence of internal labor markets, and which can be conceived of as interacting with occupational organizations is the labor market shelter. In theory, one can visualize the labor market as a collection of occupational shelters through the nature of which one can analyze in an orderly and systematic way the parameters by which we can understand both an occupation and the experience and behavior of its members. (See Caplow, 1964, pp. 142–80, for a valuable set of sketches of such shelters, though emphasizing wage theory rather than occupational organization and autonomy.)

Occupations represent the organization of productive labor into the social roles by which tasks are performed. In market economies, workers enter those social roles through the labor market, their position conditioned in capitalist economies by what Kreckel calls "primary asymmetries" between labor and capital (Kreckel, 1980, p. 529). Within that general position of relative weakness on the part of all workers, however, some are stronger than others by virtue of "secondary asymmetries," which allow them to become stable, organized groups that gain relative autonomy. In order to gain such relative strength in the market, it is essential that they gain some control over the supply of labor entering the market to perform the tasks in which they specialize, and over the substance of demand for the labor they supply. A labor market shelter represents occupational control over supply and the substance of demand. What the perfectly free market is for classical economics (see Kerr, 1950, p. 279) and perhaps for conventional stratification theory, and what the stratified market is for class theory (see Edwards, 1975), a "balkanized" labor market composed of occupationally differentiated shelters is for occupational theory.

Empirically, there are many different kinds of shelters, as is implied by the clusters found by Freedman (1976). The criteria by which discrimination is in favour of sheltered workers (and the excluded are discriminated against) are also quite variable (see Form and Huber, 1976, pp. 757–9). Since I am concerned here with identifying and following out the interaction of significant variables of occupational organization and autonomy rather than with exploring each in detail, however, I will emphasize formally negotiated shelters based on some public claim of specialized training and skill – that is, qualification (Kreckel, 1980, p. 531) – rather than those sometimes less conspicuous shelters which are created by informal and frequently publicly invisible gender, racial, ethnic, neighborhood, or kinship conspiracies. And I will more particularly emphasize the state-sanctioned quasi-monopolies to be found among some of those occupations called professions under the assumption that they will display more of the essential prerequisites and consequences of strong occupational organization than would more hidden and isolated shelters.

CONTINGENCIES OF MARKET SHELTERS

In order for an occupation to establish a monopoly, or even a lesser but stable shelter, it must in essence gain control over determining both the number and characteristics of those who can offer to provide a defined set of productive tasks for which there is a demand. Such control, however, presupposes either binding agreement by all potential consumers to use only members of the occupation for supplying a defined kind of labor (as occurs in the case of some of those occupations called crafts), or the imposition of legal controls by the polity, which either require or make it difficult for consumers to do otherwise than use only the labor of bona fide members of the occupation (as occurs in the case of some of those occupations called professions). In the former case perhaps more than the latter, the practical characteristics of the industry in which a particular occupation is employed – its seasonal character, for example, its geographic concentration or dispersion, the presence of a monopsony, or the industry's vulnerability to interruptions of production – are critical considerations. (For a provocative case study, see Zeitlin, 1979. For a more general discussion of organizational and bargaining factors bearing on shelters, see Freedman, 1976, pp. 39–65.)

In the latter case of legal controls, on the other hand, which the literature on the professions has emphasized, rather more intangible and perhaps ideological judgments figure alongside practical industrial characteristics. Restrictive licensing equally of such professions as medicine and dentistry and such occupations as barbering and tatooing seems to have depended on persuading key members of the polity that the public good would best be served by those who had a defined course of approved training thought to assure a minimally acceptable level of competence in performing a defined set of tasks (see Shimberg et al., 1973). In addition, the tasks themselves are evaluated as being of such importance to the public good that leaving them unregulated would be undesirable. Such notions of public good and functional importance to which occupations seeking support appeal, of course, must be compatible with the larger ideology connected with social control by those classes or elites which are dominant in the political economy of the society (see Larson, 1977, pp. 208–44), although it would be greatly mistaken to assume that in any complex industrial society, with all its nooks and crannies, those relations are simple, or unilateral, or functionally direct for most occupations.

A shelter in a labor market thus presupposes some method for restricting the use of a particular kind of labor by consumers. It also presupposes some method of identifying those bona fide members whose offer of labor is to be sheltered. In such organized occupations as professions and crafts, recruitment, training, and identification of competent members is largely under their control, as has sometimes also been the case for less putatively skilled occupations. Whatever the case, the modes by which members of an occupation are recruited, trained, and labeled bona fide for use by consumers are clearly important dimensions for the analysis of how a labor market shelter can be established and maintained. Recruitment, training, and placement methods also affect the quantity and quality of occupational membership, the shape of the work career, and the quality of work itself. And, by shaping the experience of the member, they also play a part in the generation and maintenance of occupational identity and commitment.

THE OCCUPATIONAL CORPORATION

Another dimension presupposed by a secure shelter in a labor market is the capacity of an occupation to negotiate collectively as an entity with either labor consumers or the polity, and to organize the institutions of recruitment, training, and work placement. This capacity presupposes at the very least some corporate organization on the part of the occupation – a union, guild, association (see Millerson, 1964), or whatever – that can be taken to represent the occupation collectively. It further presupposes a limited number of officials who can testify, lobby, and negotiate legitimately on behalf of the entire membership with the reasonable expectation that the membership will ratify and conform to any agreements reached with significant agents of the economy. The relationship of the collective membership to the formal leadership may be taken to be always problematic, however, not only because of the compromise of varied interests intrinsic to representation rather than direct participation, but also because of the division among members by varying interests due to seniority, prestige, income, and other elements of stratification present in every stable occupation, and by the varying interests and internal demarcation disputes stemming from specialization within the occupation (see Gilb, 1966). Critical to the analysis of the success or failure of an occupation to gain and maintain its shelter is the analysis of its internal stratification and segmentation, and the bearing of those cleavages on the structure of its formal organization and on the effective capacity of its leaders to undertake binding negotiations concerning its place in the labor market.

THE INDUSTRIAL DIVISION OF LABOR

Another dimension that is implied by the very notion of occupation is also critical to establishing a labor market shelter: the composition and characteristics of the division of labor in the industry or situs of which the occupation is a part, and the relation of that occupation to others in that division of labor (Morris and Murphy, 1959). To attain a strong shelter requires carving out firm demarcation boundaries – both horizontal and vertical (Kreckel, 1980, pp. 530–1) – in the face of potential overlap or encroachment on the part of contiguous occupations in a division of labor which may not be expected to accept exclusion without resistance (see Goode, 1960). Less trained occupations must be prevented from being able to claim automatic ascent on the basis of practical experience, thereby swelling the labor pool beyond the limits of security, just as puddlers attempted to prevent helpers from ascending to their position in the US steel industry (Elbaum and Wilkinson, 1979, pp. 288–9), while occupations with similar tasks and skills must be either firmly excluded or, as medicine dealt with pharmacy, securely coopted (see Kronus, 1976). Most powerful and secure is the uncommon but typologically valuable position of being dominant in a division of labor; that is, of ordering and coordinating the technical tasks of other occupations (Freidson, 1970). In coping with these issues, both the organization and the content of the division of labor, as well as the number of occupations composing it, may be taken to be variables which have important bearing on the possibility of both establishing a secure shelter in a labor market and maintaining it successfully. Part of the efforts of a successful leadership must address the relation of its members to those of other occupations composing the division of labor of which they are part, and negotiate secure jurisdictional boundaries within it (e.g., Akers, 1968; Orzack, 1977).

TASK, SKILL, AND THEIR CONTINGENCIES

The dimensions I have discussed thus far are directly connected with the process of establishing a stable place for an occupation in an economy. Insofar as they refer to the occupation's relations to the sources of ultimate control of the polity in general and the political economy in particular, they also link the occupation with the larger class system and the firms of the industry in which it works. Those dimensions are not adequate in themselves for explaining satisfactorily the organization that an occupation has or has not gained, however, for they tend to gloss over both the task and its technical contingencies, as well as the social relations of task that are generic to occupation and give it a place in industry. They furthermore gloss over the characteristics of the settings in which work actually takes place, and therefore do not provide adequate linkage between the general agreements constituting the macrostructure and the everyday life of the real people who actually perform productive labor. Without such linkage, we might be able to understand how work gets organized in a general and formal way, but we could not understand how and why it gets done in a particular way; we could chart how an occupation is organized formally, but we could not understand the source and nature of the cleavages and threats that weaken that organization, nor could we link occupation to the everyday experience of its members.

Task forms the link between organization and experience, and must be a key dimension of analysis. However, it is so laden with ambiguities as to present formidable obstacles to any fully satisfactory method of analysis. One problem with it as a variable lies in the fact that, except in the most extremely detailed division of labor, members of occupations perform a *set* of tasks rather than merely a single task (Hughes, 1971). The ambiguities of the set of tasks of even such presumably concrete manual occupations as glazier, metal-worker, and the like may be seen clearly by inspection of the "Green Book" which collates the agreements arising out of jurisdictional disputes among occupations in the construction trades (e.g., Building Trades Employers' Association, 1973). Ambiguous or not, we cannot avoid the necessity of delineating occupation in part by its tasks, and of accepting those tasks as in some sense objectively determinable even though we must recognize that the choice of tasks to emphasize and the evaluation of tasks are inevitably arbitrary and may rest on an ideological foundation (see Jamous and Peloille, 1970). Of importance for negotiating a secure shelter in a broader occupational division of labor is the capacity to single out for emphasis concrete tasks by which encroachment can be unequivocally identified – as medicine can single out and monopolize prescribing controlled drugs and cutting into the body, for example, but cannot single out "counselling" or "diagnosing." In the absence of defensibly concrete delineation of an exclusive task, an occupation can only defend the exclusive right to a title or a place on a register.

Equally important as defensible delineation of task is the claim that the task is of such a character that only members of the occupation possess the skill or qualification, by virtue of their occupational training, to perform it properly and reliably. It is difficult to sustain a claim to the exclusive right to perform a task that anyone might perform just as well. But while there can be no doubt that skill and prior training or experience play some irreducible part in the capacity to do many kinds of specialized work, the problem is that their part is so overlain with social claims and meanings that the precise outline of the irreducible contribution of skill and prior training and experience is always likely to be somewhat unclear.

Workers have to know more and do more on a job than outsiders and superordinates are inclined to believe (e.g., Kusterer, 1978). But so are workers also inclined to exaggerate the amount of knowledge, skill, and judgment that is involved in some of their everyday work (see Freidson, 1988). Like task, we must treat skill, training, and prior experience as *claims* which have indeterminate truth value, but which figure significantly nonetheless in the negotiation of shelters and in the interaction of members of an occupation with superordinates, members of contiguous occupations, and clients. From the lessons taught by the historic crafts and professions, we may presume that one condition for successful formal organization is gaining acceptance of claims to the unique qualification of members to perform important kinds of tasks requiring specially trained, esoteric skill.

By naming the tasks of an occupation, and the skill and training said to be prerequisite for their performance, one can begin to delineate the substance of the industry in which it works, its place in the division of labor of that industry, and some of the sources of its success or failure at generating an organized labor market shelter. Additional understanding of the character of its shelter stems from examining the contingencies connected with those tasks and skills. The technical contingencies of task – such as the problems of work stemming from the nature of the physical materials on which work must be done, and from the available tools and knowledge by which work must be done – not only define some of the problems of performing work, but also are invoked by workers to legitimize both their sheltered position as specially trained persons, and their resistance to the use of precise and simple criteria by which to govern the supervision and evaluation of their work (see Jamous and Peloille, 1970).

Apart from the technical contingencies of task, there are also what might be called the social contingencies or *the social relations of task*. They are linked with technical contingencies insofar as the task requires parallel or complementary tasks performed by other workers, and they are intrinsic to tasks which "technically" involve working on human beings or providing them with services. To go into detail about the social relations of occupations' tasks is not possible here, particularly since a large body of empirical material on those social relations and their variations has been built up by case studies of "industrial relations" and by those following the work of Hughes in studying individual occupations (Hughes, 1971). For the actual analysis of a real occupation, however, details are precisely what is necessary in order to build up a picture of what members of an occupation must cope with during the course of their work, how work is actually performed, and how attitudes toward work, occupation, labor consumers, and others are built up independently of formal training, the broad outlines of the occupation's shelter, and formal occupational ideology. They can also go far toward explaining rank-and-file deviation from the agreements and understandings of the formal leaders of their occupational organization by revealing the grounds of experience at work on which differences get generated.

Everyday work life is not uniform, for what is in theory the same set of tasks for many occupations is practiced in a variety of settings in which the social and even the technical contingencies of task can vary, and in which the actual substance of tasks chosen out of the whole repertory claimed by the occupation can vary. Part of this variation is a function of differentiation into specialities and segments within a complex occupation (see Bucher and Strauss, 1961), but part also is a function of differences among different work settings serving different labor consumers with different powers (see Strauss et al., 1964; Laumann and Heinz, 1979). In fact, within any reasonably large and complex occupation there are likely to be major divisions among the membership reflecting the fact that work goes on in distinctly different kinds of settings, with different social contingencies of task. Having to cope with different technical and social contingencies in different work settings, plus having to perform different tasks for labor consumers of different powers and needs, creates deeply felt differences in work experience and interest which can pose a serious challenge to the unity of the occupation and therefore its capacity to maintain its shelter in the face of occupational encroachment or consumer initiatives.

Variations in the social contingencies of task may also be seen to influence the degree and type of shelter an occupation can attain. When labor consumers are composed of a large number of heterogeneous and unorganized individuals, as is the case for medical patients, for example, the occupation can more easily organize itself for its own ends (see Johnson, 1972, p. 51). When, on the other hand, the consumers are rather few in number and powerful and knowledgeable as well, it is less likely for an occupation to be able to organize itself, though a monopsonist can deliberately choose to provide an occupation with a monopoly (Lees, 1966, p. 13), even if not allow it to pursue goals of which it disapproves. Surely the predominately corporate consumers of engineering services have something to do with the weak organization of the "profession" in comparison with that of medicine (see Larson, 1977, pp. 19–31).

THE SOCIAL PSYCHOLOGY OF OCCUPATIONAL MEMBERSHIP

Thus far, I have dealt with a number of well-known dimensions of occupational analysis, showing how it is possible to deal with them systematically by connecting them more or less directly with the process by which a labor market shelter is created and maintained by an organized occupation claiming jurisdiction over a particular set of tasks, practiced in particular settings with particular contingencies. I assume enough has been said to show how it is possible to make sense both of an organized occupation's relation to the macrostructure and of the patterned character of its members' experience and performance at work. It remains to show how those dimensions interact with the social psychology of occupational membership.

In essence, it can be argued that the labor market shelter of an occupation provides the structural resource by which the "absorptiveness" of an occupation (Kanter, 1977, pp. 25–30) can be established and sustained, and by which the member's identity, commitment, and solidarity can be understood. A primary structural resource is established by an occupational organization when it secures a shelter in the labor market. Once that shelter is given, and labor supply maintained advantageously in relation to labor demand, those who become members of the occupation can count on a relatively secure life career of performing the work of that occupation. This possibility alone tends to generate identification with the occupation on the part of its members; the frequent necessity of investing time and money in a special course of training established by the occupation intensifies the likelihood (see Becker and Carper, 1956). Only when one can count on performing it for a considerable period of time is it likely that the work of an occupation can become a "central life-interest" (Dubin et al., 1976), that the occupation can become a source of personal identity, and that its members can develop some sense of common occupational experience, identity, and interest, some "occupational community" (Salaman, 1974).

As in the case of the other dimensions, it is not possible to dwell on any detail here, but surely a labor market shelter which permits the life-long practice of a particular kind of work with some modicum of security and dignity (but by no means necessarily a high income) provides the "orderly career" which encourages commitment to both the occupation and its particular work. At the very least, it creates vested economic interest in the occupation's shelter and its defense, an interest shared with other members of the occupation and expressed as "solidarism" in collective action (see Kreckel, 1980, pp. 540–1). In the case of the historic crafts and professions, it has also on occasion sustained interest in the intrinsic rewards of the work itself, a preoccupation with the extension and refinement of knowledge and technique, and a sense of responsibility for their integrity (Carr-Saunders and Wilson, 1933, pp. 284–8) or, as Mills (1951) put it, an "ethic of craftsmanship." However rare such an ethic may be, and however vulnerable to economic interest, it is difficult to imagine it to be equally common among those participating in transient and unorganized occupations. Similarly, while we would expect the latter to feel alienated from their work, it is possible to imagine sheltered occupations to manifest *commitment* to their work.

While its mere existence is insufficient ground for explaining attitudes to work and the quality of work performance, it can be hypothesized that a shelter *permits* the development of commitments and interests that other features of occupational organization and task-performance may then actually stimulate and facilitate. The shelter may thus be seen to be at once part of the broad political economy of a complex industrial society – a special niche defining the boundaries of opportunity for members of an occupation in the labor market of that political economy – and the conditioning ground for the interaction among workers over their problems of work which establishes their consciousness, identity, commitment, and performance as they seek autonomy in the market at large, and in the concrete settings in which they perform their work.

By focusing on shelters, we establish systematic linkage between macrostructure and microstructure, and also preserve the conception of occupation as something more than mere job titles in a firm, or mere particles of class, correlates of income and education, vehicles for social mobility. Occupation can be treated *sui generis* as activities around which groups can be formed as their members seek autonomy and control over their particular and distinctive work. The variety of occupations can be conceived of as a variety of successes and failures in their "market project," some being creatures solely of their employers' demands, others gaining shelters of varying degrees of autonomy. Analysis of the conditions for success and failure links together the conventional variables of occupational analysis which have for far too long remained disconnected.

PART III

PROPHESYING THE FUTURE OF THE PROFESSIONS

6

Professionalization and the Organization of Middle-Class Labor in Post-Industrial Society

Every generation considers itself to be new and modern. And this is proper, for the contemporary is by definition what is only just being experienced in the knife-edge of the present. The problem for the participant and the analyst alike, however, is to determine whether the present is "really" new and modern, or whether it is, as the elderly are characteristically inclined to believe, just variation on settled and familiar themes. If it is merely the latter, then there is no serious point to changing our way of looking at the present or of assuming that it is leading us toward some qualitatively different future. But if it is the former, then we must ask what the genuinely new means for the future – whether it is part of a trend which leads to far-reaching shifts of emphasis in basic social institutions, or whether it is an isolated event. And if it appears to be part of a distinct trend, we must, as scholars and scientists, examine the value of our conceptual equipment for analyzing it. Unfortunately, our conceptual equipment at any particular time is far more likely to be useful for ordering the past events it was created to deal with than it is for understanding genuinely new events of the present or the future.

Our own time seems to be one in which something genuinely new is emerging. Many analysts believe that major changes are taking place in the most advanced industrial societies. Those changes are seen to be as basic and far-reaching as those which occurred two hundred years ago and which are now summed up as the Industrial Revolution. Various writers have struggled to find an appropriate name for the emergent society, but it seems to me that until future historians, from their more advantageous, backward-looking perspective, create and agree on their own epithet, Bell's term "post-industrial" is the most useful, avoiding neologism while at the same time connoting departure from the society we know (Bell, 1967). I shall use it throughout this paper.

But while many analysts seem agreed that what is new and modern in our time is something with profound consequences for the nature of society, their discussions remain fixed on substance. They are not concerned about the abstract analytical implications of those changes for the basic sociological concepts we have used to analyse the mechanisms ordering industrial society. These analysts discuss technology, including data-processing, automation, and communications, they discuss its foundation in "technique" and special knowledge, and they discuss the economy, but they do not consider the social forms by which all will be organized and dispensed. They pay little attention to social organization, apparently assuming that traditional forms will persist. But if change is to be so radical, should we expect that our present received concepts of social organization are of such universal pertinence that they can be applied without question? Is it not quite plausible that habits of thought, strategies, foci, and concepts developed for the analysis of industrial society may *not* be equally useful and well-fitted to the analysis of post-industrial society?

I shall argue in this paper that *if* what is being said about post-industrial society is true, then very basic sociological concepts for the analysis of the social organization of work must be reconsidered. One of the most basic of such concepts is that of the division of labor and, particularly, the principle of authority which establishes, coordinates, and controls specialized labor. Since the Industrial Revolution, administrative authority has been emphasized. However, in this paper I wish to suggest that a key to concepts better fitted to the emergent new society lies in the logic embedded in the concept of professionalization, which stresses a different principle of authority over labor. To show this, I shall briefly review what most writers agree are the important characteristics of the emergent society. Next, I shall point out what this view implies about the usefulness of what is by now our almost instinctive reliance on the concepts of administrative authority forged for the analysis of industrial society. Then I shall discuss how the concept of the authority of institutionalized expertise implicit in the idea of professionalization may prove far more useful and fitting than the traditional concept of rational-legal administrative authority.

THE PROTOTYPICAL POST-INDUSTRIAL WORKER

Some of the elements of the post-industrial society are predicated on the assumption that the trends of the past few decades will continue and even accelerate until a basic point of balance is passed. In this situation, formerly minor segments of the work-force will become critical. The decline of agricultural labor and the rise of industrial labor created such a change of balance between types of workers in the development of industrial society. In the present day, prophets note the decline of industrial or manu-facturing labor as a trend indicating that future workers will be engaged primarily in clerical, sales, and service work (Fuchs, 1966). Massive as the manufacturing or industrial base of the society will remain, its labor requirements will both decline and change, as machines tend themselves and other machines, and as the demand for highly trained labor expands while that for unskilled and semi-skilled labor contracts. Just as men are still engaged in agricultural work now in advanced industrial society, so will men still be engaged in manufacturing in the future, but the bulk of men will be engaged in other kinds of work, and factory labor will cease to be archetypal in the emerging age.

If this redistribution occurs, who will be the archetypal worker in post-industrial society? Most writers emphasize the significance of workers practicing complex skills for which higher education is thought necessary (cf. Bell, 1968; Lane, 1966; Etzioni, 1968). Virtually all see the new society as being "knowledge-based," but some emphasize one kind of knowledge-based worker while others emphasize another. Those such as John Kenneth Galbraith (1968), who are interested in state and corporate manufacturing and commercial enterprise, emphasize the role of the expert who plans and makes decisions, and are prone in that context to use the word "technocrat" (cf. Touraine, 1971). The workers they refer to are engineers, economists, systems analysts, and specially trained managers. Others, such as Bennis (Bennis and Slater, 1968), Bell (1968), and Lane (1966), are somewhat more general, emphasizing a broad class of professional-technical workers and the educational and scientific estate (Price, 1965) which trains them and creates their knowledge. Still others, and most especially Halmos (1970), emphasize the role of the professional and semi-professional personal service worker – the teacher, physician, social worker, nurse, counsellor, and the like who are connected with the social, psychological, medical, and other "helping" services of the welfare state.

Each writer on the post-industrial society has a particular issue in mind, and so properly emphasizes one kind of worker over another. While all workers may be alike in possessing higher education, they are educated in quite different subjects and by quite different methods, they perform quite different kinds of work, and have quite different kinds of responsibility. Higher education, as such, no matter what the curriculum and the job prepared for, does not discriminate analytic differences in function as basic as that between manager and worker. That difference is the key to understanding how work gets organized. And it is also the key to discerning how post-industrial society may differ from industrial society in ways not recognized by those who stress the role of knowledge in the abstract without asking how knowledge gets organized as work.

What is the traditional difference between manager and worker? In industrial society, managers, administrators, supervisors, or other officials of the formal productive organization exercise authority over workers. They establish the organization, determine the set of tasks necessary to attain their production goals, employ, train, assign, and supervise men to perform those tasks, and coordinate the interrelations of the various tasks so as to gain their ends. The worker, on the other hand, is the one who performs those directly productive tasks which have been organized, supervised, and coordinated by the manager. It is this by-now self-evident distinction which becomes problematic in the post-industrial society.

What is of great importance about the forecasts of post-industrial labor is that they imply that large numbers of the prototypical "knowledge-based" tasks are *productive* rather than managerial. Research scientists, teachers, and physicians, for example, characteristically perform a kind of productive labor, even if the labor is not necessarily manual and oriented to the production of services rather than goods. In contrast, other knowledge-based workers perform managerial functions, setting up frameworks of authority and communication to facilitate the performance of labor. Each has a generically different function, the task of one being to organize the labor of the other. What is different in the forecasts of the post-industrial society is that they imply that *the capacity of managers to control the productive workers* is open to serious question in ways that have not really existed in industrial society.

In industrial society, the prototypical productive worker – the lower-class factory hand – is ordered and controlled ever more systematically by management. But the prototypical productive worker of the post-industrial society – the middle-class knowledge-based worker – may be in a position to resist much managerial authority and control. Even now, the ambiguous position of knowledge-based productive labor in the present conventional industrial scheme of administration is mirrored by its anomalous classification as "staff" rather than as "line." The *jobs* or organizational positions are dependent on management for capital, supportive services, and at least some lines of communication, but the *tasks* of these workers are not. Their tasks are not created by or dependent on management, nor are the qualifications to perform them so dependent. Finally, evaluation of the performance of those tasks does not rest solely with management.

In essence, the prototypical worker of industrial society operates clearly and unambiguously under the authority of management, but the proto-typical workers of post-industrial society may work in a radically differ-ent way which limits seriously the traditional authority of management. Whereas thirty or forty years ago one could talk of the "revolution" whereby management took authority from the owner (Burnham, 1960), writers such as Galbraith can now write that the "technostructure ... not management, is the guiding intelligence – the brain – of the [business] enterprise" (Galbraith, 1968, p. 82). Being the brain is not the same thing as setting goals and being in charge, but it does make the authority of management problematic. In earlier industrial enterprises, management was the brain as well as the authority.

THE LIMITATION OF MANAGERIAL RATIONALIZATION

Apparently, neither the tasks nor the status of these post-industrial workers seem amenable to the kind of rationalization that was applied by management to the factory line worker in industrial society. Indeed, it is precisely crisis in managerial rationalization and control (cf. Berkley, 1971) which prophets of a new society imply when they point to the emergence of a growing collection of increasingly strategic productive workers whose comparatively abstract skills require long training and are surrounded by a mystique of the esoteric and the complex. Those strategic skills are of such a nature that they resist managerial rational-ization as manual and clerical skills have not been able to do. They do so in part because of their intrinsically complex character, but even more because of the occupational organization which grows up around them. Their occupational organization is a function of professional socialization rather than on-the-job training. Some of the motivation to identification with institutionalized skills and to solidarity with colleagues stems from the requirement of a long period of formal education. Long training is a socially, economically, and psychologically costly investment which vir-tually presupposes expectation of a stable life-long career, and fairly extensive bonds and common interests shared with others going through the same process. Higher vocational education does not merely insert "knowledge" into people's heads, but also builds expectations and com-mitments not easily overcome by managerial or policy rationalization. Organized specialized occupational identities get constructed. Knowl-edge gets institutionalized as expertise. The structure of meanings and commitments can override organizational goals or commitments.

The sociological rather than merely technical or economic significance of a long period of training in putatively complex and abstract skills –

that is, of "knowledge-based" skill – lies in its tendency to develop institutionalized commitments on the part of those trained. Such trained workers are inclined to identify with their skill and with their fellows with the same training and skill. They are prone to develop not merely general *skill-class,* or mass solidarity, as is sometimes the case with industrial workers in trade unions, but *disciplinary* or occupational solidarity. Their skill is not merely abstractly there as a potential, but it is institutionalized as a stable discipline or occupation. Such trained workers do not constitute a class of labor which can be treated as mere hands, to perform whatever tasks management may invent of them and then train them for. Rather, they are a kind of labor with pre-existent skills for which management may have a need, but which management must take more or less as given. Their tasks are institutionalized occupationally, and thus resist simplification, fragmentation, mechanization, or some other mode of managerial rationalization of labor.

THE LIMITATION OF MANAGERIAL AUTHORITY

If it is true that a new kind of highly educated labor with specialized skills is becoming more important to the emergent society, and that the skills involved resist managerial rationalization, what are the consequences? Even now we can see some of them. The character of managerial or administrative authority which developed in the Industrial Revolution is at present experiencing such radical changes that the traditional concepts of managerial authority and formal corporate structure are being questioned. Indeed, an increasing number of writers argue that reality has deviated so far from the concepts of monocratic, "rational-legal" administration, formal organization, hierarchical order, and bureaucracy that new concepts are needed which pick out the analytically significant elements of the emergent forms of organization. Such new concepts must, of course, perform the same analytical function as traditional ones, the most important of which is to specify the nature and source of the control and coordination of various kinds of specialized labor so that some productive goal can be reached. If traditional managerial or administrative authority has lost much of its strength, but specialization and division of labor continue unabated, what does organize labor and how is it coordinated? This question has barely been considered by writers on the post-industrial society other than on the very broad and vague level of societal or social policy goals. An answer to the question on a more concrete level is hinted at, however, by passing references to professionalization.

As I have already noted, most writers agree on the strategic importance of workers with skills requiring long formal education, skills rather more esoteric and abstract than the manual and clerical skills organized and even imparted by management in the past. The problem is how, if not by management, such special skills get organized and coordinated. A number of writers have implied the answer. Ellul wrote, "technique always creates a kind of secret society, a closed fraternity of its practitioners" (Ellul, 1964, p. 162). Skill can form the focus, in short, of an occupational group which then claims the authority of its institutionalized expertise over the performance of its work. This tendency is recognized by Galbraith in his observation that men of the technostructure are inclined to identify them-selves with their department or function rather than with the corporation as a whole (Galbraith, 1968, pp. 162–8) and by Bennis in his delineation of "pseudo-species" as "bands of specialists held together by the illusion of a unique identity and with a tendency to view other pseudo-species with suspicion and mistrust" (Bennis and Slater, 1968, p. 66). The sugges-tions all point to the development of solidarity among workers practicing the same specialized skill, an organized solidarity strong enough to resist the pressure toward integration and rationalization exerted by manage-ment. The solidarity is of specialty, as discussed by Durkheim (1964), not of skill-class. Such solidarity suggests that professionalization will be a critical element in the organization of production in post-industrial society.

"Profession," "professionalization," and "professional" are all extremely ambiguous words, much of their stubborn imprecision hinging on their confusing and sometimes incompatible multiple connotations. But there is no other word in the English language which can be used to represent an occupation so well organized that its members can realistically envis-age a career over most of their working years, a career during which they retain a particular occupational identity and continue to practice the same skills no matter in what institution they work. A similar form of organ-ization is to be found in the skilled trade or craft, though the craft cannot claim the same kind of knowledge-based skill as can the profession.

Such organized occupations can be contrasted with traditional indus-trial labor. As opposed to organized occupations with concrete and par-ticular identity, much industrial labor revolves around forms of work which are rather more appropriately called jobs or positions than occu-pations, since they are merely specially constituted tasks in a division of labor created, coordinated, and controlled by management. Those jobs are created, dissolved, and reconstituted by management on the basis of changing production goals or needs, changing technology, or further rationalization for the end of greater productivity or lower cost. They have no social or economic foundation for their persistence beyond the plants, agencies, or firms in which they exist. The persons performing concrete tasks constituted as jobs may not perform them for long, since the job can get eliminated or reconstituted. The workers are identified primarily by the general substance and level of their skill – e.g., manual or clerical, unskilled or semi-skilled or skilled – and if they are organized into such corporate associations as unions, it is more on the basis of industry or skill-class than on the basis of substantive skill and training. Such labor organizations are far more concerned with wages, working conditions, job security, and advancement than with control over tasks constituting jobs.

For industrially organized workers the substance of the work and who can do it are established and controlled by the manager or administrator. Tasks are planned around some managerial goal and men hired and trained to perform them. This is the norm for the way the Industrial Revolution has, historically, rationalized labor by first dissolving pre-industrial functional differentiation by craft and land, and then reorganizing the labor of massed, undifferentiated workers around managerial authority. But workers organized by professional or craft associations both now and in the past establish and control the substance of their work as well as who can do it. Specialized fragments of the labor market split off and become organized and stabilized around tasks which the workers have institutionalized (cf. Kerr, 1954). Organized occupations such as professions and crafts which institutionalize specialization are at once a survival and a revival of pre-industrial modes of organizing work. They are alternatives to administrative rationalization.

The key to assessing whether or not the organized occupation will gain even more strength in the future society is the degree to which all work can be rationalized and therefore reconstituted and controlled by management. It seems to be implicit in discussions of the prototypical worker of the post-industrial society that knowledge-based work, the work of middle-class experts, professionals, and technicians, is by its very nature *not* amenable to the mechanization and rationalization which industrial production and commerce have undergone over the past century. If it is true that management cannot rationalize such work – whether for technological, economic, political-legal, or even ideological or class reasons – then it can only maintain an administrative framework around it. Management remains dependent for attaining its goals on the worker but is really unable to control who performs the work and how it is done. Instead of an industrial bureaucratic structure, with authority organized vertically, management can only organize supportive services vertically, leaving authority over the work to the workers themselves. Management may set goals, but it may not set means or connect means to goals.

COORDINATION OF THE DIVISION OF LABOR

But if management cannot exercise much authority over task, how are varied tasks coordinated? How is the division of labor organized? Traditionally, the division of labor has been seen as a purely functional array of interdependent tasks performed by an aggregate of individuals possessing the necessary skills. For Adam Smith, the division of labor meant individual men competing with each other for employment to perform more or less abstractly conceived specialized and interdependent tasks. Coordination of all tasks was supposed to take place in part by the natural operation of the forces of the free market and in part, albeit implicitly, by entrepreneurs who invent cheaper ways of producing goods. Any explicit social combination of the participants in the division of labor was considered unnatural. But in reality, if only out of economic self-interest, both labor and capital were prone to organize into combinations designed to influence the labor market in ways that aggregates of competing individuals could not. While Smith's *concept* of the division of labor ruled out social organization, in the historical *reality* of the Industrial Revolution the division of labor has been continuously subject to socially organized forces and has never been a merely technical arrangement of specialized, interdependent tasks. Empirically, we must treat the division of labor as a social organization.

Historically, the social organization of the division of labor has been constituted by interaction between two radically different ways of organizing the human labor necessary to perform interdependent tasks, and of defining the tasks themselves. The common terms "bureaucratization" and "professionalization" denote, albeit crudely, those two different modes of organization. In the former case, the character of the task, who will perform it, the way it is performed and evaluated, and the way it will be related to others is created by management. The worker is recruited and organized to perform it. The worker and his labor are mere plastic materials for management, materials organized into jobs by managerial conceptions of the tasks necessary for the production of some good or service for the market. This mode of organizing the division of labor is implicit in Smith, and it is the mode characteristic of industrial society. Coordination of the division of labor in an industrial organization can easily be seen as a function of managerial or bureaucratic authority. In the case of professionalization, however, the task, who is to perform it, and the way it is performed and evaluated is controlled by the men who actually perform the productive labor. Labor is organized into specialized occupations which control their own tasks, and the division of labor is constituted as a congeries of such organized occupations. In this case, however, the mechanism by which the work of the various occupations is co-ordinated appears problematic. How can any regulation exist *between* occupations without the monocratic authority of management?

If, as is characteristically the case for *industrial* labor, the authority for the definition of tasks and their organization into jobs lies in manage-ment, then the division of labor can be seen to be constituted by the jobs which management creates, defines, and maintains. Managerial authority coordinates the relationships between the productive tasks accomplished by every job. Bureaucratization refers to a monocratic ordering of func-tions into jobs governed by particular rational-legal rules. If, on the other hand, as may characteristically be the case for *post-industrial* society, the authority for definition and organization of task comes from the proto-typical workers themselves, then the division of labor must be seen to be constituted by the occupations into which work is organized and the relationship between occupations defined and ordered by the jurisdictions established among occupations. Those jurisdictions can be established in a variety of ways, the most formal being by exclusive licensing and by contract.

Occupational jurisdictions must be seen as establishing the boundaries of institutionalized tasks and also, what is often overlooked, the occupa-tional authority to coordinate interrelated tasks. They establish, in short, their own species of hierarchical authority in the division of labor, au-thority predicated on institutionalized expertise rather than on that of bureaucratic office. Such authority gives some occupations the legitimate right to command the work of other occupations. Even now, as a class, the professions provide examples of how a structure of occupations can be ordered and coordinated hierarchically by the authority of institution-alized expertise. Medicine, for example, gives orders to a wide variety of other workers in an interdependent technical enterprise, and does so even when those workers are in the employ of others. In medicine, the division of labor is ordered and coordinated by a dominant profession rather than by management (Freidson, 1970). The division of labor thus does not need management for its coordination; an at least logically possible alter-native to management exists in the form of the occupational principle of authority over work (Freidson, 1973). Prophecies of post-industrial society suggest that there is a very real empirical possibility that the new division of labor may in fact require a shift from managerial to occupational authority.

THE SOCIAL ROLE OF KNOWLEDGE

In this paper I have argued that *if* the "knowledge-based" worker is to be prototypical in the post-industrial society, then concepts of the mechanisms by which productive labor is organized, controlled, and co-ordinated must be examined closely. I suggested that the prime mechanism of the Industrial Revolution was administrative or bureaucratic authority, the strength of which was predicated on its capacity to rationalize tasks into jobs for which it could itself mobilize and train labor. "Knowledge-based" labor, however, may be resistant to rationalization both by the very nature of the skill and knowledge it possesses, and by its tendency to organize itself into stable occupations similar to those of present-day professions. Indeed, I suggested that the mechanism for organizing, controlling, and even coordinating specialized labor to be found among professions today – the authority of institutionalized expertise – may be far more useful for visualizing the substance of the Post-industrial Revolution than reliance on now-traditional notions of rational-legal authority and bureaucracy.

Underlying the analysis in this paper is the assumption that knowledge is a problematic concept with implications which cannot be seen clearly until translated into human activity – into men who are recruited, trained, and then led to engage in the work of producing, communicating, or practicing knowledge, technique, or skill. It is assumed, furthermore, that work is analyzed inadequately if it is seen as an individual activity, that when more than one person does the same work, the possibility exists that the aggregate of workers will form a group. Should this occur, the purely rational, functional, technical quality thought to inhere in the work itself becomes incorporated into and transformed by a social, political, and economic enterprise. It loses its abstract purity and maybe even its virtue. Thus, whether or not one sees hope for a future in which "knowledge" becomes the critical guiding force of post-industrial society depends on how one can visualize the ways in which the use of that knowledge is likely to be organized and controlled.

7

The Futures of Professionalization[1]

Until very recently, it was common for some of the most notable scholars of the day to emphasize the importance of professions in modern society, and to consider professionalization to be a major social movement, transforming both society and the nature of work. Before the turn of the century, Spencer expatiated on the way in which professions augmented human life (Spencer, 1896). Almost sixty years ago the Webbs discussed professional associations as one form of "Associations of Producers" (in contrast to associations of consumers) which might provide a viable alternative to capitalistic forms of productive organization (Webb and Webb, 1917). Shortly afterwards, R. H. Tawney (1920, pp. 91–122) urged the nationalization of British industry so as to "professionalize" it, with all workers assuming responsibility for the quality of their work. In a rather different political context, Carr-Saunders (1928) pointed to the growth of professionalism as a hopeful sign of the times and, in his later work, with P. A. Wilson (Carr-Sounders and Wilson, 1933, pp. 493–4), he predicted the extension of professionalism "upwards and outwards," and the slower but continuous extension "downwards" to transform routine intellectual and manual occupations. Subsequently, T. H. Marshall (1939, pp. 325–40) noted modern society's increasing demand for professionalized services, the increasing number and type of professionals, and their changing relationship to the welfare state. By our day, Parsons (1968, p. 545) could say that "the massive emergence of the professional complex ... is the crucial structural development in twentieth-century society," and Bell (1976, p. 144) could predict that, in the emerging post-industrial society of the future, "professionals will be a major feature."

With some few and recent exceptions to be discussed later in this paper, there seems to be rather remarkable unanimity about professions

– agreement, first, that they represent a distinct kind of occupation which is of special importance to the effective and humane functioning of modern society, second, that they have been growing in number and importance throughout this century, and, third, that they will increase in number and importance in the future, into the next century. But in a very curious way we are left in limbo by such assessments and predictions, for they do not provide us with the intellectual tools by which we can connect them to concrete occupations. Indeed, when one examines such work closely, one finds sufficient confusion and contradiction in the use of the word "profession", and related words such as "professionalism" and "professionalization," so that one cannot be at all sure that Parsons, for example, refers to the same occupations as Marshall in his formulation, or that Bell refers to the same as Hughes (1971). If that is indeed the case, then the unanimity is more apparent than real, relying more on common use of the same *word* than on common agreement about what the word refers to. Thus, they may very well be at once talking to each other in general and talking past each other in particular. This makes it singularly difficult for any genuine debate to take place, and seriously handicaps the systematic accumulation of information and the refinement and elaboration of concepts characteristic of true scholarship.

We all know that there are many usages and definitions connected with the term "profession." (For one review of definitions, see Millerson, 1964, pp. 1–9.) Part of the confusion stems from the fact that people are often prone to use the word as a means of flattering themselves and others (cf. Becker, 1970, pp. 87–103). Another source of confusion lies in the fact that the word is used to refer both to concrete historical occupations and to an intellectual construct or ideal type, without consistent attention to the relationship between the two. And finally, an often unrecognized source of confusion lies in the fact that some analysts employ the term to characterize a broad social stratum including many occupations, while others use it to characterize particular occupations. Indeed, the word may be so hopelessly corrupted that its use is a positive handicap to the development of systematic concepts for the study of work and its organization (cf. Habenstein, 1963, pp. 291–300). No matter what one may wish, the problem cannot be solved by banning the use of the word: it is too well entrenched in the language of too many to be dropped out of sociological usage. Nor can the problem be solved by legislating academic usage: even if the power to legislate and enforce usage existed, there is no generally agreed conceptual rationale to justify dictating one usage rather than another. We are on our own, for better or for worse. What can be done? How can we assess the future of professionalization?

It may be that our difficulties can be at least tempered by a more considered approach to the issues of usage – that is, by being more aware of how referents change from one usage to another, and what the implications of different usages are for what we are trying to talk about. This is not to suggest that any solution lies in mere review of various definitions, for the reviews of the past do not seem to have helped much. They have not helped much, I believe, because they have attempted to review and then adjudicate the importance of all of the traits or attributes imputed to professions, treating those attributes as additive rather than parts of a system (cf. Johnson, 1972, p. 23ff.). Past concern has been more with the precise traits by which to characterize a profession than with close examination of the empirical referents and theoretical implications of any single trait, and the relation of one trait to another. The issues involved in the concept of profession, I believe, can be better clarified by examining one variable or attribute at a time, particularly those implied by some of the most common denotations of the word. Taken one at a time, they can also be used by extrapolation from their past and present distribution to trace the future of professions and professionalization. This is what I shall do here, hoping both to clarify the implications of various definitions and usages, and to facilitate the task of making sense of the contradictory readings of the future of professionalization.

Because professions do not exist in isolation from other occupations, it seems appropriate to begin the discussion with the broadest usage of the term, a usage which in essence defines both what is bona fide work, and who is a bona fide worker: it defines the boundaries of the labor force itself. Following that discussion, I will discuss attempts to define professions as a particular stratum of the labor force. The ambiguities of that definition will then lead me to discuss professions as special kinds of status groups – as organizations of workers who have gained a monopoly over the right to control their own labor. The discussion of profession as occupational monopoly will then be used as the conceptual resource by which to make sense of social psychological conceptions of professions as being composed of workers who are somehow especially dedicated or committed. Finally, I shall conclude by reassessing both the problem of defining and studying professions and the problem of predicting their future.

THE FUTURE OF MARKET-RELATED LABOR

The broadest and most general use of the word "profession" is built upon the distinction between "professional" and "amateur." In that contrast, one can see the "amateur" as one who performs a given set of tasks without conscious and calculating concern for their exchange value in the market, and the "professional" as one who performs them in a contracted market exchange by which he gains his living. In that usage, the word "profession" is a synonym of both "occupation" and "vocation" in English, and corresponds to the general usage of *Beruf* in German[2] and *profession* in French. Performing market-related labor for one's living is one's professional vocation, while performing labor unconnected with a market is one's amateur avocation.

Simplistic and primitive as it may seem, the distinction is one that establishes relatively clear boundaries between a) what is to be defined as work or labor and what is not, and b) who is to be defined as a bona fide worker and who not. Essentially, it defines work or labor as any regular activity with an exchange value. Neither the intrinsic character of the activity itself, nor the skill its performance requires, nor the physical exertion expended during its performance is salient to distinguishing professional from amateur or work from non-work. Nor does the social role involved in the activity (cf. Hall, 1975, pp. 3–7) discriminate professional from amateur. The same activity, involving the same social relations among performers, can be undertaken by either professional or amateur. What makes the activity "work" is its exchange value. What makes a performer a "worker" or a "professional" is his relationship to the market. Activities not undertaken in the context of the market may not therefore be defined as work by this definition, nor may those who perform for the intrinsic pleasure of performance or for the admiration and gratitude of others be defined as "professionals" or as "workers."

This lay distinction between professional and amateur, employing participation in the labor market as its essential criterion, also constitutes, at bottom, the foundation for official delineations of the labor force or the working force in most advanced industrial societies (Jaffe, 1968, pp. 469–4). In this sense, one meaning of "professionalization" may be said to be the process by which increasing proportions of the population come to be part of the officially defined labor force – the process by which fewer and fewer members of a population come to perform activities for the pleasure derived from their performance, for the benefit it provides others, or for the gratitude or admiration of others, and more and more come to perform them for the income it provides. Certainly there is little doubt about the very broad past trend of increase in such professionalization as capitalism has transformed the world. A large number of tasks which were originally performed on a voluntary basis by amateurs or performed for personal or household use rather than for a market are now performed by full-time workers who gain their living thereby. Thus, the trend has been toward the professionalization of tasks (cf. Mincer, 1968).

But can we project that trend into the future and forecast still more professionalization? That question is very difficult to answer, for past changes have been by no means unilinear. First, we might remember that many women and children were members of the labor force in the nineteenth century, but were later removed from factory jobs and sent back to the household or to newly constituted schools. Historically, women are *returning* to the officially defined labor force. Second, we might remember that a significant proportion of the population in such countries as the United States has in effect dropped or been dropped out of the labor force, to be underemployed or unemployed wards of the welfare state – a status that is neither amateur nor professional. Third, we must remember that, as the cost of labor has increased in most industrial countries, a number of activities that were once performed by market-related labor have been reverting back to the amateur. In some cases, economic necessity alone has motivated people to do-it-themselves; in others, a distinct ideology of self-help has encouraged people to do their own work (if we can call it work when it is technically an avocation).

The trends, in short, are very complex. What we can say of the future cannot be predicated realistically on any simple notion that one can take a finite universe of tasks and project a trend of their "professionalization." Some tasks will disappear entirely, others will be merged into new combinations, others will be returned to amateurs working alone or with others, and still others will leave the hands of amateurs and be professionalized. On balance, it does not seem to me that one can make any prophecy based on a quantitative trend toward more or less market-related labor in the future, if only because of the analytical difficulties inherent in the criterion of market relations, difficulties compounded by non-market factors introduced by the welfare state and state socialism.

Diagnostic evidence of the limitations of the concept of market-related labor may be found in the contemporary cases of two large groups of people who perform often arduous tasks of generally recognized social value, but who neither enter the labor market in order to perform those tasks, nor enter into an economic exchange relationship with another as a condition for performing those tasks. I refer to housewives and to volunteer workers. In the strict sense of the distinction I have been discussing here, such persons are not working when they perform their tasks, nor are they to be identified as members of the labor force. They are amateurs rather than professionals, and while they may occupy themselves and identify themselves by such tasks, their tasks may not be used to delineate their occupations.[3]

This is not the place for extended discussion of either of these groups of people. Certainly the case of the housewife has been receiving a great deal of attention lately, and the anomalies and inequities of her position should be familiar to most by now (cf. Oakley, 1974). It is clear that she "works" but is not identified as a worker, and that her tasks have great use-value but no market-value in the household in which they are performed. Her tasks may not be called hobbies, nor may they be said to be leisure pursuits. They do involve productive as well as consumption functions, but by market criteria neither are they work nor may she be said to be employed, to have an occupation or profession.

An equal, perhaps even greater challenge to the utility of a market definition of labor for sociological analysis may be found in the case of unpaid work taking place outside of the household – what is sometimes called volunteer work. In the case of volunteers, there is no need for identifying their activity as an occupation, because most of those performing volunteer tasks do so in their leisure time, and if not retired are otherwise engaged in market-related labor by which their occupations may be identified. The problem is how to identify their tasks as productive labor rather than as play or leisure. There is little doubt of the social productivity of much volunteer work. In the People's Republic of China, for example, unpaid labor mobilized and supervised by technical and political "professional" cadres had accomplished remarkable feats of public sanitation (cf. Horn, 1969). For a number of reasons, not the least among them the difficulty of financing the expansion and maintenance of public services and facilities in both capitalist and state socialist nations, such volunteer labor might remain important and even grow in the future. Whatever else, it is a constant challenge to the practice of delineating both work and profession by their relation to the market. Let us hope that the sociology of the future can meet that challenge by developing less arbitrary and more analytically satisfying criteria for distinguishing work from task, vocation from avocation and professional from amateur. Such criteria will be difficult to develop for, limited as it may be, the market criterion is parsimonious, is measured relatively easily, and refers to a phenomenon of undoubted importance.

THE FUTURE OF THE PROFESSIONAL STRATUM OF LABOR

The amateur – professional distinction defines the general categories "work" and "occupation." Beyond setting those broad boundaries, it cannot discriminate among types of work or types of occupation. Most sociological literature takes the market definition of work and of occupation as given and then proceeds to discriminate types of work and occupation within the officially defined labor force. Very common in the macro-sociological literature is reference to a specific "class" of professionals as a stratum of the labor force, which is treated as synonymous with society at large. To define that class, use is made of either or both of two characteristics, both of which are measured by reference to official statistics.

The first characteristic – years of formal education required for employment in particular jobs – has been used both by those concerned with the professional "class" in contemporary society (e.g., Ben-David, 1964; Bell, 1976) and those concerned with the role of professionals in complex productive organizations (e.g., Blau and Schoenherr, 1971). Essentially, they delineate professional workers as all those whose work is considered by employers to require four years of post-secondary education. In this sense, "professionalization" consists in the increase of the proportion of jobs in a society which require formal higher education. There can be little doubt that a trend of such an increase has existed in the past and that, for a variety of reasons, it will continue into the future. The same may be said for the second of the two common methods of delineating "professions" as a stratum of the work-force – that which singles out a group of workers who possess special knowledge (usually distinguished as abstract and theoretical) and skill (usually characterized as requiring the exercise of complex judgment). Patently, both formal education and skill or knowledge are closely related, for the latter may be said to have been inculcated by the former, and the former may be treated as a convenient institutional measure of the latter. In any case, the proportion of professionally skilled workers has been increasing in the labor force and is likely to continue to increase in the future. Thus, by educational and skill criteria, the professionalization of the labor force will increase in the future.

The problem with both of these definitions of profession as a stratum of the labor force lies in their helpless dependence upon the governmental and managerial processes which create the categories both in official labor statistics and in managerial tables of organization. Having no direct access to the workers or their work (and indeed, concerned less with the study of the institutions of productive work than with stratification as such), both definitions are in danger of dealing with official artifacts instead of the phenomena themselves. The requirement of formal education and the skill classification of workers may reflect institutional processes more than functional necessity. What is delineated by such definitions and measures of professions may not be the strictly functional necessities for the performance of a particular class of productive labor, so much as the institutional requirements for access to particular jobs, and institutional processes for classifying such jobs for reasons unrelated to the needs of productivity. Indeed, recent analysts such as Berg (1970) have argued that educational requirements for many jobs in the United States have been inflated beyond what is necessary for their adequate performance (see Collins, 1971, pp. 1002–19). And Braverman (1974, pp. 426–35) has argued that skill-classifications of jobs have also been inflated well beyond the actual skill and judgment they require. Thus, while "professionalization" is, by measures of formal education and skill-classification, increasing, this increase may not reflect significant changes in the real education and skill required for effective productivity, may not reflect, in short, technological need for the "centrality of theoretical knowledge" so important to the rationale of Bell's delineation of post-industrial society. The definition of "profession" may thus refer more to how the powers that be in society or in productive organizations are prone to *classify* jobs than to the nature of the jobs themselves and the work experience of those who fill them.

A perhaps more serious deficiency in this usage of profession lies in the variety of occupations it includes, a variety of far-ranging and systematic differences so great that all those in the stratum cannot be seen to share anything more than higher education (no matter where or what substance) or a general skill-classification (no matter what the particular skill): nothing of any further significance is held in common. It is much too broad a classification to aid one to understand the differentiation of work and the processes of production (see Braverman, 1974, pp. 403–9). The definition includes a large minority of the labor force, including both the traditional professionals and technicians. It in fact embraces what is designated as the "professional and technical" ranks of labor in official classifications in the United States, and what is designated as the "intelligentsia" in the Soviet Union (see Churchward, 1973). It includes much if not all of what some (see Mallet, 1975; Touraine, 1971) have called the "new working class" and constitutes the growing segment of the labor force which Bell (1976, pp. 15–18) sees as the major feature of the emergent society of the future.

Even a casual look at the array of occupations included in this broad "professional" class reveals its analytical diffuseness. It includes physicians, engineers, dental technicians, clergymen, schoolteachers, reporters, nurses, airline pilots, social workers, photographers, professors, chemists, and a large and varied proportion labelled "others." So gross is the class that even Bell (1976, pp. 213ff and 375) felt obliged to stratify it internally so as to separate an internal "professional class" from "semi-professions" and technicians. What joins all those occupations together into a single professional stratum is trivial compared with the nature of the differences between many of them. Neither general level of skill imputed by employers nor the amount of formal education required by employers tells us enough to allow us to analyze and explain the markedly different life-chances and work-lives of the occupations included in it. The problem with this usage of "professional" thus lies in part in the empirically and theoretically problematic character of the criteria of formal education and imputed skill, but also no less importantly in the analytical limitations of class analysis itself. Class analysis is simply too gross to analyze the division of labor and the institutions of production in a society. To understand better the division of labor and the institutions of production, and to understand the crucial differences *among* occupations, I believe, requires instead an emphasis on the degree to which they, as occupations rather than classes, have gained the organized power to control themselves the terms, conditions, and content of their work in the settings where they perform their work.

THE FUTURE OF OCCUPATIONAL MONOPOLY AND DOMINANCE

A criterion of professionalization other than skill or education is provided by a number of recent writings which all converge on the same emphasis. In work carried on in the tradition of occupational analysis (see Stewart and Cantor, 1974, pp. 1–7), the attempt has been made to find strategic ways of distinguishing among occupations with almost equal education and skill but with markedly different working conditions – ways of distinguishing, for example, between pharmacists and optometrists in the contemporary United States (Freidson, 1988) – and ways of analyzing markedly different situations for the "same" occupation in different historical periods (Elliott, 1972, pp. 14–57) and different national settings (Johnson, 1973, pp. 281–309). What seemed critical in explaining those differences was the presence or absence of the organized power of the workers themselves to control the terms, conditions, and content of their work – what Johnson (1972, p. 45) called *collegiate control*, or "professionalism." Another way of delineating this approach is to be found in Weber's discussion of group monopoly (Weber, 1968, pp. 339–48, and Berlant, 1975, pp. 43–63).

The existence of such control over work by the workers themselves cannot be explained by the mere length or content of formal education or by some intrinsic character of skill. Rather, control presupposes a successful political organization which can gain the power to negotiate and establish favorable jurisdictions in an organized division of labor, and to control the labor market. Variation in control may be seen as the critical difference between such occupations as pharmacist and physician. Both are nominal members of the "professional class," both have complex skill, both have a higher education in the United States, and both have exclusive licenses by which they monopolize certain task. But there is a critical difference between them: the pharmacist can work only at the order of the physician, and thus may be seen to be in a critically different position in the division of labor. It is possible to reserve the term "profession" for that form of occupational organization which has at once gained for its members a labor monopoly and a place in the division of labor that is free of the authority of others over their work. Work as such, and the skills it entails, while not irrelevant, are not the focus for discrimination so much as the organized place of an occupation in the labor market and in a division of labor. A particular kind of work – practice of the tasks of healing, for example – can be organized as a profession at one point in history and not at another, and in one nation and not another.

In assessing the analytical importance of occupational monopoly and authority as central criteria for differentiating labor, one must remember how pervasive can be its consequences. The recent position of medicine is a case in point (see Turner and Hodge, 1970, pp. 38–41). The profession has been able to determine how many physicians are trained, who is selected to be trained, how they are to be trained, and who is to be licensed and thus to work. In that way it has controlled the labour market for its services. Furthermore, it has exercised supervisory power over a growing array of technical workers the para-professional workers who may not work without authorization or whose products (such as laboratory analyses, X-rays) are unusable by anyone but physicians. In that way it has dominated a division of labor. Its control both restricts the supply of its own labor and subordinates related labor in the institutions in which its members work.

Most of medicine's control has not been exercised directly in negotiation with clients or employers, but rather indirectly, through licensing, registering, and certifying legislation that establishes constraining limits around what can be negotiated among workers and with managers in concrete settings. As the Webbs noted some time ago (1917, p. 41), professional associations have found "legal enactment even more advantageous in securing their own ends than the Trade Unions have hitherto done, and the organization and direction of political activity have become important features of the modern Professional Association." Those organized powers of professional occupations have been real and are well known. Economists have deplored their interference with the labor market and thus, as labor monopolies, their purported cost to the public (Friedman, 1962); political scientists and lawyers have deplored their role as "private governments" (Gilb, 1966; Lieberman, 1970).

Legislation is a more effective method of controlling the circumstances of work of the self-employed worker than is collective bargaining, but even employment of the worker does not in itself reduce the effective possibilities of occupational control. The effectively organized professional occupation controls even the determination and demarcation of tasks embodied in jobs supported by employers. There is no intrinsic reason why management in any particular organization must be the agent, as it has been traditionally in industry, to determine what kind of worker must be hired for a particular job, what tasks those in and around that job can perform, and who can supervise and take responsibility for the proper performance of those jobs. Through their influence on regulatory agencies, the organized professions (and the crafts) are often responsible for writing the job descriptions for their members and determining the employer's training and educational requirements as well as the kind of special skill imputed to the qualified worker. They have done this independently of the employing organization, and the employing organization has been required by the state to follow those professionally determined guidelines in order to gain state charters or licenses to operate. When an occupation gains effective organization, therefore, it can raise powerful barriers against the process of rationalization which management has been fairly free to advance in the case of those less-than-professionally organized technical workers who were recently discussed by Harries-Jenkins (1970, pp. 53–107).

Given this definition of profession as an occupational monopoly with a position of dominance in a division of labor, what is the likelihood of professionalizing more occupations in the future? What of the new technical occupations – those with more education and complex skill than most workers? By and large, Touraine seems accurate in describing them as largely powerless, and with few hopeful prospects (Touraine, 1971, p. 58). But this does not seem to be so because of the character of their higher education, knowledge, or skill. Nor does it seem to have much to do with their salaried status. Rather, such occupations seem to have few prospects because they are part of productive domains which are already organized and controlled either 1) by dominant professions and their allies, or 2) by managerial agents of either the state (in socialist nations) or corporate capital. In the massive and still growing domains of health, welfare, law, and education, the division of labor is organized around the central authority of dominant professions (Freidson, 1988, pp. 47–84). In manufacturing, sales, financial, service, and other such enterprise, the division of labor is organized by what Johnson referred to as "corporate patronage" (Johnson, 1972, p. 46) – control by managerial authorities guided by elaborate information, plans, and advice drawn up for them by a small corps of professionalized experts who constitute what Galbraith called the "technostructure," and who are often mislabelled "technocrats."

In the former instance of professional dominance, the growing corps of technical workers is organized *around* the delineating and supervising authority of key professions. When they are licensed, certified, or registered, the legitimacy, even the legality of their work hinges upon their nominal supervision by that dominant profession; in many cases, only the dominant profession can order, interpret, evaluate, and consume the service they provide. They are thus bound into an occupationally subordinate position even though many have organized themselves into occupational associations and trade unions and have claimed many of the attributes ascribed to professions. Some of them may break away to occupy a niche in the division of labor that is parallel and unsubordinated to their erstwhile occupational superiors, but most, in spite of their many "professional" attributes, are certain either to remain, by my usage, paraprofessional workers, or to become transformed by managerial authority into technical workers with fewer of the trappings of professionalism. Trade unionism, I would guess, will succeed in improving the terms and conditions of their work, but will be unlikely to change their position as workers whose work is ultimately at the disposition of others (cf. Mann, 1973, pp. 20–1).

In those industries where there is managerial dominance, the technician is also unlikely to gain control over his work because, apart from the general training he brings with him into his job, his work tends to be a function of the needs of a particular job defined by a particular organization. This specificity of task, over which he has little control, prevents his actual working skills from being generalizable across a wide variety of jobs, thereby hampering both individual job mobility and the possibility of developing collegial solidarity across employing organizations (Mallet, 1975, pp. 68–75, saw "sectoralism" or *internal* solidarity as a possible outcome). Furthermore, unorganized to begin with, he is likely to be able to wield little power to prevent periodic managerial rationalization and the adoption of new techniques which threaten him with the spectre of his own obsolescence, or replacement by a machine. Under those circumstances, his development of organized control over his own work is unlikely. Indeed, as Goldner and Ritti (1967, pp. 489–502) noted for the engineer, technician *par excellence*, "professionalization" may constitute in reality only a flattering symbolic reward by management to conceal career immobility and even demotion in those circumstances in which true career success is gained by leaving one's occupation to join the ranks of management.

Finally, there is the matter of the future of the present-day occupations which now have extensive control over the terms, conditions, and content of their work. This may not be a question we can answer by simple linear projection because different professions provide services to clientele who are constituted in significantly different ways, and perform tasks with markedly different implications for institutional control. Perhaps more important is a fairly recent threat to professions created by rising expectations for greater productivity – that is, for the wider distribution of more professionally produced goods and services through the population. This has led to the generation of political forces which are pressing toward important changes in the organization and delineation of the work of present-day professions. While some decline in relative prestige and income is entirely possible in the future, and while *portions* of presently professional work may very well return to the control of lay persons or become controlled by management, none of those changes has any intrinsic or inevitable connection with loss of occupational monopoly or position in the division of labor, and most writers do not anticipate such a loss in the future. Very recently, however, a few writers (e.g., Haug, 1973; Haug, 1975; Oppenheimer, 1973) have pointed to trends which they employ as evidence that the future will bring changes in status so extreme as to lead to either deprofessionalization or proletarianization. Much of their argument is empirically unverifiable, and, as is characteristic of the literature in general, it is not entirely certain that they are all talking about the same occupations, but some of their argument is based on three long-standing trends which are unquestionable, and which therefore deserve close attention. Let us examine those trends and their implications for assessing the future of professionalization.

First the trend toward specialization *within* the established professions – a trend almost certain to continue – is argued to be contributory to deprofessionalization or proletarianization in that increasingly narrow specialists can be expected, like the classic factory worker, to be doing the same work over and over again, without knowledge or control of the whole productive process of which each speciality is a mere part. True as far as it goes, such reasoning is based on confusing two profoundly different processes of developing and organizing specialization. In one, very common in the history of crafts and professions, *the workers themselves* specialize and negotiate with their fellow workers for a niche *within* the occupation's division of labor. They do not lose organized control over their work. In the other, characteristic of the experience of the factory worker, *a superior authority* breaks a task down into its simplest units, requiring the least possible skill to perform, and then hires, trains, and supervises workers to perform them in a division of labor it creates. In both instances specialization does indeed occur, but in the former case it is the worker who invents, chooses, and controls his task, trains for it in depth, and pursues its minutest complexity on the basis of increasingly esoteric skill, while in the latter case it is management that creates a task which has been broken into specialized activities requiring little training or skill and the use of workers who are cheap and readily interchangeable (cf. Braverman, 1974, pp. 85–121). Both are indeed "specialization," but an increase in the development of the former within the professions cannot be said to be analogous to the development of the latter, which dissolves traditional occupational jurisdictions. Evidence of managerial creation and control of work would have to be demonstrated before claims of deprofessionalization or proletarianization could be supported. No such evidence has been produced. The bald fact of an increase in specialization without reference to evidence about the way it is developed and organized thus has little analytical relevance to the issue.

Second, the trend toward increasing complexity in the division of labor of which professionals are merely one part has been adduced to sustain the prophecy of deprofessionalization or proletarianization. The trend toward a more elaborate division of labor is as indubitable as that toward specialization *within* professions, and represents part of the same process, but it, too, means little when treated as a mere quantitative phenomenon. Specialization and the division of labor have indeterminate analytical significance without consideration of their social organization (Freidson, 1976). It is true that, when one who once worked by himself comes to work as part of a larger division of labor, he becomes one interdependent part of a larger whole, but as the political theory of centuries has observed, interdependence does not mean each part of the whole has equal authority. In present-day health care, a professionalized industry in which the division of labor has grown increasingly complex for fifty years or more, there is little or no evidence that physicians have been losing significant elements of their monopoly over ordering and supervising the work provided by other occupations in the division of labor. Interdependence does not necessarily corrode dominance. The empirical examples of exceptions to professional dominance cited to support prophecies of the deprofessionalization or proletarianization of physicians are drawn from special experimental programs in artificial (usually academic) settings, or from temporary arrangements observed in times of institutional or national crisis. Provocative and worth study as they may be, such exceptions are cross-sectional in nature and do *not* constitute trend data on which sound prophecy can be based.

Finally, there is the long-remarked (cf. Marshall, 1939; Lewis and Maude, 1952) trend away from self-employment and towards employment in large organizations. As an indicator this also is much too mechanical to have analytical value in and of itself. For one thing, priests, rabbis, and ministers in organized churches have almost never been self-employed. The same may be said for the university teacher, at least since the demise of the medieval university, and for the modern research scientist. Does this mean that all this time they have really been members of the proletariat? Employment does indeed indicate nominal dependence on another agent to provide one's income, but so also does self-employment. The analytical issue is not employment or self-employment as such so much as the nature of the process by which the content, terms, and conditions of work are established. If workers have a monopoly in the labor market, and the power to control their own work, they can dictate the content, terms, and conditions of their employment as well as of their self-employment. Without monopoly and dominance their position when self-employed is hardly less desperate than when employed, as anyone familiar with the history of medical and legal self-employment should be aware. Furthermore, presently available large-scale data on employment and self-employment – particularly in the case of traditionally self-employed professions – is unreliable because of the artefactual character of the designations. Of the increasing proportion of American physicians who are now classified as employees, a significant number are share-owners of an incorporated practice organization who are on a salary solely for legal and tax convenience. This does not imply that they have become a proletariat any more than does the fact that workers in worker-managed enterprises are usually paid wages. The fact of being employed or self-employed, then, is too ambiguous a datum to serve as useful evidence bearing on the future of professional monopoly and dominance.

What, then, can we say of the future of professional monopoly and dominance in a division of labor? First, it seems difficult to see any trend by which many more occupations will move into such a professional position (cf. Wilensky, 1964, pp. 137–58). The trend in industrial societies has indeed been toward more licensing, registration, and certification of occupations, providing them with a monopoly in the labor market, but there does not seem to be a trend toward occupations assuming new positions of overall dominance in a division of labor. Second, it seems difficult to see any trend toward significant expansion in both numbers and functions of present-day established professions that does not at the same time imply radical changes in their constitution. The trend instead seems to be toward a redefinition of both function and jurisdiction. In all industrial countries, the cost of the comparatively long period of training now given professionals has become too great to allow them and only them to meet individual and public demand for all the services they now monopolize. This would be so even were their compensation to be reduced to a considerably more modest level than at present. Sooner or later, many of the more common and putatively less complex skills now monopolized by professionals will be transferred into the hands of less expensively trained workers who will be allowed some form of limited practice. This could take place both by the use of non-professionals, and by the sharpening and deepening of the stratification presently existing in the professions, with the lower stratum, increased in size, receiving shortened training and considerably more restricted rights to practice.

If the reorganization of jurisdiction and task occurs, the essential analytical issue for the future of professions lies in the way in which this will come about, who will guide the process and specify the options and who will control it. Judging by the experience of state socialist nations which have attempted drastic changes in the political and legal status of the established professions, political ideology and power can effectively enforce the choice of broad goals and means available to professionalized work, but the professions have remained in control of the knowledge and technique by which those goals and the broad means connected with them are advanced. It seems unlikely that in the course of reorganization there will be a reproduction of the process that occurred in manufacturing, with present-day professional workers losing control of the knowledge and technique connected with their work. Even if the number of their members falls and their present-day tasks are taken over by non-professionals, there is likely to remain in the future an important place for the professions, at the very least as planners and programers of the reorganization of their erstwhile work, as researchers and teachers, and as consultants to and supervisors of the workers who have replaced them in the provision of direct services.

THE FUTURE OF COMMITTED LABOR

Thus far, my discussion has been limited to positional and structural characteristics which deal with relations to the market, strata within the entire labor force, and occupational organization as it is manifested in a labor market and a division of labor. These modes of analysis all lack reference to human beings, and to the commitments, relationships, and values that are, at bottom, what they purport to analyze. In addition to this analytical deficiency, one may note the absence, thus far, of any reference to one of the most commonly cited characteristics employed to define professions – the orientation to ethical service of others. Many scholars have emphasized such dedication: to cite just a few examples, Goode (1960, p. 903) has stressed as one of two "core characteristics" of professions an orientation to serving the public good. Halmos (1970) claimed altruism. Tawney (1920, p. 94) and Carr-Saunders and Wilson (1933, pp. 284–6) emphasized the significance of the professional's sense of responsibility for the integrity of his work. In general, such discussions do not refer to the social organization of professional work so much as to the motivations and values of professional workers.

Elsewhere (Freidson, 1988, pp. 77–82) I have discussed the problem of determining the empirical referents of such imputed attributes of professional workers, and I have questioned their validity as empirical statements about professionals. Whether or not the substance of those attributes is empirically accurate, however, the *class* of variable they represent is essential to address in any systematic analysis of work and workers, for values and motivation cannot be ignored. The problem with traditional discussions of "ethicality" lies not in the unimportance of the topic, but in their level of abstraction and in their tendency to treat the topic as if it were something merely to be added to a list of other attributes, without relating each to each. While this is not the place for a detailed exposition, and while I do not claim that it is the only useful method of relating traditional attributes to one another, I wish to suggest here that the social psychology of professions and professionals can be discussed coherently and systematically as derivations from the social organization of professions.

In essence, it can be argued that the social organization of professions constitutes circumstances which encourage the development in its members of several kinds of commitment. (On commitment, see Becker, 1970, pp. 261–73.) First, since an organized occupation provides its members with the prospect of a relatively secure and life-long career, it is reasonable to expect them to develop a commitment to and identification with the occupation and its fortunes, if only on self-interested, economic grounds. Such *occupational commitment* is markedly different from what is found in prototypical wage labor, whose commitment is not to a particular *occupation* but only to whatever job provides the most material benefit. Second, since an organized occupation by definition controls recruitment, training, and job characteristics, its members will have many more common occupational experiences in training, job career, and work than is the case for members of a general skill class, who are recruited, trained, and employed in a considerably more heterogeneous fashion in the course of their work lives. Such shared experience – sometimes referred to as occupational culture or occupational community (Salaman, 1974) – in conjunction with sharing the occupation's privileged (and sometimes threatened) position in the labor market and the division of labor, may be seen to encourage commitment to colleagues, or collegiality. Such *occupational solidarity* tends to be exclusive in character, rather than extending across occupations to a working class. Third, we may see professional organization encouraging *work commitment*. In so far as jurisdictional boundaries are comparatively stable, they allow the performance of a set of particular tasks for a lifetime. This provides the opportunity and stimulus for the worker to develop a committed interest in the work he performs. Work can become a central life interest for professionals far more easily than for blue-collar workers (cf. Dubin, 1956, pp. 131–42, and Orzack, 1959, pp. 125–32), for the latter cannot be assured of performing the same tasks from one job to the next, let alone perform tasks that they create and control themselves.

Occupational organization may thus be related to workers' commitment to and identification with their occupation, their occupational co-workers, and their work. But what does this have to do with dedication, altruism, service orientation, or craftsmanship? (On craftsmanship, see Mills, 1951, pp. 220–4). Can they, too, be said to have some plausible connection with occupational organization? When this is discussed in the literature, the consensus seems to be – paralleling the claims of the professions themselves – that professions recruit members who are devoted to serving others, create training programs which instill dedication to serve others, and organize work settings in such a way that altruistic and craftsmanlike work is assured by informal processes of collegial control. That is to say, the theory is that the content of the institutions sustained by professional organization is such as to encourage and maintain dedication in members.

Dedication implies that what is unique to professions is not the fact of having a material relationship to a market – as in the case of the professional/amateur distinction discussed earlier in this paper – but rather the fact of being a literal amateur – of working for the love of others and for the love of the work rather than for the love of money. But in the world as we find it, market relations and the social organization of the means of production are more apparent to the observer than is dedication. Empirical evidence does not support the claim of a distinctive dedication which takes precedence over individual and collective material interest. In a recently reported study of a group of doctors (Freidson, 1980), it was shown how etiquette – an expression of occupational solidarity – was given priority over efforts to realize the ideals of dedication to service and to craftsmanship. Without denying that on some occasions and in

some individuals those ideals are empirically realized, there is little evidence that they are distinctive for professionals or correlated with professional organization. Indeed, I would suggest that the notions of dedication
to service and of craftsmanship are more usefully treated as elements of
an ideology than as empirical characteristics of individual and collective
professional behavior. Taken as ideology, they have empirical status as
claims about their members made by occupations attempting to gain and
maintain professional monopoly and dominance.

Certainly it is evident that ideologies of craftsmanship and public service
are advanced by workers attempting to gain and maintain control over
the determination of their own work and working conditions (see Jamous
and Peloille, 1970, pp. 111–52 and Holzner, 1972). Since such control
hinges on gaining access to power which is not inherent in the work
itself, an ideology of professionalism must be ecumenical rather than
parochial (see Dibble, 1962), designed to persuade those in power that
members of the occupation are the best arbiters of the work, that the
work is in the public interest, and that the workers are dedicated to doing
good work and using their privilege for the good of others rather than
for their own interests alone. That ideology may be said to be an important component of the process by which occupations seek to gain and
maintain their control.

There is, however, more use for the ideology of professionalism than
just the advancement of the ends of workers in an organized occupation.
It may also be used to motivate workers in the *absence* of occupational
control over work. Involvement in and commitment to work, and an
orientation toward service, have been found among non-professional
workers whose occupational position prevents them from controlling
their own work. Indeed, those working under the direction of professionals may very well manifest greater devotion to serving others than do
professionals themselves (see, e.g., Hall, 1968, p. 97, and Engel, 1973).
Organizational superiors can use the ideology to make career immobility
and even demotion palatable to workers (Goldner and Ritti, 1967), as can
professionals in the course of passing down "dirty work" to subordinate
occupations (Emerson and Pollner, 1976, pp. 243–54). The ideology is
not only attached to the armamentarium of professional occupations,
therefore, but also employed by occupation leaders aspiring to professional status, by members of occupations subordinate to professions,
and by members of occupations such as engineering which have an uncertain status in a managerially dominated system. The ideology may be
used by political, managerial, and professional authorities to distract
workers from their objective lack of control over their work, to lead
them to do the work assigned them as well as possible, and to commit
them to means and ends others have chosen for them.

In sum, it is possible to observe that occupational commitment may be plausibly treated as a function of professional organization, varying directly in strength and frequency as occupational organization varies. The same may be said for work commitment. So also may it be said for occupational solidarity, though the strength of the association may be diminished by internal differentiation into specialties and segments within a profession. The futures of each of these commitments may thus be expected to be tied up intimately with the future of occupational monopoly and dominance. Commitment to serving others, however, and to doing good work, cannot be connected so plausibly with occupational organization, and remains analytically separate from it except as an ideology that aids its development and maintenance. Espousal of the ideology by individuals may be empirically present even when the professional organization of work is absent, for it does not seem to depend upon professional monopoly and control for its existence. Thus, even though professional organization should decline in the future, the use of the ideology of professionalism could very well increase.

THE FUTURES OF PROFESSIONALIZATION

I began this paper by noting that a large number of eminent writers over many decades have seen a trend toward the increase of professions in the future. I expressed doubt that they all agreed with each other on much more than the use of the same word, and suggested that they may in fact be talking past each other even when they appeared to agree, let alone when they disagreed. I suggested a careful look at the varied referents of the word, and in the body of my paper did so, examining the varied referents both for their analytical value and for assessing the trends in their development in the future.

With my discussion of profession as an ideology, as a claim of dedication advanced to protect an interest, I came to the end of the catalogue. I have not been exhaustive of all the attributes which have composed all the definitions of the term, but I believe I have touched on the most essential. Even if I have overlooked some of importance, I trust I have made the point that what one predicts as the future of professions is based on one's conception of what they are, in interaction with the evidence of trends. For a term such as "profession," used in so many ways, there cannot be sufficient consensus in usage and definition to make it possible to predict only one future. There can only be many futures, each a function of choice of definition and each correct within the limits of the available data and its own definition.

One might observe furthermore that two different predictions can be at the same time accurate in the light of available data and completely contradictory of each other. This can be so because the criteria or attributes employed in one prediction may have no relationship to those employed in the other, so that each can use data that vary independently of the other. Thus, defining professions as occupations with higher education and imputed complex skill yields a predication of continuing increase in the future; defining professions as self-employed occupations yields a prediction of continuing decrease in the future; defining professions by monopoly and dominance in a division of labor yields a prediction of at best slight increase and possible mild decrease. Definitions may also be related to some but not all others: taken as dependent variable, commitment to occupation, fellow workers, and work may be seen to vary with occupational organization, but it is likely to vary slightly with and perhaps even independently of education and imputed skill. Dedication to service and to craftsmanship, on the other hand, may be seen to have no simple and direct relationship to any of the other criteria of professionalization discussed here: as ideologies, they seem to be available for the use of any agent seeking to control work and motivate and direct the worker.

Finally, I might note that in this paper there is another perhaps more important theme running alongside the issue of defining and predicting professionalization. It argues that a fruitful way of developing theoretical coherence in the field of the sociology of occupations lies in adopting as one's central problem the analysis of the organization of control over work, and its consequences for work, workers, organizations, and society. Part of the virtue of such a focus lies in its compatability with other bodies of information and theory which have heretofore run largely separate from occupational sociology as a discipline. When individual occupations are seen as part of a division of labor composed of many occupations, much of organizational theory becomes relevant as an explication of particular ways of organizing and coordinating an institutional division of labor. So, also, does much of the work in industrial sociology. This focus, then, can join occupational sociology to other specialties, and advance intellectual synthesis. Perhaps more important, on the level of general theory, focus on the issue of control over work facilitates the critical use of at least some of the perspectives and analytical tools developed by Marxist theory, which contains at its core the same emphasis on control even though its preoccupation is more with analysis of class than of occupation. But that is all programmatic: what is important here is the exploration of the analytical meaning of the various attributes employed to delineate professions, and the direction it points toward future analysis of an important even though ambiguous phenomenon of industrial society.

NOTES

1 This is the revision of a plenary address at the Annual Conference of the British Sociological Association, Manchester, England, on 9 April 1976. This paper is based on work partially supported by the Russell Sage Foundation. It has benefited from critical comments and suggestions by Howard S. Becker, Arlene K. Daniels, Celia Davies, William A. Form, Marie R. Haug, Carol L. Kronus, John B. McKinlay, Caroline Persell, Margaret E. Reid, and Dennis H. Wrong.

2 It will be recognized as Max Weber's definition of *Beruf*, which the translator interprets as "occupation" (see Weber, 1947, p. 250).

3 It is true that on official forms it is proper to list "housewife," "student," and "retired" as one's "occupation," but that practice is more a matter of denying the stigma of unemployment than of claiming an official position in the labor force.

8

The Changing Nature of
Professional Control

The professions have long occupied a special position in sociology. Nominally, they are productive trades – such as butchers, bakers, and electricians – and are part of the social division of labor. But professionals have always been treated as more than merely specialized workers. Since Herbert Spencer's work (1896) or before, the professions have been singled out as occupations that perform tasks of great social value because professionals possess both knowledge and skills that in some way set them apart from other kinds of workers. It has also been thought that professionals are distinctive because they bring a special attitude of commitment and concern to their work, leading R. H. Tawney (1920, pp. 91–128) to urge the cultivation of "professionalism" as a means of reorganizing and reorienting the conduct of those engaged in industrial pursuits.

According to many sociologists, the professions are also subject to a self-regulating form of social control that has not been typical of most occupations in modern times – i.e., a middle-class version of worker self-management prevails. Apart from the entrepreneurial businessman, whose work is presumably subject to control by the invisible hand of the capitalist market-place, most workers perform their jobs in industrial and commercial settings where social control is exercised formally by employers and their representatives and informally by fellow employees during the course of everyday work. Furthermore, the work they do is formulated and evaluated by their managerial superordinates. Professionals, on the other hand, have been represented as independent of significant formal control by non-professionals and responsible largely to their own professional associations and to fellow professionals. The courts can exercise control over professional behavior after the fact, of course, when civil suits are brought against individual practitioners for negligence or malpractice.

Nevertheless, the emphasis in the traditional sociological literature has been on the self-governing character of the professions. Indeed, the Webbs (1917) assessed the professions in depth, searching for a model of worker self-governance (or producer cooperatives) that might provide a viable alternative to the more hierarchical practices they considered typical of capitalism.

Traditional professional self-regulation is exercised on a formal level by the professional association, which can discipline its members by threatening expulsion from its ranks and loss of the associated privileges. But as Carr-Saunders and Wilson (1933, pp. 395–6) correctly observed, formal expulsion or discipline of any sort has been rare. "Of more importance to the social control of the professional is the silent pressure of opinion and tradition . . . which is constantly around him throughout his professional career" (Carr-Saunders and Wilson, 1933, p. 403). Parsons, too, noted professionals' characteristic reliance on informal controls. Like Carr-Saunders and Wilson, he explained it as a result of their need to avoid the imposition of a rigid orthodoxy of norms on what should be a creative, even risk-taking, exercise of refined judgment (Parsons, 1951, pp. 470–1). Barber (1962, p. 195) characterized the professions as a company of equals which lacks a formal hierarchy and command that "issues detailed directives and enforces rigid control" and whose members are controlled by conscience.

Over the past twenty years, however, there has been increasing evidence that this characteristic depiction of social control within the professions has become too far removed from reality to be useful even as an ideal type. Not only have observers been concerned that organized professional associations have flouted the public interest (e.g., Gilb, 1966; Lieberman, 1970), but it has become evident that the informal method of social control prevalent among professionals has typically been guided by norms that prevent that control from being exercised judiciously and systematically (Freidson, 1980; 1988).

In addition to this evidence, which has emerged from a critical examination of the empirical process by which professionals purport to exercise controls over deviant performance, a number of political and economic events have occurred that imply that new forms of social control are developing. Organizations where professionals work – universities, law firms, social agencies, hospitals, and accounting firms, for example – have become larger and more complex, thus changing at least some working conditions. From the 1960s on, scandals have tainted the public image of scientific research, medical research and practice, legal practice, and judicial neutrality. For a time, the number of malpractice suits against physicians and lawyers increased markedly, and various kinds of government regulation have been imposed in some areas of professional work. Meanwhile, several types of legal action have been taken to prevent the professions from engaging in self-interested efforts to protect themselves from competition. The emphasis in sociological writing has therefore shifted from analyzing the professions' special knowledge and ethicality – as revealed in the process of professional education, for example – to examining their concern with establishing and maintaining a specially favored market position (Larson, 1977) and investigating their relationship to the power of the state, patrons, and clients (Johnson, 1972). A new theme has also emerged, namely, that professionals have become subject to forms of social control that erode their very status as professionals.

In this paper I shall attempt to assess contemporary modes of exercising social control over professionals in the United States. The basic question is whether the changes that have taken place have transformed the position of professions in the political economy in general, and in the workplace in particular, to one considerably less distinctive than that prevailing when traditional sociological conceptions of the professions were formulated. Some contemporary writers claim that the professions have lost so much of their power that they have become subject to the same formal, hierarchical lay controls as other occupations. Let us examine their arguments.

THEORIES OF CHANGING PROFESSIONAL STATUS

While there are no fully articulated, formal theories that address this issue, it is useful to examine two overlapping approaches – the theses of deprofessionalization and of proletarianization. Proponents of both argue that the professional's status in the United States has changed markedly and that the social control exerted over him or her has also been transformed.

The deprofessionalization thesis, which is associated most closely with the work of Marie R. Haug (1973; 1975; 1977), is fairly pragmatic. Essentially, the argument is that the professions are losing their position of prestige and trust. Haug emphasizes several attributes which, taken as a whole, she thinks have accounted for that prestige and respect in the past – e.g., possessing a monopoly over a body of knowledge that is relatively inaccessible to lay people; having a positive public image that stresses altruistic rather than self-serving motives; and having "the power to set their own rules as to what constitutes satisfactory work" (Haug, 1973, p. 196). Haug argues that these characteristics are disappearing and, as a consequence, the special prestige and authority enjoyed by the professions is eroding. Becoming mere secular experts, professionals are no longer protected from the necessity of negotiating and compromising with a skeptical clientele, and they are losing their jurisdictional monopoly over a defined area of knowledge and a given set of tasks.

Threats to the professions' monopoly over defined bodies of complex knowledge and skill stem from a number of sources. Insofar as their formal knowledge can be stored in a computer, it loses its esoteric character because anyone can retrieve it. The computer, furthermore, can be used to assess professional performance according to the authoritative standards stored within it. Another threat to the professions' monopoly over specialized knowledge stems from the lay population's increasing levels of education, which makes people less inclined to see this knowledge as mysterious and more likely to be critical and challenging in their dealings with professionals. Finally, the increased complexity of the specialized division of labor within which professionals work makes them dependent on other specialists in new fields who claim authority for themselves and contest control over some portion of the formal knowledge and skill that the established professions formerly monopolized.

The experiential knowledge of the personal service professions, which allowed their members to claim authority on the basis of more comprehensive experience than any single lay person seeking help for individual problems could possibly have amassed, is similarly threatened. These threats arise from an increase in consumers' formal education, but more importantly, from the rise of special consumer self-help groups and of "indigenous" or lower-level para-professional workers. In the case of consumer groups, the women's movement and associated women's health-care groups are especially prominent, but many self-help groups concerned with particular diseases, disabilities, and other problems are also important. Insofar as the members of such groups exchange information and experience with one another, they can claim an extensive experiential knowledge that rivals the professional's.

The effects of these challenges to the professions' monopoly of a specific body of knowledge and skills are central to Haug's analysis. In discussing professionals' alleged altruism, she points out how much publicity has been given to the disproportionate increase in physicians' incomes after the passage of legislation that paid many patients' bills with public funds and how the climate of opinion has become increasingly hostile. These changes create greater demands for accountability and for the protection of client's rights, which at once reflect the professions' loss of the trust and prestige they once enjoyed and contribute to this trend. Thus, all of those factors that bolstered the professions' autonomy and enabled them to set their own rules may soon disappear. "In a time when 'professionals' offer only expert information, with the client in a position to seek alternatives, we will begin to see a consumer model, rather than a patient or client model, of the entire transaction and the concept of profession as now formulated will be indeed obsolete" (Haug, 1977, p. 226).

The key to Haug's position lies in her emphasis on the consumer and her relative lack of emphasis on work. The proletarianization thesis emphasizes the circumstances of professional work in large organizations. This thesis stems from Marx's theory of history, in which he asserts that over time the intrinsic characteristics of capitalism will reduce virtually all workers to the status of the proletariat, i.e., dependent on selling their labor in order to survive and stripped of all control over the substance and process of their work. Wage labor, or employment rather than self-employment, is the common denominator of proletarian status. As Braverman put it, "the formal definition of the working class is that class which, possessing nothing but its power to labor, sells that labor to capital in return for its subsistence" (Braverman, 1974, p. 378). In contrast, Oppenheimer (1973, pp. 213–14) describes self-employment as a position in which "the source of income is a more individually-regulated sale of a product or a service under fairly loose market conditions established by face-to-face bargaining, rather than the sale of labor time (in advance of the creation of anything); and where the whole income goes directly to the worker without any bureaucratic intermediary except perhaps an agent (as in the case of an artist)." Therefore, professionals who come to be employed are proletarianized (cf. Esland, 1980, pp. 229–32).

But there is more to it than that. Employment is an important factor because it implies losing the capacity to control the terms of work. At its foundation is the issue of power or control, and there is more to control than merely setting the economic terms of work. There is also the question of being able to determine what work is to be done, how the work is to be done, and what its aim is to be. Thus, in the case of professionally trained workers, Aronowitz asserts that "they neither control the production process, whose object, specifications and methods are determined from above, nor their own work, which is defined rigidly within the occupational hierarchy" (1973, p. 305). What is being emphasized is not the mere fact of employment, but rather the consequences of working in a large organization where tasks are assigned rationally and ordered by hierarchical supervision – in short, in a bureaucracy. As Oppenheimer put it:

> The bureaucratized workplace ... tend[s] to replace in the professionals' own workplace factory-like conditions – there are fixed jurisdictions, ordered by rules established by others; there is a hierarchical command system; jobs are entered and mobility exists on the basis of performance in uniform tasks, examinations, or the achievement of

certification or "degrees"; work tends to become specialized, hence extensive division of labor develops. . . . The gap between what the worker does, and an end product, increases. (1973, p. 214)

Presumably, professionals are no longer able to govern themselves by their own informal methods of using peer influence and exercising the powers of their associations; instead, they are controlled by others. Echoing Haug, Oppenheimer points to the imposition of new administrative measures aimed at greater professional accountability and notes the pressures stemming from clients' demands for better services.

APPRAISING THE DEPROFESSIONALIZATION THESIS

While there is no logical reason for this, Haug's deprofessionalization thesis stresses cultural and political, more than economic and organizational, phenomena. Indeed, Haug seems to highlight the cultural and political events of the 1960s and early 1970s and assume that they would persist and even intensify in the future. But many of these movements have simply collapsed; others have become so conventional that they are barely recognizable; and still others, if they have not disappeared entirely, have at least become considerably attenuated and altered by counter-movements.

Proponents of the deprofessionalization thesis singled out events that seem particularly vulnerable to the effects of historical changes. An emphasis on the strength of the consumers' movement – most particularly of self-help groups and consumer-oriented segments of the women's movement – is central to the thesis. But community and self-help groups have a high mortality rate and often a highly transient group of participants. Apart from formally organized groups run by "program professionals," the consumer movement today is much less strong than it was in the early 1970s. Furthermore, while hostility to (or at least a suspicion of) professionals' motives continues to exist in the United States, it is diffuse and far weaker than that directed against others. The existing evidence shows that the public is much more dubious about the motives of politicians, "big business," trade unions, and others. Lipset and Schneider's (1983) careful analysis of a variety of surveys taken over decades documents an overall decline in confidence, but public trust in medical, educational, and other professional institutions has dropped comparatively little. Nor is there any evidence that their relative prestige has declined.

It is true that a series of important legal and legislative events have occurred over the past five years that have weakened the professions' capacity to protect themselves from competition. A number of recent Supreme Court decisions have effectively prohibited professional customs aimed at fixing prices and otherwise preventing price competition among colleagues and have held professional associations responsible for the actions of their constituent committees. Nonetheless, there has been no perceptible movement toward actually eliminating the quasi-monopolies or cartels provided by licensing, accreditation, and registration practices, nor any inclination to interfere with the professions' exercise of authority over their own technical areas of expertise (cf. Kissam, 1980).

Similarly, while all professions have, over the years, ceded control over certain areas of work to erstwhile competitors or subordinates, there is no noticeable trend toward a steadily shrinking jurisdiction. In the prominent case of medicine – a profession which has been confronted by a bewildering variety of challenges over the decades – there is little evidence that physicians are even close to running out of work. Indeed, if anything, continual new advances in technique make even more medical work possible in areas that were previously dealt with far more simply.

It is in such a context that we must evaluate whether or not the "knowledge gap" has narrowed. Even if the public has more formal education than in the past, it is either a general education or, when it is specialized, it is spread across many different fields. The average consumer is capable of evaluating much more specialized technical information today than was the case yesterday, but, as this capability has grown, the quantity and quality of specialized knowledge has also increased. While today's lay clients can be the informed, critical consumers of the services of *yesterday*'s professionals much more easily than in the past, it is an entirely open question whether they can effectively play such a role when dealing with the services of *today*'s professionals, whose knowledge and technical competence have continued to expand.

The professions thus continue to possess a monopoly over at least some important segment of formal knowledge that does not shrink over time, even though both competitors and rising levels of lay knowledge may nibble away at its edges. New knowledge is constantly acquired that takes the place of what has been lost and thereby maintains the knowledge gap. Similarly, while the power of computer technology in storing codified knowledge cannot be ignored, it is the members of each profession who determine what is to be stored and how it is to be done, and who are equipped to interpret and employ what is retrieved effectively. With a continual knowledge gap, potentially universal access to stored data is meaningless. In sum, while the events highlighted by proponents of the deprofessionalization thesis are important, the argument that members of the professions are losing their relative prestige and respect, their special expertise, or their monopoly over the exercise of that expertise over time is not persuasive.

APPRAISING THE PROLETARIANIZATION THESIS

As I have already noted, proponents of the proletarianization thesis emphasize economic and organizational factors, the most elementary of which is the worker's status in the labor market. Like both conservative (Lewis and Maude, 1952) and liberal (Marshall, 1939) writers, supporters of this thesis assert that the long-term trend is for professionals to be employed, rather than self-employed (cf. Johnson, 1973, pp. 131–2). Like artisans and yeomen before them, it is argued that this trend reflects a process of proletarianization, since being employed by other people diminishes one's capacity for independent, autonomous work.

In order to assess the validity of this proposition, two questions must be answered. First, is there such a trend away from self-employment both for individual professionals and for professions as a whole (i.e., has the number of professions characterized by self-employment declined)? There is no evidence that either trend is occurring in the United States. While the proportion of self-employed workers in the US labor force as a whole has declined considerably during the twentieth century, this statistic reflects the declining number of people working in agriculture. If one examines the statistics for all non-agricultural workers, one notes that the proportion of self-employed has been extraordinarily stable over this period, save for a temporary increase during three decades during and after World War II (cf. Tausky, 1978, p. 2). The overall stability masks changes in the employment status of certain groups, for during this century there has been "a pronounced *rise* in the number of [self-employed] professionals and salesworkers and a corresponding *decline* in the number of proprietors" (Bregger, 1963, p. 37, italics added; see also Ray, 1975, p. 49 and DiCesare, 1975, pp. 23–4).

There is thus ground for doubting that a decline in de facto self-employment by professionals has occurred, and it is possible that there has actually been an increase in self-employment. Whatever the trend for the aggregate of *professionals*, however, there is no doubt that the number of *professions* characterized by self-employment has not declined. In fact, employment has typified most professions since their invention, so that a trend *toward* employment is impossible to observe (see Kornhauser, 1962, p. 4). Looking at the traditional professions – medicine, law, the military, the clergy, and (connected with the clergy historically) university teaching – we see that three of the five never involved self-employment, though professionals in these fields did not necessarily enter into a wage contract. Instead, they operated with the understanding that they could obtain an income from collecting bribes, loot, tithes, rents, student fees, etc. When we examine the occupations assigned to the modern professional-technical category, we see that members of the overwhelming majority of the newer professions have also been typically employed, rather than self-employed. It is true that there is a growing trend toward the employ-ment of the members of two traditional professions that were mostly characterized by self-employment in the past – lawyers (but not judges) and doctors – and of members of the older professions of dentistry and architecture. The norm for professionals, however, has always been employment.

The second question to be addressed is whether employment status bears a reasonably close relationship to economic autonomy. The answer to this question is also negative. When we examine the conditions sur-rounding self-employment in actual historical circumstances, it is impos-sible to argue that the self-employed enjoy greater economic security, higher economic rewards, and more autonomy at work than the em-ployed. Owning property or the means of production, whether it is a professional practice or a shop, is not important in and of itself in assur-ing control over one's economic fate and autonomy in one's work. Surely the more critical matter is one's relationship to the market, capitalist or otherwise. If one's goods or services are so highly valued on the market that consumers are clamoring for access to them, then one can exercise considerable control over the terms, conditions, content, and goals of one's work. But if one's goods or services are not in heavy demand, then one will be confronted by indifferent consumers and at best will live "a life of dignified starvation," as a medical journal characterized the eco-nomic condition of two-thirds of the physicians in New York City in 1889 (Shryock, 1947, p. 116). Whether one is employed or self-employed is beside the point. Given a strong position in the market, one can be employed and "write one's own ticket" nonetheless.

Overall, then, employment status is not a good, direct measure of control or lack of control over one's work. The prime argument of the proletarian-ization thesis that we must still assess is the assertion that bureaucratization – i.e., the organization of professional work into a complex division of labor ordered by a hierarchy of positions – has led to the loss of profes-sionals' traditionally asserted right of self-direction.

BUREAUCRATIZATION AND PROFESSIONAL CONTROLS

I have pointed out that it is typical of professionals to be employed rather than self-employed. Furthermore, they are usually employed by organizations – e.g., by schools, hospitals, law firms and legal service organizations, social agencies, colleges, industrial firms – rather than by individuals. In addition, over the past few decades the organizations employing professionals appear to have become larger and more complex. They are often integrated into a still larger public or private system which is frequently called a bureaucracy. In contrast to popular usage where the word bureaucracy connotes inefficiency, in academic usage it connotes efficiency through the meticulous supervision and control of its members and the careful planning of activities. In the context of industrial production, those espousing the proletarianization thesis find an analogue of bureaucratic control in management's "Taylorization" of work tasks, i.e., through the development of a detailed division of labor and the creation of an elaborate hierarchy of supervision designed to control the performance of the assigned tasks (see Braverman, 1974). Aronowitz, Oppenheimer, and others advancing the thesis of the proletarianization of professionals obviously have such a parallel with industrial organization in mind. Bureaucratic organization is assumed to be antithetical to the freedom of activity traditionally imputed to the professional.

There is a fairly large literature referring to the conflict between bureaucratic administration and professionalism. The underlying assumption is that professionals owe allegiance to their peers and to their profession. They seek to control their work in light of their own standards, while resisting the necessity of taking orders from bureaucratic superiors who assert the aims of the employing organization (for a review of areas of conflict, see Scott, 1966). A number of studies have attempted to demonstrate with varying success that professionals are dissatisfied, even alienated, in bureaucratic organizations. But not all organizations where professionals work possess all of the characteristics of a bureaucracy. Empirical studies of such organizations – e.g., hospitals, law firms, accounting firms, and social agencies – have led to the creation of a variety of concepts representing hybrid forms of organizations that deviate from the bureaucratic model in order to accommodate their professionals. Such terms as advisory bureaucracy (Goss, 1961), professional bureaucracy (Smigel, 1964), and professional organization (Montagna, 1968; Scott, 1965) are familiar to students of the literature. These studies, as well as more recent developments in organizational theory, call into question the validity of the assumption that large organizations employing professionals are sufficiently bureaucratic to allow one to assume that professional work within them is ordered and controlled by strictly bureaucratic means.

By and large, most organizations that employ professionals deviate far more than those that do not from the bureaucratic ideal or, more generally, are more likely to violate the premise that organizations operate as rational systems concerned with maximizing efficiency. Indeed, it is no accident that three of the four representative theorists advancing non-bureaucratic models of organizations whom Scott linked together as proponents of an Open Natural System Model (Scott, 1981, p. 128) arrived at their ideas through the empirical study of organizations whose primary productive workers were professionals. The notion of an organization as an "organized anarchy" developed in part over the course of a study of the governance of universities (Cohen and March, 1972). The author of the most influential analysis of organizations that contradicts the conventional notion that they function effectively as a result of tight bureaucratic linkage and control of units and who argues that they should be viewed merely as loosely coupled systems elaborated his argument using references to schools and school systems (Weick, 1976).

None of these theoretical developments provides any actual empirical proof either that bureaucracy, in the form of pervasive scientific management, does not exist in many organizations employing professionals or that no form of systematic control is exercised over them. They do, however, raise strong doubts about the propriety of assuming – without careful, case-by-case analysis of the empirical evidence – that the controls that are exercised place professionals in a position directly analogous to that of the industrial worker, i.e., being subject to close supervision, having their skills expropriated, lacking discretion in the performance of their work, and the like. Indeed, by examining the framework of law and established practice surrounding the organization and performance of professional work, we move farther and farther away from that analogy.

Let us examine the central issue of autonomy or discretion in the performance of work. All workers everywhere practice some discretion in their work, and, as Kusterer (1978) has rightly argued, more knowledge is required to perform even detailed labor than is generally assumed by superordinates. Furthermore, classic industrial relations studies have documented over and over again the power of informal controls among workers in tempering and even sabotaging formal plans. But professionals differ from other workers in the degree of control that they exercise. In US labor law, professional workers are distinguished from ordinary rank-and-file workers because they are expected to exercise judgment and discretion on a routine, daily basis in the course of performing their work, i.e., discretion is a recognized and legitimate part of their work role. This characteristic, along with such others as their common training, credentials, and pay differential, is considered sufficiently distinct to justify treating them as special kinds of workers who have the right to choose a collective bargaining agent independently of other employees (see Gorman, 1976).

In addition, professional workers are subject to a different system of supervision. More often than not, supervisors of industrial and non-professional white-collar workers are people who have been trained as managers; they usually are not members of the rank and file who have risen in position and assumed greater responsibility. The former are not required to be at least nominally competent in performing the productive labor of those whom they supervise. For a great many professional employees, on the other hand, members of their profession routinely fill the supervisory, managerial, and often even executive positions. In industrial firms employing scientists and engineers, supervisory, managerial, and even higher positions in the hierarchy are filled primarily by employees with professional credentials (see Schriesheim et al., 1977). At the very least, the first line of hierarchical supervision of professional employees is *always* filled by a professional. For most professionals – accountants, librarians, social workers, nurses, physicians, lawyers, and schoolteachers, among others – the managerial levels above the immediate supervisor are also filled by qualified professionals because it is mandated by law, required for institutional accreditation or chartering, or effectively sustained by custom and convenience. Indeed, for some kinds of organizations providing professional services, it is either a legal necessity or a requirement for accreditation for even the chief executive officer of the organization to be a bona fide member of the profession. Non-professional business managers and administrators may become increasingly indispensable, but the professional executive officer exercises ultimate control.

Thus, while rank-and-file professional workers may have to take orders just as blue-collar or clerical workers have to, these orders are given by a superordinate colleague, not by someone trained in management or some other field. Where the work of the professional employees is formally delineated in some detail – "formatted" in the case of engineers (Ritti, 1971, pp. 18–43) – it is not done by outsiders who have expropriated the professional's skills, but rather by members of the same profession who have specialized in the accomplishment of such tasks. While this formatting does reduce the use of discretion and judgment by *individual* rank-and-file professional workers, it does not represent a reduction in the control of professional work by the *profession* itself, for other professional workers create it and supervise and manage the rank and file. It is therefore entirely inaccurate to say that the professions as corporate bodies have lost their capacity to exercise control over their members' work, even though individual professionals may have. While there are some new formal controls that are now exercised over the professions, concepts such as deprofessionalization and proletarianization are too far off the mark empirically to illuminate the character and implications of these controls. Let me try to delineate them in the remainder of this paper.

THE FORMALIZATION OF PROFESSIONAL CONTROLS

While the nature of professional control has changed, it remains largely dominated by the professions themselves, although it is limited, as is always the case, by the resources allocated to the support of professional work by the state, by the governing boards of firms and other institutions, by managers, and by individual clients. Professional controls in the past were largely informal, sustaining a live-and-let-live relationship among colleagues and preventing open conflict between professional elites and ordinary practitioners. Recent events have considerably weakened the grounds for such a relationship, while reinforcing and formalizing the differences in prestige and authority that have always existed within the professions. If there is any historic parallel to this situation, it is not to be found in the relations between capitalists and industrial workers so much as in the relations between masters and journeymen during the later days of the pre-industrial guilds (see Thrupp, 1963).

The first element that has changed the relationship among presumptive peers is suggested by current efforts to apply anti-trust laws to the professions. Nominally, these efforts attempt to substitute regulation by the competitive process of the market for self-regulation. Effective regulation by the market presupposes that there are no barriers to competition, i.e., no "restraints of trade," so that any form of collusion aimed at fixing prices, restricting consumer knowledge of price and other kinds of product information, or excluding competitors from the market is prohibited. Therefore, over the past decade a series of legal cases mounted as Sherman anti-trust or as First Amendment (freedom of commercial speech) actions has significantly altered the economic framework of professional practice for that small number of professions which have numerous self-employed practitioners. The courts have struck down professional bans on advertising that is not false or misleading, including publicizing the prices of routine services and goods, and on competitive bidding. Price-fixing in the form of standardized or minimum fees has also been swept away.

While court decisions have significantly reduced the professions' capacity to restrict competition among their members, neither judicial nor legislative actions have seriously diminished the barriers to competition created by occupational licensing laws. With minor exceptions, in the United States these matters (cf. Shimberg, 1982) fall under the jurisdiction of states and localities, not of the federal government. Broad, national action to eliminate or reduce licensing is therefore difficult to mount. Indeed, while there have been revisions in the licensing laws in one state or another, there has been no overall movement toward eliminating licensing itself, despite a great deal of discontent with the process. Some potential competitors to the established professions have been licensed in certain areas – nurse practitioners, midwives, and denturists, for example – but the scope of their work has been carefully limited. There has been nothing resembling the deregulation of competition *among* professions. Therefore, the major role market forces now play lies in relations among colleagues *within* given professions.

It is assumed that the economic consequences of this limited deregulation will be lower costs to the consumer, in part because consumers will select practitioners who charge lower fees, and also because new forms of practice will evolve. Through price-cutting, attractive advertising, and an increase in scale it has recently become possible to develop commercial chains for the provision of tax accounting, optometric, dental, legal, and medical services which are staffed by professional employees and directed by professional managers. It is much too early to tell, but it is quite possible that costs will fall and that the average income of professionals will decline compared with other groups over the next few decades.

The potential consequences of an increase in intraprofessional competition are more than merely economic, however. Traditional professional codes of ethics designed to restrict competition among colleagues were not solely economic either in their intent or their consequences. By banning overt, public appeals aimed at attracting a clientele by making invidious distinctions among professionals – appeals which, in the past, included outright deprecation of the competence of colleagues – these codes also helped sustain a certain solidarity within the professions. Price competition always existed – there were always celebrated as well as humble practitioners and the former charged far higher fees than the latter. When all were limited to a single method of announcing their availability to their potential clientele and prevented from making any *public* reference to charging higher or lower fees, however, the fiction of a company of equals could be preserved. Deregulation now allows, perhaps requires, the public display of differences among colleagues. If enough professionals take advantage of this opportunity, the professions may no longer be able to sustain their public image of solidarity and uniform competence. Indeed, the solidarity they did have may disappear.

Another traditional custom that helped to preserve professional solidarity was the avoidance of public and formal criticism of colleagues' competence and ethics. As more than one commentator has observed, it used to be difficult to get professionals to testify against a colleague in malpractice suits. Furthermore, the disciplinary boards maintained by professional associations, as well as those attached to state licensing boards, seemed to act slowly, if at all, in response to consumer complaints. They seldom censured their colleagues and revoked their licenses even less frequently. Political pressures have now forced the professions to be more active in such affairs, thus setting colleague against colleague. In the case of medicine, which has been subject to the greatest political pressure, it is now mandatory for all physicians who hospitalize their patients to be subject to a formal review and evaluation of their decisions by a committee of colleagues. The live-and-let-live etiquette of the past can no longer preserve the facade of equality in probity and competence. Physicians and other professionals must now judge each other, and, more importantly, do so formally and sometimes publicly. The conspiracy of silence, as well as the conspiracy of tolerance, has been seriously challenged. As a consequence, trust in one's colleagues' discretion and good will may also be undermined.

The fiction that colleagues are essentially equal in competence, authority, and power and that they basically share the same interests has also been weakened, particularly in the case of professional organizations that are large enough to require full-time administrative officers. The professionals who serve in executive, managerial, and supervisory roles are clearly delineated by their formal rank, and their authority is distinct from that of their rank-and-file "colleagues." Professional stratification in organizations involves differences in official authority and power that in turn produce varying perspectives on the professional enterprise. Rank-and-file professionals are primarily preoccupied with performing their work according to their own view of the intrinsic practical problems and of the necessary means of coping with them on a day-to-day basis (Lipsky, 1980). In contrast, supervisory professionals are accountable for the aggregate performance of the workers under them and they tend to have an organizational perspective. They identify as much, if not more, with the type of professional organization they represent as with the practicing profession.

As the threat of legal action, government regulation, and, in commercial enterprises, investor pressure for higher profits all increase an organization's accountability for the performance of its professional workers, those in the administrative elite will be more likely to assume a less collegial and a more superordinate relationship with their subordinate colleagues. Given the professional credentials of the administrative stratum of the profession, its members are at least nominally qualified to issue directives governing the work of the rank and file. In doing so, they violate the traditional etiquette of an earlier day (Goss, 1961) and so mark their distance from their nominal colleagues. The collegium becomes formally and overtly divided into those with administrative power and those who perform the productive labor.

By itself, the administrative elite is in a position to assert economic and administrative, but not technical or cognitive, power. They may be technocrats (Heydebrand, 1979), but they do not produce the professionally legitimate technical knowledge that they use to order, assess, and direct the work of the rank and file. The source of such knowledge is another elite segment of the professions composed of those who devote themselves on a full-time basis to research.

The most important difference between the modern professions and the crafts and earlier guilds lies in the way in which the former have systematically developed a relationship with the university. The professions control innovation largely by having a special class of members in professional schools who are devoted to research, experimental practice, and theorizing. This group constitutes the knowledge elite of the professions, and its members both teach professionals-in-training the latest knowledge and techniques and explore new areas. Making decisions about public policy issues has increasingly required scientific advice. This advice is provided by the knowledge elite, which is called to testify, to serve on committees recommending guidelines to govern professional practice, and to formulate acceptable standards for evaluating professional performance.

Lacking its own authority of expertise, the administrative elite must invoke the standards and guidelines of the knowledge elite in its directives aimed at formulating and evaluating the work of the rank and file. Since the standards of the knowledge elite are grounded in the abstract world of logic, scientific principles, and statistical probabilities rather than in the concrete world of work, in experimental designs and controlled laboratory findings rather than in the untidy, uncontrolled arena of practice, and in circumstances that are considerably less subject to the constraints of time, money, equipment, and other resources than is true of everyday practice, it is not hard to understand the skepticism of the rank-and-file professional. Indeed, historically, resentment and tension between town and gown, between practitioner and academic, have existed coterminously with the university itself as well as with its professional schools. With the formal invocation of academic standards as a means of legitimizing the increasingly self-conscious, formal, and public control of everyday professional practice, the tension between the rank-and-file practitioner and the knowledge elite cannot fail to grow as well, creating a deeper division between them than existed when practitioners were free to ignore the standards established by the latter, if they so chose.

THE IMPLICATIONS OF FORMALIZATION

I have tried to stress that none of these tensions is historically new for the professions. As long as there have been professions, there has been competition among its members. So, too, there has always been stratification, both of intellectual authority and of economic power. What is new today is the magnification and formalization of these relationships into a considerably more overt and consequential system of stratification within the profession which can no longer be protected by the face-saving norms of traditional professional etiquette. Nonetheless, so long as the formulation, direction, and execution of the control of professional work remains in the hands of members of the profession, it is not intellectually useful to employ either of the concepts of proletarianization or deprofessionalization. But when one elite formulates the standards, another elite directs and controls, and other professionals perform the work, something important has happened to the organization of the profession as a body and to the relations between its members which may have serious implications for its corporate character in the future.

In a well-known article, Goode (1957) characterized a profession as a "community," a group that shares a common experience and identity. While it is true that professions are divided internally by specialization and intellectual orientation into segments (Bucher and Strauss, 1961) and by the differences in interest, power, and prestige connected with the clientele being served (Laumann and Heinz, 1977), Goode's characterization is relevant for professions such as law and medicine. They have a long tradition, a distinct (though inaccurate) public image and identity, and a fairly homogeneous system of professional training. While they have been internally divided both by stratification and by specialization, and the membership in their professional associations has never been complete and has fluctuated a great deal, they have nonetheless sustained a community in Goode's sense, i.e., they have maintained a degree of solidarity that allows us accurately to characterize them as single professions. The divisions within them have not been great enough to lead to exclusive, warring associations that share no consistent common interest. It is this community, however, that is likely to be seriously threatened by the formalization of professional controls. Rank-and-file practitioners could conceivably split off from researchers and administrators and only participate in those associations that reflect their interests, leaving the elites to participate in their own.

While this possibility may be a novelty for physicians and lawyers, it is not a new development for the broad aggregate of professions in general, most of which are already divided in this fashion. Consider schoolteachers: their administrative superiors – principals and superintendents – usually have had training as teachers in schools of education and some years of experience in classroom teaching. Indeed, such training and experience are often prerequisite qualifications for their positions.

Similarly, the experts who formulate the guidelines and standards employed in schools are usually faculty members of schools of education, or are professionally qualified staff members of state boards of education. Even though they perform different functions, all may be seen as part of the same profession. The divisions among the three strata are so great, however, that in effect they are separate. There is even militant trade unionism among the rank-and-file practitioners, which is a rare occurrence among professions in the United States (see Marcus, 1973). Medicine, law, dentistry, and other professions that have not been subject to formal controls up to now may move in the same direction.

Nonetheless, it is by no means inevitable that professions that undergo a formalization of collegial relations, with a division into administrative elites, knowledge elites, and rank-and-file workers, will break up into distinct and separate corporate entities. But it does seem unavoidable that, with or without collective bargaining, the level of conflict will intensify, because the formalization of social control creates organized groups with different perspectives, interests, and demands. It also poses new and unaccustomed obstructions which reduce practitioners' capacity to perform their daily work in a manner that satisfies them (quite apart from whether they receive the compensation to which they believe they are entitled). Notwithstanding, there is little evidence that the special status of the rank-and-file professionals will deteriorate so much that they will find themselves in the same position as other workers. Even though they will be subject to more formal controls than in the past, they will probably continue to have distinct occupational identities, rather than being mere jobholders. In all likelihood, they will also exercise considerably more discretion than other workers in performing their work, and will be able to participate in formulating standards and evaluating their own performance through some type of peer review. Finally, they will still enjoy at least occupational kinship with their superiors.

RECONCEPTUALIZING THE PROFESSIONS

In conclusion, it is essential to point out that a major source of the deficiencies in the theories of deprofessionalization and proletarianization lies in their ambiguous conception of the professions. In their own way, proponents of each theory implicitly conceptualize the professions as collections of fully autonomous, highly prestigious, individual entrepreneurs who can essentially do what they please. Neither corporate organization nor legal and political status – both of which play an important role in sustaining privilege and power – nor any other institutional characteristics that influence labor market status figure in this conception. Such an incomplete conception is neither analytically coherent nor empirically salient, even as an ideal type, to most professions since the nineteenth century. The problem lies not so much in these particular theories as in the state of theorizing about the professions in general, which they reflect quite faithfully.

As I pointed out in Chapter 1, sociological theorizing about the professions has typically never gone more than halfway toward two possible positions. On the one hand, one can theorize about professions as concrete, historic forms of organization which some largely middle-class occupations developed in the nineteenth and twentieth centuries. These forms vary markedly from one country to another, though they preserve some significant commonalities in English-speaking nations. Adequate theorizing therefore requires a close analysis of concrete institutions and social categories, foregoing any effort to develop general, positivistic concepts. On the other hand, one can conceptualize professions as a special kind of occupation that is singled out and defined on the basis of abstract, theoretical considerations – as organized occupations that enjoy a special shelter in the labor market, for example, or as occupations whose members maintain control over their fate (Child and Fulk, 1982). To adopt this alternative, however, requires dispensing with history in the sense that it is the abstract conception of the occupation, not the fact that some occupation may be commonly regarded as a profession in some nation at some point in time, that determines what one studies and the variables one elaborates. Pursuing both of these tasks, which are essential when performed separately, will greatly advance our future understanding of the professions and their role in modern societies.

PART IV

CHOOSING PROFESSIONALISM AS SOCIAL POLICY

9

Are Professions Necessary?

At present, I think it is fair to say that scholarship concerned with the professions is in an intellectual shambles. In the United States today there is little, if any, of the broad consensus on mode of discourse that held sway among academic sociologists until the 1960s. Interest in the topic has become more widespread and complex in the meantime, extending beyond the academy. Some of that interest has been politicized into policy positions and interest group movements. Some of it has been manifested in extensive intellectual discussion in journals of ideas and opinion. And some of it is embodied in the current preoccupations of recent social history, particularly that focusing on the Progressive Era. The tone of most of this literature is hostile to the professions, but, because it is essentially unanalytic, much of it remains on a level of criticism so diffuse that one is at a loss to understand its implications. Nor is the literature even united in the object of its criticism, for there is no general consensus on what the word "profession" refers to, what occupations and types of occupations it addresses. Thus, almost any attempt to make sense of that literature is bound either to break apart on semantic shoals or to have to limit its own discussion and relevance to the narrow channel opened by its own necessarily arbitrary definition.

The extravagance and confusion of recent discussion begs for sifting and evaluation. This is what I should like to try doing here. But, given the highly varied referents of usage, not to speak of the highly varied issues preoccupying discussants, a narrow focus will not do. What I propose to do here is first establish a framework within which evaluation can take place, a framework built by indicating the most basic characteristic of all occupations, professional or not, and then specifying the progressively more particular characteristics that many and finally only a few of these occupations called professions may be said to possess. This strategy, I believe, can avoid confusion by equipping us to locate the key referent of most writers' usages, and to pinpoint the issues connected with it. Given that framework, I will go on to review what I believe to be the most basic elements of contemporary criticism of the professions and attempt to evaluate them.

"PROFESSIONS" IN THE MODERN LABOR FORCE

Let me begin by assuming that, whatever else a profession is, it represents a kind of work that people do for a living. Thus, the professions are part of a labor or work-force. As conventional American delineations of the work-force indicate, the twentieth century is witness to a marked and steady rise in the proportion of the work-force that is classified as "professional-technical" workers. Since 1900, there has been a drastic decline in farm workers, a rise and then leveling off in blue-collar, semi-skilled workers, a growth in the proportion of clerical and sales (or white-collar) workers, and a rise both of managers and of professional and technical workers. Only the crafts (or skilled blue-collar workers) have been stable, remaining in much the same proportion of the labor force throughout the century.

This set of trends is familiar to readers of such books as Daniel Bell's *The Coming of Post-Industrial Society* (1976). But what does it mean? What distinguishes the "professional-technical" stratum from, let us say, the clerical and sales stratum? The US Census occupational classification scheme which distinguishes between the two is really much too crude and ambiguous to provide us with a satisfactory answer to that question. It is true that its categories can be arrayed in a rough hierarchy of relative prestige, education, and income, so that we can say that "professional-technical" workers are "higher" than clerical and sales workers. But that does not tell us very much. Insofar as we are treating professions as occupations by which people gain a living, we can understand them better by being able to link their relative prestige, education, and income to the institutional circumstances surrounding the way they work, circumstances which both reflect and contribute to their relative position and which help us substantively differentiate them from other occupations.

Insight into the institutional circumstances of working for a living is provided, albeit stereotypically, by notions of the dual labor market originated by Michael Piore (Doeringer and Piore, 1971, pp. 163–83) and most recently discussed in detail by Richard Edwards (1979). Those notions identify markedly different conditions of employment by which we may distinguish among various occupations, conditions which can be used to explain variations among occupations in power and prestige. Briefly, Piore sketched two major sectors of the working population based on their relation to the hiring and promotion policies of employing firms – that is, their place in "internal labor markets." One – the *secondary sector* – need not concern us here except as a point of contrast. The secondary sector includes within it all those people who are employed spasmodically, with low wages, dirty and unskilled work, and close and arbitrary supervision by superiors. Here we find the unskilled worker, the transient, underemployed, and other low-paid members of the labor force – the young, women, black, and Spanish-speaking minorities. The jobs they do are varied and impermanent: they have few if any job rights or privileges; they are unorganized by unions and the like. By no stretch of the imagination can anyone working in the secondary sector be called "professional."

What Piore called the *primary sector* of the dual labor market is central to our concern here – that segment of the labor force which has steady employment, some form of job rights and job protection. The *lower tier* of the primary labor market is composed of blue- and white-collar workers who have stable positions and who are protected by seniority rules in large firms. They tend to be locked into their particular employing firms by that seniority and by the equity they have in the fringe benefits and promotion and retirement prospects that go with it. Their future hinges on the organization they work for. Their work is governed by elaborate work rules and formal administrative procedures and is being increasingly mechanized. The precise nature of their jobs is both determined and supervised by administrative planners and managers and tends to be specific to the unique needs of the employing firm. Few if any writers would call any of these workers "professionals." It is the *upper tier* of the primary labor market that contains all those workers who by any stretch of the imagination may be called professional, but it also contains some who may not be. This upper tier is characterized by lifetime, relatively secure, and stable work careers in particular identifiable occupations. On the whole, life-tenure in a particular occupation is made possible by institutional practices which require particular *credentials* testifying to training considered necessary to work. One cannot get the job in the first place without such credentials. By and large, occupations in this upper tier are of such a character as to be useful to more than one firm, and so in good economic times members of these occupations may and do move from a job in one firm to a better job in another. Unlike those in the lower tier, their careers are not restricted to the possibilities of promotion within a particular firm. Furthermore, they are subject to far less close supervision than those in the lower tier. They have considerable discretion or autonomy in doing their work. And when they are supervised, many of them are as likely as not to be supervised and evaluated by a member of their own occupation – by a colleague serving in an administrative capacity.

Our problem of delineating professions arises when we think of all the kinds of workers to be found even in this proportionately small upper tier of the primary sector. They are all full-time, often lifetime specialists. But among them are to be found workers who are never considered professionals – *the crafts*. The crafts are blue-collar workers. They differ from the professions in their reliance on practical on-the-job apprentice training, or sometimes training in secondary vocational schools. They have little or no contact with higher education and its emphasis on theory and verbal abstractions. But they are credentialed and they have lifetime careers in their work. Their skills are sufficiently general that they can move from employer to employer, and are not locked into the jobs provided by any single firm. *Technicians* also belong in this tier of the primary labor market, for they too have specific training for a specific set of job titles. Unlike the crafts, some of them have training in two-year if not four-year colleges, a fact which sometimes leads writers to address them in concert with professions. Third, there are those most often called *professions*, for whose work some kind of higher education is required, though the amount and kind of specialized rather than general education varies widely. Finally, there are those usually called *managers*, a group which has been claiming professional status in the United States for many decades with rather limited success. They are more likely to be promoted up from the white-collar ranks than are professionals, crafts, or even technicians, and while specialized educational credentials are not generally required for employment as managers, a general college education is increasingly being expected.

Given these distinctions, it is possible to point out that virtually all those who write about the professions have in mind some of the occupations in this upper tier of the primary sector of internal labor markets. What is common to all of them is that the people in them characteristically enter some kind of training institution prior to seeking work, and are often employed on the strength of their training credentials. Where they differ, however, is in the nature of the training they undertake, and in the degree to which their credentials are essential for employment or not. As I have already noted, most crafts do not receive training in institutions of higher education while technicians receive little, if any, higher education. Some training credentials, such as those of crafts, technicians, and occupations such as nursing, dentistry, and medicine, reflect highly specialized vocational training, while others, such as the general BA degree of managers, reflect little or none. Furthermore, credentials differ markedly in their capacity to assure employment – some are so strongly supported by legally enforced rights granted by exclusive licenses that no one can work without them, while others, such as a general BA degree, are used as criteria of employment solely because of the good will, convenience, or prejudice of the labor consumer or employer.

It is in discriminating among all the occupations in the upper tier that we find critically important differences among writers on the professions. Collins (1979), for example, addresses the whole range, assuming that any form of credentialism, no matter how tenuous, is sufficiently important to be exclusive and discriminatory. Crafts are arrayed along with those who have received at least some higher education. Most writers, however, exclude crafts because their credentials do not presuppose higher education. Many other writers, the Ehrenreichs (1977) and Gouldner (1979) among them, cluster managers with professionals in the new middle class, even though credentialism based on training is far weaker among managers. Bell (1976, p. 213ff), on the other hand, excludes managers, and delineates a general professional-technical grouping which is itself internally differentiated into a hierarchy at the top of which are "creative scientists and intellectuals," followed by practising professions, semi-professions, and the like, down to technicians at the bottom. Analytically oriented sociologists such as Wilensky (1964), Etzioni (1969), and Goode (1969) have reserved the label for a relatively few well-established, prestigious and strongly credentialed, exclusive occupations such as medicine, law, and certified public accounting. Writers such as myself (1970; 1988) and Terence Johnson (1972) have emphasized the capacity to control and regulate themselves as the mark of such occupations.

All writers agree, even if only implicitly by their selection of illustrative occupations, that, whatever else they are, professions are full-time *specialists*, their members being committed to their work as their source of income rather than being either part-time dabblers or amateurs, or people who work at one job one year and another the next. Furthermore, their specialized work is considered skilled, not like casual labor that any normal adult can be expected to know how to do, and not like semi-skilled labor that any normal adult can be expected to learn after brief instruction. In cases where their work involves consultation, they might be called experts, and their specialized knowledge and skill called *expertise*. In addition, these occupations can all be characterized by some form of *credential* testifying to the formal training thought to be prerequisite for competent performance or, as in the case of general education, for providing the background necessary for training on the job.

The type, content, and amount of such prior training varies greatly, as do the training institutions, occupational associations, licensing laws, certification and accreditation institutions, employment policies, and other elements connected with credentialism. Only a small proportion of those credentialed occupations can be considered self-governing or *autonomous*, however.

THE SPECTRUM OF CRITICISM OF PROFESSIONS

I wish to suggest that the denominators connected with various notions of professions, from least to most exclusive, are expertise, credentialism, and autonomy. Those who have attacked the professions over the last decade or so have all referred to one or another of those dimensions, or to institutional and ideological factors which are closely connected with those dimensions. Indeed, when we examine that literature in terms of those dimensions, we find odd, but revealing political bed-fellows. Let me start with the most conventional critical position.

The mildest critics of the professions are the *reformers of professionalism*, among whom we find political conservatives, liberals, and radicals. Their common position on the professions is one that is familiar to all of us. They all accept the basic idea that sustains the special position of professions – that there are certain kinds of specialized work which are sufficiently important to society and sufficiently difficult to do well to warrant protection by credentialism and its supporting institutions. The professions, therefore, are criticized neither because they are credentialed specialists, nor because it is felt that most of their claims to special knowledge and skill of value to society are essentially false, but rather because they are felt to be functioning defectively and perhaps receiving greater rewards for their work than is appropriate. They are thus in need of reform and not abolition.

While all those in this camp agree on the need to preserve the essential elements of the professions, however, the solutions they recommend vary because of their different diagnoses and prescriptions. Conservatives, and spokesmen for the professions, emphasize reducing the interference of the state and reforming the professions from within – paying more attention to recruiting the right kind of person to professional school, reforming professional education, and strengthening self-regulatory processes within professional institutions. Liberals, among whom we may count most of the traditional writers on the professions who laud them but who are not unaware of their failings, are likely to emphasize the importance of maintaining and strengthening state regulatory processes and consumer pressures while reducing the capacity of professional institutions to resist those "external" forces. Radicals, on the other hand, are likely to emphasize the importance of the political economy in which professional work takes place, arguing that it is the power of capitalism and its orientation to private profit which corrupts professional goals and performance and seduces professionals away from serving the public good. Under some as yet unrealized socialist regime, they believe, professions will be liberated from the yoke of false consciousness and capitalist exploitation and will be able to devote themselves whole-heartedly to the true public good without elitism and in concert with all other workers and citizens.

A second group of critics even more varied than the first may be delineated by a common position of urging *abolition of credentialism*. With few exceptions, their implicit target is not all those occupations that can be called professions but only those whose credentials are exclusive. Managers, for example, are not referred to. The critics' positions range along the entire political spectrum – from conservative to radical. On the one hand, such neo-classical economists as Milton Friedman (1962) believe that, if exclusive licensing of the professions were abolished so as to create a genuinely free labor market, the intensified competition among and within occupations would lead to improving the quality of work, developing innovative ways of performing it, and reducing its cost to the consumer. Also arrayed against exclusive occupational licensing is a loose collection of populists, anarchists, and consumer advocates who wish workers to be free to do what work they desire without constraint, and consumers to be free to seek products and services from whomever they wish, by their own choice and criteria.[1] They too urge a free market solution, though on moral rather than on economic grounds. In the case of medicine, the profession that has by all odds received the greatest amount of attention and criticism, this group of critics attacks constraints on seeking services from unconventional practitioners, on buying and using whatever drugs one wishes, and on the freedom to undertake diagnosis and treatment oneself by self-help and mutual aid rather than being forced to use professional services.

An entirely different group attacks credentialism on grounds of efficiency rather than of economic or personal freedom. It is composed of policy-makers and high-level managers whom Robert Alford (1975) has called the corporate rationalizers. They see professional institutions as obstructions to the efficient allocation and coordination of labor for specific productive ends. They attack the notion that professions have the right to refuse to perform all but a defined core of professional tasks, and the right to prevent any other workers from performing any portion of the tasks they claim, no matter how trivial or unskilled those tasks may be. They attack the rigidity or inflexibility of the allocation of tasks which accompanies the idea of credentialism, and in essence they seek for themselves the power "rationally" to design, allocate, and coordinate the tasks around professional services, and to determine who can perform them in the light of their own policy goals and their own administrative needs.

Allied with this administrative attack on professional licensure, though with different aims, has been the "new careers" movement which represents workers rather than management, and most explicitly sub-professional workers. Spokesmen for that movement have argued that the credentialism of professions constitutes a restriction on the possibility for upward mobility, preventing workers from moving upward from one occupation to another on the basis of accumulated work experience, on-the-job acquisition of skills, and practical rather than theoretical demonstration of competence. The present system prevents, for example, a practical nurse from being promoted to registered nurse without having to return to school for the full course of training which would provide her with RN credentials.

Those I have described are arrayed in favor of the abolition of credentialism – particularly the most stringent kinds of credentialism involving licensing, regulation of the market, and exclusive training programs. They are institutional abolitionists. One other important critic is an abolitionist also, but in a considerably more profound and radical way which requires special attention. I refer to Ivan Illich (1980). As I understand him, he goes beyond attacking the social forms by which expertise is institutionalized into professions. He attacks the very idea of expertise, no matter what its institutionalized form, though he illustrates his attack by reference to the strongest "dominant professions." He is a generic abolitionist who wishes to *abolish occupational expertise itself.* What he attacks is the dependence that is created when individuals or firms produce advice, or a service or product which people come to regard as indispensable. Unlike Adam Smith and Karl Marx, who deplored the human consequences of specialization for workers, he deplores the consequences for consumers. Instead of seeing professional institutions as a mere restriction on individual choice, he attacks professions for being by their nature *disabling* to consumers. As he sees it, by their very existence experts discourage people from learning how to do things for themselves and from relying on themselves and their community. Thus, the mere existence of experts discourages the use of people's potential to rely on their own resources, and so discourages the full development of human capacities.

Clearly, the critical positions I have described box the compass. At one extreme there are those arguing for reform of the professions without making any basic change in their characteristics as credentialed, full-time occupations. In the center are those who suggest abolition of the credentialing institutions of professions, but not of the full-time specialized tasks they perform. And at the other extreme there is argument against the preservation of the specialized occupations themselves – argument for the abolition of occupational expertise itself. How can we evaluate these positions? What are the issues underlying them, and what are their implications? Let me take up each major position, one by one, beginning with the most radical.

IS EXPERTISE NECESSARY?

Let us begin with the least common denominator of professions. Whatever else they are, professionals are experts: indeed, "profession" as opposed to "amateur" connotes not only earning a living by one's work, but also superior skillfulness, or expertise at doing a professional as opposed to an amateurish job. There are some tasks which almost everyone in a given society at a given point of history can perform merely by virtue of being an adult who possesses such conventional skills of everyday life as being able to dial a telephone or drive an automobile, and there are others which can be performed after only brief training or instruction. There are still other tasks which require either extensive training or experience or both, and, in this case, the performers are true specialists with skill and knowledge – that is, with expertise – which is distinctly theirs and not part of the normal competence of adults in general. This is not to say that the capacity to learn such skills is beyond most or even all others outside the occupation, but only that in order to learn them those outside must take the time to go through the training and practice necessary for adequate performance. Normal adults without prior training or experience cannot expect to do such work effectively. Is such specialized expertise necessary?

For the sake of argument, let us assume that all people have the same potential ability and that all are therefore capable of learning all the special skills that constitute the universe of work in our society. Given this, it becomes possible to say that when they do not use one of those potentials and instead rely on or submit to an expert for advice, service or goods, their "liberty to learn or to heal or to move on their own" (Illich, 1980, p. 62) has been shrunk, and a potential for independent action has been extinguished. The existence and employment of specialized experts, therefore, can be seen as disabling to consumers.

Furthermore, for the person who is an expert, specialization itself, performing the same work day in and day out, can also be seen to be disabling, since the person has the potential to do many things but does only that one thing: his preoccupations are narrow and limited. Karl Marx, concerned with producers rather than with consumers, expressed great hostility to the idea of a person doing only one kind of work all his life, even when that work is less mechanical and degrading than the narrowly specialized tasks performed by the proletariat in the detailed division of labor of industrial firms.[2]

Is it possible, however, to conceive of a society in which people do not serve as full-time specialists? The answer is obvious: people can do everything for themselves without depending on specialists for satisfaction of the full range of their needs only so long as their needs are very modest and their mode of life very simple. Long before the Industrial Revolution the accepted standard of living and the complexity and size of the great urban centers virtually required specialized expertise. This has been so not because people were not in principle capable of learning how to do everything, but rather because in practice there is not enough time in any one person's lifetime to go through the process of learning every particular form of expertise serving the varied, expansive needs of a dense multitude. Furthermore, a great many specialties – particularly such manual specialties as surgery – require frequent and recurrent practice for maintaining competence, while many others require time to keep abreast of new knowledge. Apart from the time it would take to be trained in every specialty, there is not the time in a single person's life to perform or otherwise be preoccupied with each specialty often enough to sustain competence.

Since the beginning of the Industrial Revolution, the exponential growth of knowledge and technique has made the possibility for any individual to learn and perform every specialty even less conceivable than it was before. Perhaps it is recognition of this that led Illich to stress that the reduction of needs and of the goods and services available to a society is prerequisite to abolishing the "disabling professions." However, he does not follow out the drastic implication of his position. In order truly to abolish disabling experts, one would have to abolish all but small, largely economically self-sufficient communities and accept a very severe reduction in the number of needs permitted to their inhabitants. Without reducing population to seventeenth-century levels, or without assuming a complex technology and economy which covertly relies on experts to form a supportive technological structure around such communities, the abolition of full-time, specialized experts is really inconceivable. One can conceive of abolishing some, even many types of experts, but one cannot

take seriously the radical position which urges the abolition of occupationally organized expertise itself. One is left, therefore, in a reformist
position of considering how to reduce dependence on experts, how to
eliminate all "unnecessary" experts, and, for those who are left, how to
minimize the scope of expertise and the magnitude of its privilege.
Credentialism, of course, is one protective source of such privilege.

IS CREDENTIALISM NECESSARY?

Given the necessity of accepting some role for occupational expertise and
skill, we must recognize the fact that in order for expertise to exist as a
stable and reliable activity it must be institutionalized in some fashion. In
any large and complex community there must be some conventional way
by which people can identify an expert without having to rely on word-
of-mouth testimonials, on prior personal experience, or on time- and
resource-consuming, risky, trial employment. This is particularly the case
for relatively esoteric experts who cannot be evaluated by everyday criteria
or by recurrent contact and use. The most elementary source of such
identification is the occupational title claimed by a person; but since anyone can claim a title, when the stakes to the labor consumer are high, one
might expect institutional devices which add plausibility to claims of competence and which therefore facilitate choosing among various claimants.
Expertise in a complex society is inseparable from some form of credentialism, for there is too much to know to be able to know it directly;
one has no alternative but to rely on indicators such as credentials. Credentialism often presupposes some organized system of conventional
training, but at the very least it presupposes some method of certifying
and titling prospective specialists by occupational associations, by the
state, or by prior employers, consumers, or teachers. Even if they do not
provide testimony predicting performance accurately, their role in facili-
tating the process of choice among all actual and possible claimants makes
them attractive to labor consumers (cf. Spence, 1974). It is difficult to
imagine how expertise in a large and complex society, which has a fairly
elaborate technological foundation, can be employed without reliance on
some form of credentialism to testify to minimal capacity to perform a
given kind of work.

From the point of view of the labor consumer, then, credentialism may
be seen as a necessary device for narrowing the range of choice and
therefore simplifying the intrinsically problematic process of choosing a
particular kind of specialist in a world in which there are many kinds.
The real world of advanced industrial society does not and cannot

approximate the primitive conditions of a perfectly free labor market (or of primitive communism), so that inevitable problems of information and evaluation require arbitrary institutional solutions. The issue is not whether credentialism as such is necessary, therefore, but rather whether credentialism is necessary for the choice of a particular kind of knowledge and skill and whether particular forms of credentialism are necessary. Obviously, unreliable and invalid forms of credentialism may be rejected, but not credentialism itself for at least some kinds of expertise.

But there is more to credentialism than we can see from the point of view of the labor consumer. There is also the point of view of prospective workers. Even in so modest a form as a letter of reference, credentialism is intrinsically exclusionary, for if one person has a letter and the other has not, the other may not be able to gain the opportunity to work. Many critics have focused their attack on the exclusionary character of credentialism, for credentialism creates a "social closure"[3] by which potential competitors are excluded and work opportunities restricted solely to the credentialed. Credentialism is thus said to produce inequality.

This is not the place to address in detail the analytical problems connected with the exclusionary side of credentialism, but it does seem appropriate to point out that, insofar as credentialism excludes the competent and protects the incompetent, we can agree that it is both unjust and inefficient. But what if credentials were sufficiently valid and reliable to be able to predict competent performance? The consequence of such a circumstance is that those without credentials, who might very well be able to perform as competently, are excluded from access to work merely by virtue of the lack of a conventionally accepted credential. Exclusion is, I believe, an inevitable consequence of a division of labor. The absolute number of people who can practice a particular form of expertise as "professionals" rather than as "amateurs" and hobbyists is always finite, limited by the need or demand for it. Insofar as work is specialized, it has limited use-value, so need or demand is similarly limited. A thousand great opera singers would not be able to perform leading roles regularly because there are not enough appreciative audiences for every one of them. Thus, not only is it impossible for everyone to have the skills of all experts, but it is also impossible for everyone to be able to practice the same kind of expertise. By its very nature as specialization, expertise can be practiced successfully and well, on a regular "professional" basis and as career, by only a limited number of people. That number may very well be smaller than the number capable of performing it well. What may be reasonably criticized about credentialism, therefore, is not the *fact* of selectivity and exclusivity, but rather only whether the *grounds* for exclusion are just or fair.

It also seems appropriate here to note a second underlying issue of credentialism – that the coin of exclusion has a reverse side of inclusion and protection. It creates, in Marcia Freedman's apt choice of terms (1976, pp. 113–29), a "shelter." Without a shelter which provides the reasonable expectation of sufficient security to be able to count on a career of work at a particular kind of expertise, why should one undertake training for it? It is possible to argue that a labor market shelter created by credentialism is an essential institutional device for motivating people to invest the time, effort, and lost earnings into the period of training necessary for acquiring particular kinds of expertise. And furthermore, if a particular kind of expertise is so unprotected that one cannot be sure that one will be able to practice it regularly, as a career, how can one become committed to it as a central life-interest? Credentialism thus creates the sheltering conditions by which it is possible to conceive of maintaining a committed relationship to work that is the antithesis of the alienation that Marx ascribed to the semi-skilled worker in a detailed division of wage-labor. And indeed, only if all work were reduced to easily learned skills in a detailed division of labor is it possible to conceive of people being so freely interchangeable among jobs that credentialism can be considered an artificial barrier; only if all workers lacked any commitment at all to any particular kind of work could we conceive to them freely and routinely moving from one kind of work to another.

In all, it should be clear how complex is the issue of credentialism. Without denying the validity or importance of arguments about the unjustly discriminatory character of particular instances of credentialism, one must nonetheless assert the necessity of some form of credentialism both for the facilitation of choice of specialists by labor consumers, and for the creation of commitment to and continuous involvement in a specialized career on the part of experts. Specialization is intrinsically exclusionary. It does *not* follow from this conclusion, however, that any particular kind of work must be credentialed. It is quite possible that many jobs requiring credentials today can be performed as reliably by people without them, though whether or not labor consumers wish to take the trouble to develop screening devices of their own is an open question. Furthermore, while some form of credentialism may be necessary, other forms may not be necessary at all. The solution of the problem of exclusionary credentials, therefore, must be sought in the abolition of inappropriate forms of credentialism for some kinds of work and complete abolition for other kinds of work. Absolute abolition of all credentialism cannot constitute a solution to the problems posed by the institutionalization of expertise in the division of labor.

A solution to the problems of credentialism thus requires what the critical literature so far fails to provide – distinctions among various kinds of work and among various forms of credentialism instead of global generalizations. There are important differences among various forms of credentialism which produce marked differences in the careers and conditions of work of various professionals. As I have already noted, virtually all those writing about professions as a broad class presuppose a large group of occupations whose members obtain their relatively prestigious and well-paid work in the upper tier of the primary internal labor market by virtue of having credentials testifying to some form of higher education. This very general form of credentialism is a far cry from the legally sustained, exclusive credentials of such professions as medicine. Medicine is relatively independent of the institutions in which its members work, and in fact controls much of what goes on in those institutions. Through its research and training institutions, the profession both creates and transmits its own knowledge and skill; it selects those it will train and its credentials are supported by licensing laws which the profession has successfully pressed the state to institute and enforce. It is the authoritative arbiter of what is health and illness, and of what is acceptable and unacceptable treatment. Only its members have the legitimate right to evaluate one anothers' work and set standards for its performance; self-regulation through peer review is the characteristic method of social control they claim to employ. The amount of discretion its members have in performing their work is so much greater than is ordinary that the term "autonomy" both for the organized profession and its members is not inappropriate.

This external, occupationally generated constraint which enables medical professionals to carve out a broad area of discretion even in circumstances of employment is markedly different from that which characterizes the vast majority of occupations assigned to the general professional class. Many of the people in these occupations are employed on the basis of a general BA degree, or an area of modest concentration declared a "major" within a general educational program. This training is only mildly, if at all, influenced by their occupation as an organized enterprise, and their general degree, or credential, is influenced even less. The effectiveness of their credential depends almost entirely on the good will and convenience of their employers. The substance of their work – their very occupation – is both created and evaluated according to criteria advanced by their employers. The leeway, flexibility, and freedom they may have in their jobs is a function of permissive personnel policies meant to reduce turnover and dissatisfaction in status-sensitive middle-class people rather than a function of occupational power. And their performance is controlled by essentially hierarchical, bureaucratic means, tempered by genteel etiquette that avoids the naked rhetoric of command in favor of the velvet-gloved rhetoric of suggestion and guidance. While such "professionals" as a class do often have elements of discretion in accomplishing their tasks, they are hardly so significant as to warrant the use of the term "autonomy."

IS PROFESSIONAL AUTONOMY NECESSARY?

Consideration of such matters as professional autonomy and discretion in the context of credentialism virtually requires us to return to the issue of expertise, or specialized knowledge and skill. The justification for credentialism of any sort rests upon the assumption that there are some kinds of expertise which are so valuable or potentially dangerous, or which are so complex and esoteric, that labor consumers are unable to choose competent practitioners without the aid of formal testimonials to competence and reliability. The same may be said of labor market shelters: they are justified by the social value of the work and the dangers attendant on its abuse. Consequently, the shelter both encourages the committed performance of bona fide experts and protects them and the public from purported incompetents. And so it is also for discretion at work: the knowledge and skill it is said to entail is asserted to be so esoteric as to warrant no interference by laymen, and so complex, requiring so much judgment from case to case, as to preclude governing it by an elaborate system of detailed work-rules or by supervision exercised by a superior official. In this sense, the issue of autonomy is closely connected with the issue of expertise itself, most particularly those kinds which are said to have very special characteristics.

Comparatively few occupations are organized in such a way as to manifest what I have called professional autonomy, or what Terence Johnson (1972) called collegiate control. Taken as an ideal type, complete autonomy is sustained by an occupational monopoly embracing several dimensions. It is first of all an economic monopoly: the profession controls recruitment, training, and credentialing so it can regulate directly the number of practitioners available to meet demand. This has obvious implications for income. Economic monopoly is viable, however, because professional autonomy also includes a political monopoly over an area of expertise; the profession is accepted as the authoritative spokesman on affairs related to its body of knowledge and skill, and so its representatives serve as expert guides for legislation and administrative rules bearing on its work. Furthermore, the profession has an administrative or supervisorial monopoly over the practical affairs connected with its work: its members fill the organizational ranks which are concerned with establishing work standards, directing and evaluating work. "Peer review" rather than hierarchical directive is the norm. Clearly, as I have defined it, professional autonomy represents a privileged position of some significance. Is professional autonomy necessary? Should it be abolished?

Here, as for the other questions I have raised in this paper, we cannot arrive at any thoughtful answer without postulating certain goals. If we want a society characterized by a richly varied culture, we cannot do without some forms of expertise. If we want to stabilize and focus expertise into an identifiable and reliable occupation that consumers can employ without the sometimes costly risks of trial and error in an entirely free labor market, and that workers can enter with some assurance of being able to find work, we cannot do without some form of credentialism. What goal is relevant for adjudicating the question of professional autonomy? I believe two are important. First, I think we can agree that we would like to support methods of constituting and organizing work which are not deforming and degrading to the producers of goods and services. Second, I think we can agree also that we would like to support the production of goods and services which are not disabling to consumers.

On the matter of work which is deforming and degrading to those who perform it, I need not say much. The revival in popularity of the Marxist critique of capitalism, with its notions of how workers have been reduced to a proletariat without control over their work and its fruits, and degraded by a meticulously detailed, deskilled division of labor, is familiar to us all. Ideal typically, professional autonomy is the antithesis of proletarianization: the workers themselves determine what work they do and how they do it. Professional autonomy allows workers to emphasize discretion in their work, to assert their own judgment and responsibility as the arbiters of their activities.

As I have already noted, professionals characteristically justify their autonomy by asserting that their work is sufficiently complex and uncertain as to require the exercise of discretion and judgment from case to case. That is to say, the claim is that each item to be produced, each person to be served, is sufficiently individual to require judgment and discretion in deciding how to perform the appropriate task, that a very special kind of expertise is required to do the job adequately, which in turn demands autonomy. The claim is that neither professional products nor professional services can be standardized.

In fact, this claim is not true. Any service or product can be standardized and mechanized. A shoemaker can claim correctly enough that every foot is different and thus that every shoe must be custommade by him, exercising judgment and discretion adapted to each individual's feet. But history has shown us the success of developing standard sizes and standardizing the production of shoes. As is the case with shoemaking, so also is it in the pursuits of medicine, law, and other ostensibly professional enterprises; they too can be broken down into small units and reduced to standard problems and standardized services. Just as the consumer's feet are made to accept standard shoe sizes, so consumers' problems can be made to conform to standard solutions. Of course, it is also true that when we reduce the producer's discretion in dealing with individual consumers, we risk proletarianizing the producer and forcing the consumer into inappropriate categories. Such a consequence may not seem serious for shoes, transistor radios, or uncontested divorces, but it might seem serious to us in the case of other goods and services. When at least some of the consumer's needs are reduced to standard categories, thus reducing the consumer to a standard object, this may seem oppressive and disabling. I think it can be argued that the producers of some goods and services should be able to exercise discretion and judgment not only for the sake of their own humanity, but also for the sake of the humanity of the consumer.

Of course, what has generated so much hostility to professional autonomy is its historic abuse; economic self-interest has seemed to overweigh service. Furthermore, in some cases professional authority has been so strong that professions have been able to impose on consumers their own conception of what is needed, and to intimidate and oppress the consumer in those instances where face-to-face service is involved. However, these problems are amenable to management by means which do not presuppose the total abolition of autonomy. Consider the economic dimension: even if we assume that some sort of economic protection is necessary both to preserve the integrity of a body of expertise and to commit people to a lifelong career of its accomplished practice, it does not follow that it is necessary for the profession to be the one to establish and maintain that protection. Surely that represents the most obvious conflict of interest. There might very well be defensible grounds for assigning professionals greater rewards than technicians or blue-collar workers, but it need not be up to the professions to determine their own rewards.

Similarly, a political monopoly over the *goals* of professional work does not seem necessary to sustain its integrity and value, though at least a very strong voice, if not an absolute monopoly, in the selection of technical means would seem necessary where it seems that the expertise is indeed valid and valuable. Goals, after all, are not a function of technical expertise, but rather of human values and of choices, which all are entitled to make by virtue of their humanity. Needs, in the sense that Illich uses the word, may be treated as values rather than as objects of technical expertise, and so may be considered subject to determination by all participants in society and not only by professions.

Finally, there is what I regard to be central to professional autonomy – sufficient authority over work to be free to undertake discretionary action as a matter of course. This presupposes some significant degree of economic and political protection of the profession so as to prevent the kinds of destructive tyranny that clients exercised over the considerably weaker professions of the past, and to stave off as well the pressure toward routine standardization – toward proletarianization – which powerful proprietors or managers are inclined to produce. Insofar as professional work remains discretionary and adaptive, its technical judgments are not easily or fairly evaluated by anyone other than a colleague. Thus, the characteristic mode of supervision and evaluation of professional work should remain collegial, involving peer review. But this does not mean that all other sources of evaluation and pressure are properly excluded. Only part of any kind of work is technical, based on truly esoteric knowledge and skill; only part of what enters into discretionary action is technical rather than social and moral. In order to put technical knowledge and skill into practice one must establish social and moral relationships with those involved in its application, lay and otherwise. It is in supervising those social and moral areas of work where technical peer review is overly narrow that evaluation and control by those outside the profession becomes essential. Outsiders, lay and professional, are the ones who are appropriately engaged in assuring that internal peer review actually does go on within the profession, that it is practiced honestly and effectively, and that more than a narrowly collegial point of view is taken into account. Within such a framework of external pressures, it becomes possible to conceive, first, of expert work in which there is sufficient autonomy to encourage commitment rather than alienation; second, of sufficient discretion to allow the production of goods and services which are adapted to individual consumers rather than forcing consumers and their needs into mechanically standardized categories; and finally, of work which transcends being merely self-serving and which can be of genuine value in enriching and improving the lives of its consumers.

ARE PROFESSIONS NECESSARY?

Are professions necessary? Given the essential ambiguity of the term, the question cannot be given a sensible answer. One can hide by saying, "It depends on what you mean by the word," or one can answer it arbitrarily by reference to a meaning with which one is comfortable but which may be irrelevant to what others have in mind when they attack the professions. Or one can restate the question, which is what I have chosen to do. Is expertise necessary? Yes, one can have no doubt that some kinds of expertise are necessary for a large, complex society with a rich material and intellectual culture, though the particular kinds of expertise that are necessary are open to debate. Is credentialism necessary? Yes, given desirable expertise, some kind of credentialism is necessary in a society that wishes to protect its lay members from the costs of inadequately informed choices and to protect as well the commitment and integrity of those who practice the expertise. Which occupations need to be credentialed, however, and what forms of credentialism are appropriate are open to debate. And finally, is a form of credentialism necessary which so protects an occupation that it can be essentially autonomous in determining both the needs of its consumers and the methods by which those needs are to be served? No, such sweeping autonomy is not necessary in a society which values individual choice and self-determination. Neither economic nor political autonomy is justifiable, though sufficient autonomy to permit significant areas of discretion at work is necessary if we wish to avoid both the alienation of practitioners and the standardization or objectification of consumers.

Clearly, the issue of the professions cannot be addressed in sweeping terms; it is one about which we must make a series of linked choices and decisions. That necessary discrimination is precisely what is lacking in most of the recent critical literature on the professions. Much of it relies instead on the rhetorical force of romantic anger at the oppression and degradation to be found in our time. While it is properly concerned with advancing the possibility of a society in which human potential is better developed, the very absoluteness of the criticism prevents serious thought about the social means by which we might realize that possibility.

In both the nineteenth and twentieth centuries we have witnessed post-revolutionary societies which have abolished on grounds of egalitarianism the protective institutions of professionalism, only to see them creep back in. My suspicion is that this re-emergence occurs not because of counter-revolutionary political winds, or because of class politics, but rather because of a generic problem that has little or nothing to do with political issues of equality and unjust privilege. At the foundation of professionalism, as I have tried to show, is specialized knowledge and skill thought to be of value to human life. At the foundation are issues created by the division of labor. Generically, specialization represents not inequality, but functional difference. Specialization poses problems to human society which cannot be dealt with successfully by the invocation of egalitarianism. Knowledge and skill cannot advance the necessary and desirable ends of sustaining and enriching life without being institutionalized in some fashion. The problems facing us cannot be dealt with by the abolition of the practice of knowledge and skill nor by the abolition of the institutionalization of that practice. Rather, we must discriminate those claims to knowledge and skill that are genuinely valuable from those that are not, and create and maintain forms of institutionalization which allow both knowledge and skill to be used to mutual benefit while preventing their becoming a source of exploitation and injustice.

NOTES

1 While he does not think of himself as a neo-classical liberal, Collins (1979) seems to embrace a free market alternative to credentialism.
2 Marx and later Marxists have devoted most of their attention to a critique of the detailed division of labor of capitalist factories without attention to the more general "social division of labor" which is addressed here. The absence of such attention creates an enormous deficiency in the capacity of Marxist literature to go beyond critique to the formulation of viable alternatives to capitalism. This weakness stems from Marx himself. On his hostility to specialization, see Avineri (1968, pp. 122–3). On the idea of the division of labor in Marx, see Giddens (1975, pp. 82–91). For discussion of Marx by a philosopher who sees in professionalism the source of a good life, see Haworth (1977, pp. 113–19).
3 This concept of Max Weber's has been discussed at length by Frank Parkin (1979). For a somewhat more articulated elaboration of the idea, see Kreckel (1980).

10

Professionalism as Model and Ideology

Professionalism is under attack today. In the case of law, both radicals and liberals accuse the profession of elitism, discriminating against minorities in recruitment, training, and employment, and failing to protect the interests of the poor and the underprivileged. Its members are charged by, for example, Auerbach (1976) with being hired guns who protect the interests only of those able to pay them handsomely – namely, the rich and the powerful. Others, far more politically influential over the past decade or so, argue from the point of view of both the consumer movement and that of neoclassical economics that law is a business like any other and should be subjected to free competition in the market-place, unprotected by any special privileges. When the leaders of the profession invoke ethics and the values of professionalism, critics declare it a self-serving ideology that masks the reality of naked self-interest. At their most charitable, they consider professionalism to be an antiquated survival of an earlier day that has no relevance to the work of those called professionals today. Does the idea of professionalism have any relevance to us?[1] Is it at all defensible in light of the patent deficiencies of its institutions? What are the central issues of professionalism?

These questions cannot be answered easily because much of the debate about professionalism is clouded by unstated assumptions and inconsistent and incomplete usages. Most important, it is not informed by a systematic method of thinking. In this paper I hope to be able to clarify the issues by first distinguishing the characteristic limitations of the most common usages employed in the debate and noting the absence of a systematic analytic or ideal model of professionalism. I will then sketch such a model and discuss its relationship to the alternatives that underlie most attacks on the professions. Finally, I will discuss how the professions can be defended by the use of an analytic model and the implications an effective defense would have for the regulation of the professions.

VERSIONS OF PROFESSIONALISM

The idea of profession or professionalism is developed in a number of distinctly different ways. First of all, it is a naturally created social label applied by lay people to a limited number of occupations that are considered to be in some way superior to ordinary occupations. This is the lay or folk idea (Becker, 1970, p. 92). It is a very loosely organized construct, including within it criteria of relatively high prestige, extended, specialized training, and being paid for one's work. It might be useful to call it the *commonsense* idea of professionalism.

The commonsense idea of professionalism is developed passively: it is not elaborated, systematized or refined self-consciously so much as it grows out of everyday, social usage. Among professionals themselves, as Nelson and Trubek (1992) rightly argue, its substance varies with the arenas in which they work and their perspectives on them. When it is expanded and articulated by those who think about it self-consciously, it changes. In English-speaking nations, where professions have often been self-organized rather than created by the state, the idea of profession is elaborated by their leaders in the course of making a claim to professional standing and used as a political tool for dealing with legislatures, the media, and the public at large. It is this larger policy arena that concerns me here. In that arena it is used to represent the profession not only to outsiders, but also to its own members. Commonsense usage is expanded to emphasize those characteristics of an occupation that justify special standing and privilege: it becomes a *profession's* portrayal of profession. Its content is determined largely by the political and ceremonial needs of the profession, and it is used primarily to advance and defend its position. While many versions emphasize the same things – for example, probity and public service – its ideological character, particularly in those substantive areas where the profession's internal politics of self-interest is threatened, precludes its development into a systematic and consistent whole.

Most of the debate that surrounds professions compares the actual performance of their members with either the ideological claims made by those supporting them or the commonsense expectations of the public and the commentators. Comparison between promise and performance reveals discrepancies that lead some critics, for example, Roth (1974), to reject the relevance of the idea of profession for understanding occupations with professional standing and others to attack professional standing itself. But what is rejected is professionalism either as a commonsense idea or as the professions' ideology, neither of which is developed as a model or analytic concept.

The needs of analysis are different from the needs of either common-sense thinking or ideology, for neither of the latter is impelled to create a systematic, logically coherent model of all essential characteristics based on a stated rationale or principle. Commonsense thinking need not concern itself with contradictions between various usages so long as it can segregate them from each other by invoking them in different contexts. Ideological and ceremonial conceptions of professionalism are shaped primarily by convenience and necessity and need include only those elements that defend threatened interests by denying accusations of damning characteristics and claiming laudable characteristics. This variation in emphasis on the part of those who speak for professions is clearly shown by Solomon's analysis (1992) of the responses of leaders of the Bar to the crises they perceived over a thirty-year period.

By contrast, an analytic model attempts to seek out and resolve contradictions in order that it be logically consistent, and to include within its framework all that is necessary to create a systematic whole. It can be a model only when it does not attempt to describe reality and instead attempts to create a conceptual yardstick against which the empirical world can be compared. It attempts to create a systematic way of thinking about reality by picking out what is most consequential or important about it. It is most satisfying when its terms explain what they address, but if not, nonetheless shows plausibly how they hang together, how the model works.

MODELS OF PROFESSIONALISM

An important but often overlooked characteristic of analytic models in the social sciences is that, while they can be used in a purely neutral fashion, they can also be used prescriptively to represent what should exist and to guide practical efforts to realize them. They too can be ideologies employed to focus and organize political activity. Indeed, the most effective ideologies are those based on models that are sufficiently abstract to allow their application to a wide range of issues and circumstances. They are the sources both of systematic explanation of what is wrong with the world and of the guidelines by which wrong can be righted. The most persuasive attacks on professions come from those who themselves, explicitly or implicitly, are advancing an ideology based on an analytic model. For them, professions are attacked not merely for deficiencies in their performance but because their existence stands in the way of realizing another model.

The basic policy question underlying discussions of professionalism is *how the work of those we now call professionals should be organized and controlled.* Two quite different models for organizing work can be fairly easily recognized as the foundation for the most powerful criticism of professionalism today. One is advanced by neoclassical economists who attack professionalism as a barrier to what *should* exist – namely, individual freedom of workers in the market-place to offer whatever goods and services they desire and of consumers to decide to buy whatever they wish. The implicit and often explicit analytic model, which is wholly logical and utopian in character, is that of the perfectly free market. A quite different model is implicit in critiques of professionalism that stress order, efficiency, and comprehensive service: many conservative and some radical critics attack professionalism as a barrier to the attainment of a planned system of efficient services that would exist if it were subject to the centralized, monocratic control of either private corporate capital firms or (representing the people) agencies of the state. The underlying model is that of rational-legal bureaucracy.

There is in theory a third model implied by the critical position of some of those who criticize the professions for elitism and who advance an egalitarian ideal whereby all workers collectively, rather than managers or experts, determine what work is to be done, who is to do it, and how.[2] However, a plausible model for the exercise of collective or egalitarian control over work seems to presuppose a very simple division of labor in which all work is sufficiently unskilled to be easily learned, performed, or understood by all workers. There is no provision for the elaborate forms of specialized work that are characteristic of large, complex societies with an advanced standard of living.[3] Perhaps this theoretical difficulty is responsible for the paradox that much of the criticism of professionalism by radicals seems to advance the implicit alternative of the individualistic free market that underlies capitalism (e.g., Collins, 1979, pp. 197–204). Without presenting a plausible alternative model of their own, egalitarian and populist critics sustain their position solely by rhetoric.

There are, then, two clear alternative models for envisioning how professional services can be organized after eliminating professional privileges – Adam Smith's free market and Max Weber's monocratic, rational-legal bureaucracy. But no analogous model of professionalism figures in policy debates in the same way and on the same level of abstraction. Nonetheless, as Gordon and Simon (1992) note, professionalism can be conceived of as a distinct alternative to the free market and bureaucracy. Let me sketch out the essentials of such a model and then discuss its relevance to the debate.

AN IDEAL-TYPICAL MODEL OF PROFESSIONALISM

Professionalism, like the free market and bureaucracy, represents a method of organizing the performance of work. It differs from the free market and from bureaucracy in that it revolves around *the central principle that the members of a specialized occupation control their own work*. By control, I mean that the members of the occupation determine the content of the work they do. Absolute control presupposes controlling the goals, terms, and conditions of work as well as the criteria by which it can be legitimately evaluated. By contrast, in the free market, consumer demand and the free competition of workers for consumer choice determine what work will be done, who shall do what work, how, and for how much pay. In bureaucracy, the market for labor and its products is institutionalized by rational-legal methods: the executives of organizations decide what product will be made or service offered, who shall make it, by what methods, and how it shall be offered to consumers.

Given this fundamental criterion of occupational control over work, one can build a model around the circumstances and characteristics that are necessary for occupations to gain and maintain such control. This requires attention to methods of controlling recruitment and training, entrance into the labor market under conditions that allow gaining a living from performing the work, and the procedures and criteria by which performance is organized and evaluated at work. In the professional model, both individual consumers and executives or managers (who are corporate or organizational consumers of labor) are excluded from such control. But since specialized knowledge and skill have no intrinsic connection with material (as opposed to cultural) capital or power, an occupation can fend off control by individual or corporate consumers of their work only by having power delegated to it by the state. An essential element of an analytic model of professionalism must therefore be to specify the activities and institutions that obtain the delegation of state power and subsequently maintain the conditions that assure its continuation.

In order to have power delegated to it, an occupation must be organized as an identifiable group: it cannot be a mere aggregation of individuals who claim to have the same set of skills. Only if it is an organized group, or if someone speaking for it manages to establish a corporate identity for its members, can it be dealt with collectively as a defined social category. The profession becomes an organized, corporate body either by the action of its own members independently of the state, as has commonly been the case in English-speaking nations, or by the actions of the state in creating specialized civil servants, as was more common in countries on the European continent. However the occupation becomes organized, those holding power must be persuaded that the body of knowledge and skill ascribed to the occupation is of such a special character as to warrant privilege. A number of claims have provided the ground for privilege – the functional importance of the body of knowledge and skill for the well-being of some significant segment of society, its intrinsic cultural importance, its unusually complex and esoteric character, and its superiority over the knowledge and skill claimed by competing occupations. Perhaps the most powerful claim is that there would be grave danger to the public if there were no control over those who offer their services – that the work provides access to "guilty knowledge" (Hughes, 1971, p. 288) that only those who can be trusted should have, and that serious consequences to the individual or the public at large can result from poor work. Central to effective claims is the idea that the profession's skills are so complex and esoteric that lay people are not well enough informed to be able to choose the competent over the incompetent, or to judge the quality of the work and even its outcome.

Beyond being persuaded that the occupation's body of knowledge and skill is worthy of special protection, the state must also be persuaded that the occupation as a corporate body is organized in such a way as to be able to control itself without abusing its privilege. The occupation must display institutional arrangements that make self-regulation plausible. Such arrangements include methods of recruiting new members selectively and restrictively by using screening criteria of ability or probity, and the maintenance of training institutions that are sufficiently standardized to permit assuming that all who complete their training successfully will be of at least minimally acceptable competence. Additional assurance can be provided by requiring examinations of those who have completed their training before allowing them to work. Not only competence but also trustworthiness must be assured. The claim may be that recruits are selected who have "good character" in addition to potential competence. Codes of ethics may be created both to display concern for the issue and to provide members with guides to proper performance at work. Peer or collegial review to assure adequate performance at work may be established, as may regulatory institutions such as disciplinary committees. Floating above all such claims and activities, of course, is the ceremonial rhetoric of the leadership.

With their material interests secured by their control over their work and their protected position in the market-place, members of professions are able to develop a deep life-long commitment to and identification with their work: it becomes a "central life-interest" (Dubin et al., 1976). Concerned with advancing the discipline to which they have become committed, some will experiment, innovate and do research to expand their body of knowledge and skill both for its own sake and to find new practical applications for it. And to protect the integrity of their profession and its work, they will monitor and correct each other's work and discipline or even expel deviants when necessary.

Collegiality is a central element of the professional model (Waters, 1989), distinguishing professionalism from both the unfettered individualistic competition among workers in a free market and the formal hierarchies of rational-legal bureaucracy. Protection from competition by other workers aids in the development and maintenance of such collegiality, of course, but bitter competition between members themselves and between various specialties within the profession is always possible. In order to promote a professional community professions attempt to limit potentially divisive economic competition among their members by promulgating rules designed both to temper the spirit and substance of intra-professional competition and to establish a basic income floor for all its members. Established within the profession is an egalitarian, collegial atmosphere in which the greatest rewards are symbolic. As Parsons (1939) pointed out some time ago, professionals are not distinguished from people in business by being altruistic rather than self-interested. They, too, are self-interested, but their goal hinges more on gaining the symbolic rewards offered by their colleagues than on gaining a high income. Professional honors are accorded to those who advance the discipline by unusual achievements in its daily practice, in innovation, and in employing it to make an important contribution to the public good.

THE VIRTUES OF PROFESSIONALISM

All this should sound familiar, for it is composed of bits and pieces freely borrowed from the major writers on the professions. But here those bits and pieces are brought together in a systematic way, and are not advanced as empirical facts. They are advanced as a model of the elements that together allow people to control their own highly specialized work in the spirit of service to others and the advancement of their discipline. The model specifies the conditions for professionalism, just as those of the free market and rational-legal bureaucracy specify the conditions for "universal opulence" (in Adam Smith's words) and formal rationality respectively. None of those models faithfully describes the way professions, markets, and bureaucracies actually perform. All are both ideological and analytic in character, advancing a desired ideal as well as an analytic construct.

Both economists and planners for state and corporate enterprises are well aware of the way empirical versions of the professional model obstruct their aims. Understandably, they have not dwelt on its virtues. Rather, they dwell on the virtues of what they claim will be gained by their own alternatives once the obstruction of professionalism is removed – more goods and services at lower prices and greater variety, more innovation, more predictability and reliability, greater efficiency, and the like. In contrast, those speaking for the professions today have employed a purely reactive, mostly commonsense and ceremonial defense.[4] But once one conceives of professionalism as a model, one can identify potential virtues that commonsense thinking alone overlooks.

The professional model is based on the democratic notion that people are capable of controlling themselves by cooperative, collective means and that, in the case of complex work, those who perform it are in the best position to make sure that it gets done well. It contains within it the assumption that when people can control their own work, and when their work, while specialized, is complex and challenging, they will be committed to it rather than alienated from it. According to the terms of the model, people find intrinsic value and interest in the work itself, which leads them to want to do it well. Furthermore, they constitute a kind of community in that they interact on grounds of strongly held common interests both in maintaining their professional position and in performing the work they do (Goode, 1957). Thus, they are alienated neither from their work nor from each other, nor, insofar as they believe they advance the good of others through their work, are they alienated from society. In short, as Gordon and Simon observe (1992), the ideal of professionalism provides many of the conditions that neutralize those specified in Marx's analysis of alienation from work under capitalism.

There is an additional activity of some importance that is encouraged by professionalism. It provides a milieu which encourages intellectual innovation – the development of new knowledge, skills, and ideas. But that innovation is not restricted merely to developing new modes of satisfying the perceived needs or demands of consumers in a market-place, nor of those who control organizations. More important, because it is insulated from the need to be immediately responsive to the demands of others, it can go beyond the status quo and so depart from received opinion as to be revolutionary. The amount and kind of innovation that is possible are richer and more varied than would otherwise be the case.

Research and theorizing that threaten the foundation of the practical work of normal science become possible, as does questioning the legitimacy of conventional practices and policies.

It may seem inappropriate to impute to professionalism the function of critical thinking and the creation of new ideas and knowledge. The former function is usually assigned to those whom social scientists call intellectuals, while the latter is assigned to scholars and scientists. To many, the professional is someone who merely applies available knowledge to the solution of practical problems – the practicing doctor and lawyer being prominent exemplars.[5] Intellectuals, scholars, and scientists, in turn, are not considered to be professionals. How one chooses to use a word is, of course, a somewhat arbitrary matter, but if we wish to take into account the institutions that make such activities as the "disinterested" pursuit of knowledge for its own sake possible on a regular and predictable basis by a large number of people, then we must include scholars and scientists among professionals. They could not exist without such institutions. Neither could most intellectuals.

Ever since the nineteenth century and the decline of the gentlemanly amateur scholar/scientists who relied on personal or patronage resources for their living, the institutions of professionalism, tied to universities, have been responsible for creating the shelters within which modern intellectuals, scholars, and scientists can do their work. Like the practicing professions, they control the recruitment, training, and employment of their members. Furthermore, most cannot make a living by scholarship or research any more than most intellectuals can do so by their writing. The university teaching jobs that they control provide them with their living. Those jobs require daily concern with the issues of scholarship and research and provide the free time in which to pursue rather than merely teach them. Following Parsons (1969), then, I would include scholars and scientists among those occupations today that resemble the ideal model of professionalism.

There is more to it than including scholars and scientists among the professions, however. It must also be recognized that the conventional practicing professions also produce new knowledge and techniques by exploring their own concepts and theories rather than merely serving others' demands passively. The traditional professions have been graced by individual practitioners in the past who made new discoveries or who have raised their voices against the accepted practices of their time, and there remain some who do so today. But the closer reality comes to the model of professionalism, the more such activity becomes possible on a routine, institutionalized basis primarily by members of the profession who serve in the special role of teaching.

Practitioners, of course, are heavily involved in the day-to-day activity of serving others, so one cannot expect most of them to be routinely engaged in scholarship, research, or the like. But professions control the recruitment, training, and certification of their own members, and insofar as the process is institutionalized so as to assure some standardization of the outcome, formal schools will perform those functions, with special members of the profession serving as faculty. Insofar as they are full-time faculty, those in professional schools are in the same position as conventional scientists and scholars in universities – supported economically by the practice of teaching in circumstances that leave them a fair amount of free time to theorize and do research. They, too, are insulated from the practical demands and needs of the outside world and in a position to develop ideas and make discoveries independently of it. Like scholars and scientists in universities, concerned with the development and practice of their specialized body of knowledge and skill, committed to the goals or purposes of their craft, they may pursue the unexamined logical implications of what is known and extend them well past immediate practical necessity.

While these institutional grounds for independent thought and research that professionalism provides are much too important to ignore, it is obviously dangerous to exaggerate the degree of independence that is possible. Quite apart from the impossibility of ever being entirely free of the perspectives and prejudices of one's historical time and place, a practical limit on independence is posed by the impotence of knowledge and the dependence of its bearers on the dominant powers for their protection. What they do collectively, therefore, cannot deviate so far from the interests of those powers as to threaten them overtly. But the collectivity provides a general shelter within which highly critical modes of thought can develop well past what is conventionally accepted.

These innovative cognitive activities characteristic of professionalism provide a source of growth and enrichment in knowledge, values, and technique that could not be produced by workers who are wholly dependent on satisfying the demands that others formulate, and who are concerned primarily with serving their own material interests. While the extension of old ideas and the conception of new may lead to the creation of new demands that increase the number and value of professional jobs, it is only the most vulgar view that implies deliberate intention to do so. In any case, without meaning to imply that professions have a corner on the market for Truth, their capacity to pursue new knowledge, techniques, values, and ideas from a relatively independent point of view is a valuable virtue. It can make an important contribution to the possibility of developing a more humane, richer, and effectively functioning society.

THE INADEQUACY OF THE PRESENT DEFENSE

This conceptual construct, professionalism, advances a kind of blueprint for organizing work in a manner that can be argued to be more desirable than the others. It sketches a coherent alternative, shows how and why it deviates from the free competition and rational order advanced by the others, and justifies its deviation by its virtues. It shows the interrelationship between various attitudes, activities, and institutions and given ends. Thus it provides the resources not only for a defensive ideology employed merely to fend off criticism, but also for an aggressive or offensive ideology directed at extending and strengthening professionalism in the real world so as to get closer to the ideal model and its benefits.

In current debate, few if any from outside the professions have defended them. Indeed, most who are not members of conventionally recognized professions have joined in the attack even though a great many of them are academics whose position is sheltered by professional institutions. Among academics, most sociologists attack professions for exclusionary practices that contribute to inequality, often sounding like advocates of a free market. Political scientists (e.g., Gilb, 1966) attack them as private governments unresponsive to public needs. Historians (e.g., Auerbach, 1976) attack the elitist and exclusionary nature of their past activities. And economists understandably attack them as monopolists who interfere with the free operation of the market. Among those prominent in practical policy affairs – planners and heads of state agencies in the public sector, and executives, managers, and investors in the private sector – professions are more often than not seen as obstructions to their goals.

Most of those who attempt to reply to such criticism have been members of the conventionally recognized practicing professions – some in their capacity as officials of professional associations, and some especially prominent in other ways. This has made for a focus on individual professions rather than on the principle of professionalism, and encouraged reactive and defensive rather than assertive tactics. Those who defend their own profession do not defend other professions and even join others in attacking them – representatives of medicine and law, for example, often attack one another publicly. They have shown little awareness that all professions share a common interest that is threatened by exponents of the alternative models. Furthermore, because the defenders are usually official or quasi-official representatives of their professions, they cannot escape being prisoners of the conflicting interests to be found in the politics of their own associations. They can neither openly concede patently indefensible abuses as anything other than anomalous or rare, nor propose or agree to corrective actions that are unacceptable to some important segment of their profession. The consequence is that their defense has been weak, partial, inconsistent, and in some cases even misleading.

Because all professions in the United States today can count on a fair degree of respect and trust, albeit ambivalent and varying in degree from one to another, many of their claims are likely to be accepted by the public and the politicians who sanction their privileges. But when the position of the professions seriously interferes with the economic and political interests of capital or the state, capital and the state have the power to change public opinion and reduce support for professional institutions. Like all workers, intellectual or no, professionals have no tangible power of their own. They possess only their knowledge and skill, the essence of their labor. Therefore, the professions are highly vulnerable to political and economic pressures. Medicine, the most prestigious and wealthy of them all, provides an instructive example of ultimate weakness in the face of the power of the state and of capital. It is being forced to change in ways that were inconceivable twenty years ago, and it is possible (though not probable) that law will share its fate in the future. While I certainly do not believe that the professions are on the way to settling into the position of a true industrial proletariat – indeed, not even industrial workers in the United States may be said to be in such a position – it is quite possible that the conditions of professional work will move further away from those specified by the ideal-typical model I have sketched here. A decline in relative income is likely, but that has little relevance to professionalism as such so long as it does not drop to truly penurious levels.

Present defenses, I believe, can do little to prevent the changes going on in the United States today. I have already noted that the leaders of the professions are the intellectual prisoners of a purely reactive ideology as well as the political prisoners of the conflicting interests that characterize their associations. As Schneyer's analysis (1992) of the process of creating the 1983 American Bar Association Model Rules of Professional Conduct shows, the official reforms that are pressed are limited mostly to what is acceptable to a heterogeneous membership. They are also limited by an ideology that is insufficiently systematic to provide adequate intellectual guidance, and seriously distorted by reliance on elaborations of traditional, commonsense conceptions of professionalism. The ideology they employ is an intellectual patchwork created from selected fragments of idealized history, moral precepts, pious exhortations, optimistic interpretations of the profession's members' capacity and inclination to serve the public good generously, and obsession with symbolic matters of tradition, convention, and propriety such as advertising, unionization, and the like. The worn thread that holds the patchwork together is almost always spun from a naive, commonsense conception of human action in which the knowledge, values, and attitudes of individuals provide the major source of motivation and direction for their behavior. And so their main emphasis is on reforming the way recruits are selected and trained while paying little attention to changing the institutional and economic structures within which their members do their work. As the model of professionalism specifies, the two are interdependent: the latter provides the resources that either corrupt or reinforce the consequences of the former.

I wish to suggest that an aggressive ideology advancing the terms of the analytic model of professionalism can perform far more effective service for the professions' defense than a commonsense version. It can do so, first of all, because it is better equipped to argue the greater desirability of professionalism than the alternatives implied or asserted by exponents of the free market or of rationalized corporate or state authority. It is able to acknowledge monopoly without apology, for monopoly in and of itself is a vice only if one assumes that a free market is a virtue, and that a monopoly exercised by an independent body of specialized workers cannot serve the public interest better than a mono- poly of authority exercised by functionaries of capital or the state. It can observe that there is no reasonable basis for expecting people to serve the public good if they cannot be assured of a reasonably secure (but by no means necessarily luxurious) income for themselves and their families. And it can argue that a monopoly held by an occupation whose members are committed to maintaining the integrity of a craft that is of value to others is a more desirable and less destructive solution to an important social problem than is the free play of unbridled material interest or the reduction of all work to formally specified procedure proposed by its critics. The practical issue then becomes regulating the conduct of those who possess the monopoly so as to assure adequate performance, and not eliminating monopoly itself.

Following the model, however, a truly consistent and principled ideologue will go on to specify what must be done by the professions in order to come close to realizing the virtues claimed for the ideal model. A principled ideologue for the free market cannot serve as an apologist for concentrations of economic power that prevent the free play of indi- vidual choices to produce, offer, and buy services and goods on the basis of material interest. A principled ideologue of rational-legal bureaucracy cannot condone the use of anything other than competence to decide who shall hold a position or any exception to the rule-governed exercise of authority employed to gain the ends specified by the ultimate authorities.

By the same token, a principled ideologue of professionalism cannot condone a monopoly that serves primarily to protect rather than seek out and control the incompetent, the venal, and the negligent among its members, any more than condone a monopoly in which all are free to maximize their incomes at the expense of a public which has nowhere else to turn.

A principled defense of the professions, in short, is offensive as well as defensive. In contrasting its ideal-typical model with those of its critics, it asserts it as no more or less utopian than theirs, and argues that the characteristic pathologies to be found in empirical forms of the other models are even less desirable than those to be found in professionalism. It is aggressive in joining the attack on the pathologies that stem from material self-interest in the market-place, and from the reduction of work and its products to formal procedure in bureaucracy. But it can be no less aggressive in joining the attack on the practices of professionals that compromise the integrity of the model. Only by maintaining its own integrity can it succeed in leaving no doubt of its superiority over the atomistic play of individual self-interest or the iron cage of formal rationality.

NOTES

1   Another question of some intrinsic value is why all this criticism of professionalism arose when it did. For a lively chronicle of the rise of such criticism among sociologists and historians, and a tentative explanation of it, see Metzger (1987).

2   See, for example, Gordon (1977). In Wright's considerably more sophisticated analysis, expertise is recognized as a source of exploitation, but it is not considered *intrinsically* exploitative so long as "ownership rights in skills have been equalized . . . [when] differential incomes and control over the social surplus cease to be linked to differential skills" (Wright, 1985, p. 85). This position is extremely rare among left-oriented critics, who tend to be hostile to specialized skill.

3   Rothschild and Russell's review of studies of democratic participatory productive organizations (1986) finds that they all tend to have a simple division of labor. My guess is that the primary source of difficulty for exponents of egalitarianism lies in their inability to recognize that functional differentiation need not represent inequality, and in their conflation of two quite different things – the authority of political, economic, and administrative power with the authority of expertise. While many, Foucault (e.g., 1980, pp. 146–65) being the most prominent, would impute "power" to expertise, they refer to the influence of discourse or persuasion and semantically conflate it with the power of material sanctions, which they recognize as quite different.

4 For a discussion of the ideal of professionalism in law in light of the approach of economists, see Simon (1985).

5 They too, however, are in a position in which they exercise judgment that is independent of their clients', balancing the interest of the client against that of other clients and the public at large. For a sophisticated and sensitive analysis of the independence of practicing lawyers, see Gordon (1988).

11

The Centrality of Professionalism to Health Care

Professionalism is most in need of defense in the case of medicine, for the latter's crisis continues and is intensifying. The percentage of Gross National Product that the United States spends on health care is well above that of any other nation, and the cost is becoming unacceptably high. In the absence of control exercised over institutional budgets and physicians' prices, as is done in Canada and elsewhere, the key to containing cost is the physician, because it is the physician who authorizes or "orders" the use of most other services and health-related goods. Therefore, many efforts at controlling costs in the United States have been aimed, directly or indirectly, at influencing the physician's practice patterns. But few if any have been an unequivocal success. What, then, should be done?

I shall address that question here by noting that some policies designed to lead the physician to be more economical in providing and ordering services contain within them conflicting and incompatible assumptions. I shall try to clarify those assumptions by suggesting that they can be reduced to three logically or ideal typically "pure" and mutually exclusive methods of organizing, motivating, and controlling the performance of work. I shall argue that the critical question for the future lies in choosing one of those methods as the central focus for policy support, and using the others solely as supplements. Arguing that a desirable health-care system must be based on trust in professional workers who are free to exercise discretionary judgment, I shall conclude that policy should aim at strengthening professionalism and employ elements of the other models – especially those of the free market – with great caution.

THE CONFLICTING ASSUMPTIONS OF COST
CONTROL POLICIES

Many financial mechanisms and administrative procedures have been developed by both public and private insurers to contend with excessive costs. Taken together, they make a number of contradictory assumptions about the way practice patterns are influenced. This becomes apparent when we take as an example the use of Diagnosis Related Groups (DRGs) as the basis for reimbursing hospitals, and the review framework by which they are administered.

The use of the Diagnosis Related Group involves reimbursing hospitals a flat sum for each patient they care for (see Vladeck, 1984). It is based not on the cost incurred by the hospital for each patient no matter what the diagnosis, nor on the individual diagnosis, nor on the number of days individuals actually occupy a bed and use hospital facilities, but rather on the DRG into which individual diagnoses fall. The hospital is reimbursed at the same flat rate for a variety of individual patients who have different, though related, diagnosed problems, and who have different degrees of complications connected with those problems. The flat rate is set statistically, by the cost of the average number of days in hospital and the average variety of services and facilities. If, in fact, a patient must stay longer than the norm and use more than the usual services, the hospital must absorb the above-average cost. If, on the other hand, the patient can be discharged earlier than usual, and use fewer services and facilities than the average, the hospital can pocket the difference in cost. In any case, cost is controlled by the flat-rate prospective payment. What are the assumptions underlying it?

The immediate, superficial assumption underlying this method of reimbursement is that the hospital will receive adequate reimbursement for an average mix of patients, and that it will be motivated to eliminate unnecessary days and services in order to avoid costs above and beyond the set rate of reimbursement. Indeed, because it is possible for the hospital to keep the difference between its own lower cost and the fixed rate, and therefore make a profit, it is assumed that its members will be motivated to undertake cost-saving efficiencies that go beyond those required to break even. These manifest assumptions rest largely on the plausible belief central to economics that people are motivated primarily by the desire to avoid financial loss and increase financial gain.

But there are also other assumptions. One is that the hospital administration will be motivated to put pressure on its attending physicians – either by its own actions or by the actions of its medical staff or a staff committee – to minimize both the days in hospital of patients and their use of services and facilities. It is assumed that work in hospitals is arranged in such a way that administrators and members of the medical staff have both the power and the inclination to exercise significant influence over the behavior of individual physicians. That is, physicians' choices are not purely individual, but rather are embedded in a social organization that influences those choices.

Still another assumption is that the diagnoses at the heart of the method are made on the basis of some objective and stable set of criteria. However, there is often more than one way of categorizing or diagnosing a patient's problems, including the choice of what is primary and what secondary. There is some evidence that physicians select a target outcome and choose their diagnoses accordingly. Thus, should they want their patient to spend more time in hospital than is the norm for one DRG, they select a diagnosis in another, related diagnostic group which provides the reimbursement that pays for such a length of stay. For example, a discharge diagnosis of difficulties due to pre-existing heart disease can be shifted instead into related codes which include acute myocardial infarctions and chest pain, for which there is higher reimbursement. This phenomenon has been called "DRG creep" in the trade (see Simborg, 1981). It suggests how vulnerable the system is to those who create its records. The service is not exactly and irrevocably specifiable independently of the discretionary judgment of the "worker." And the way that judgment is employed to fill out administrative forms and medical records is no doubt subject to a variety of motives and influences.

It is also important to note that, while the DRG method deliberately creates financial incentives for cost-saving, it would not be employed if it were assumed that financial gain were the sole criterion for decisions. The method assumes that professional standards and ethics limit the incentive to increase income or profit, so that concern for the well-being of the patient, as well as concern for the integrity of the service itself, will take precedence over gain. Underneath it all, therefore, such a policy does not assume that either physicians or administrators will act in a purely calculated, materially self-interested fashion.

Finally, I may note that the DRG method of payment does not rely on complete trust either in individual or organizational financial incentives or in professionalism. It also relies on a complex administrative structure of reviewing claims for payment. The procedures for review, payment, and adjudication of ostensible violations of the stated rules are formal and bureaucratic, and are maintained not only for accounting purposes but also for establishing and administering sanctions in the event of the discovery of untoward activities. The method assumes that an administrative structure standing outside individual hospitals and consultation rooms can effectively check practice patterns by reviewing the official records reflecting the actions and claims of practitioners and the organizations in which they work. Underlying it is, of course, the above assumption that the records are objective and reliable.

TYPIFYING LABOR MARKETS

It should be apparent that the health-care system is based on a number of quite different, even conflicting assumptions, and that its elements are organized by a variety of quite different, even conflicting methods. On the one hand it assumes that physicians and others can be motivated to change their behavior by purely self-interested, material incentives. On the other, it assumes that response to financial incentives by physicians will be constrained by an ethical concern for the well-being of those to whom they provide services, and a professional concern for doing good work. Reliance on economic incentives is predicated on the actions of individuals freely making calculated choices, but those actions take place within formal organizations such as hospitals and HMOs which structure choice in ways that preclude considering them to be wholly free or individual. Furthermore, practice takes place within a broader administrative and fiscal framework that organizes routine and systematic procedures for reviewing and approving or disapproving claims and decisions by the use of standardized administrative criteria. And the primary providers – physicians – are embedded in a social system composed of colleagues in various collaborative and supervisory positions, and of administrators in various positions of organizational and agency authority.

Clearly, there is no single, consistent set of assumptions that guides the financing and organization of health care, but traces of several different sets, each one of which is markedly different from the others. Since the logic of none of them is fully developed, and policy is typically created opportunistically, piece by piece, there is real danger that conflict between elements of one set will cancel out the benefits expected of elements of another. In order to be clearly aware of that possibility, it is useful to examine the fully elaborated logic of three methods of organizing work into labor markets.

I believe that the best way to conceptualize the organization and financing of health care is to treat it as a labor market. However, in order to do so, we must recognize that there is more than one way of organizing a market. I suggest that there are three distinct ways of doing so. There is, first, the free market, in which workers compete freely to be chosen and paid by employers or clients. Second, there is the bureaucratic market, which is hierarchically organized and controlled. And, third, there is the professional market, which is organized and controlled by the specialized occupations themselves. In the first the consumer is in command; in the second the manager or executive; in the third the specialized worker. In order to understand how those markets work, it is essential to specify the incentives each relies on to motivate and direct the energies of their participants, and the values attached to work. Consonant with the logically ideal and therefore relatively simple structures of the models, differences in incentives and values may be put starkly.

In the free-market model, the common interest of all participants is in monetary price and gain. Workers have no necessary interest in the kind of work they do or in the way they do it, nor are they bound to any particular workplace. Indeed, if one job pays more than another, they will promptly move to it. All that is important to them is maximizing the income they gain from their work: they will perform their work only as well and as rapidly as is necessary to maximize income. Furthermore, they act solely as individuals, each competing with the other without any sense of common interest or inclination to organize themselves collectively.

The primary concern of those who consume their labor is with the price of goods and services, and they seek the lowest price. Given the extent to which the model requires that the individual consumer be fully informed about the nature of the goods and services available and rationally calculate value and advantage, the quality of goods and services is assumed to be reflected in their price. The same may be said of those who contract with workers to produce a particular good or service: they are driven by competition in the market-place to keep the price of their products as low as possible, and, since their aim is to increase their income or profit, they are driven to reduce costs by various efficiencies, including minimizing the wages of labor and using the cheapest possible production techniques and resources. Price and profit are the central measures of success, with efficiency defined by the minimization of price in the production of a particular good or service.

Actions are much more constrained in the bureaucratic labor market, and incentives and values different. The emphasis of those officials in command is on the reliable and predictable production of specified goods or services. The price of such goods or services, while obviously a consideration of some importance, is nonetheless subordinate to their reliability and the predictability of their supply. Quality is defined by formal rules and standards which guide the review and evaluation of the performance of the workers. The individual consumer can choose only among those goods and services that the governing officials of the bureaucratic labor market – national, sectoral, or local – have decided to produce, and must pay the specified price for their standardized quality without necessarily being able to trade off lower quality for lower price. Workers can compete for jobs in the bureaucratic market by gaining the qualifications required for them. Once employed, they compete for advancement by conforming to the rules of the organization and gaining whatever additional qualifications are required for mobility. And they can gain the security of some version of tenure or seniority and thus a lifetime work career in the organization. While monetary incentives have some importance, the predictability and security of working conditions provide their primary incentive. They gain those benefits by conforming to the formal standards established and enforced by the hierarchy.

In the occupationally controlled or professional labor market, the relationships among the participants and the incentives for their work are yet again different. The choices of worker by both consumers and employers are limited to those allowed to work by the corporate occupation or its representatives. While there is some economic competition among members of the occupation within their sheltered position in the labor market, their occupation's emphasis is on community and "brotherhood" or collegiality. The tendency to establish a basic income floor, if not the full equilibrium of a "single price," reduces considerably the incentives of material interest.

Their income being somewhat protected both from the pressures of individual consumers or employers and from vigorous competition from others inside and outside their occupation, their central commitment is to do the work well and to gain the approval and respect of their colleagues. Their evaluation of one another's work does not emphasize the criterion of cost: what is applauded is the quality and virtuosity of work irrespective of cost and even outcome. Inspired and perhaps irreproducible management of a rare and little-understood problem takes precedence over the reliable management of routine cases. Committed to their work, they believe it to be both intrinsically valuable and of benefit to others. In performing it, therefore, they believe they are contributing to the well-being of others, and that their commitment to their work represents commitment to serving the good of others.

CONTRASTING INCENTIVES AND VALUES

Put baldly, one can say that in the free-market model the prime incentive is material gain, and value is measured by money. Its legitimacy is established and sustained by imputing efficiency to it; its prime benefit is low cost to the consumer and profit to the provider. In the bureaucratic model the prime incentive is security, and value is measured by reliable conformity to established standards. Its legitimacy is established and sustained by imputing legality, or rule-conformity, to its products. In the worker-controlled or professional model the prime incentive is the respect or approval of colleagues, and value is rooted in the quality of work. It gains its legitimacy from the authority and value of the knowledge and skill of the workers which justify the cost of their work, even when it does not succeed.

In each case workers compete with one another, but they compete for different things and by different means. In the perfectly free market, competition is over price and profit or gain, which depends on satisfying the demands of consumers no matter what they may be. In bureaucracy, competition among workers revolves around conformity to established standards and rules in order to gain the approval of superordinates. In professionalism, competition is focused around the virtuosity and quality of work that gains the honor and respect of colleagues and symbolic rewards such as awards and citations, in which financial gain is a marginal consideration.

THE DIMINISHED ROLE OF THE CONSUMER

When we use the three logical models to sort out the strands of the American health-care system today, it becomes immediately apparent that the perfectly free market has very limited relevance. Under ordinary market circumstances customers are free to patronize those who will give them what they want, whether or not it is professionally approved. But in health care the patient is not an ordinary consumer. Indeed, consumers are even less free in the market-place today than they were yesterday.

Throughout the history of Western medicine, most conventional analyses have concluded that, owing both to the complex and esoteric knowledge involved in medicine, and to the emotional and physical incapacitation that often accompanies illness, patients are not in a position to be adequately informed and fully rational consumers who are capable of looking after their own interests in the medical market-place. It is for those reasons that restrictive licensing which limits the patient's freedom to choose health practitioners is justified.[1]

Today's health-care system adds a structural restraint on the patient's freedom of action. These days it is out of the question for the vast majority of consumers to finance their own health care out of pocket: some sort of group-based insurance, whether involving fee-for-service or capitation payments, is essential, as is partial financing by employers or government.

What this means is that, while patients may be the primary end-consumers, they are in a poor position to make direct and free individual choices of what they believe they need. "Third-party" health insurance carriers, whether private or public, are the powerful consumers, as are large-scale employers who negotiate contracts with insurance carriers or with health providers. Those brokers of health care dictate the range of alternatives and limits for individual consumers' choice of financing and delivery plans, as well as choice of treatment once covered by a plan.

For patients, choices in the health-care labor market are not made freely from day to day or illness to illness as each occasion to consume arises, based on experience from previous occasions, for insurance plan coverage has already set the direction and limits of choice. True choice of alternatives is made periodically when enrollment in or renewal of plans is made. And when that choice is made, it is based on what is at best a dim awareness of the full implications of complex contractual instruments specifying what complaints or conditions are or are not "covered," which health-care occupations and which members of those occupations can be consulted, issues of "co-insurance," "deductibles," and the like. The choice, furthermore, is speculative, being addressed to the terms of *future* care at a time when one is not sick and has no immediate sense of concrete need. Once the choice is made under such poorly informed conditions, a complex and economically powerful administrative system controls what they may choose when they feel the need for a service, granting them the use of a particular service only so long as it is covered as part of the package and deemed to be necessary.

THE MISSING PREREQUISITES FOR A FREE MARKET

It should be clear that to the past view of how patients' choices are limited by ignorance and disability must be added further limitation by today's organized methods of financing and administering care. Even less than yesterday can we conceive of the patient as a well-informed, well-equipped consumer who is free to make choices and bargain as an autonomous individual in the market-place. But without a well-informed, rational consumer who is free to make choices, one absolutely essential requirement of the free market model is missing. And given occupational licensing, which prevents free entry into the labor market and also limits the range of consumer choice, another essential element of the model is missing. There is very little chance that these conditions will change. Its fundamental terms being missing from the health-care system, the free-market model is relevant to it more as a source of ideological critique than an analytical guide. The health-care system is not structured by the free economic competition of all who wish to sell services and goods, with consumers free to choose what they wish. And the nature and substance of whatever choice consumers have is limited by the increasing concentration of economic resources into the hands of relatively few public and private organizations that pay for health care and, to a lesser degree, organize it.

The health-care system of today is best made sense of as a mix of the bureaucratic and professional models, with elements of the former rapidly growing in importance as the administrative structure surrounding practice expands. It is only *within* the organized and regulated structures of the system that competition can exist, and it need not necessarily be directly grounded on material gain. Policies that try to introduce the material incentives and values connected with the free-market model into a system from which the essential conditions for anything resembling a free market are absent will not only fail, but will also threaten the conditions upon which the effective functioning of the system depends. The same may be said for policies that so intensify elements of the bureaucratic model as to stifle those of the professional model that is at the heart of the present system. When fully developed, each model is hostile to the other. Each must be considered a logical alternative to the other. Policy must choose one to advance, and employ elements of the others only as corrective supplements that do not undermine it. And for all the patent faults that real rather than ideal professionalism has shown, I wish to suggest that it is a more desirable model for health-care policy to advance than either bureaucracy or the free market.

PRESERVING TRUST AND DISCRETION

Consider the basic grounding of the models, and their relationship to the nature of health care. The free-market model entails the unfettered competition of individual workers concerned with maximizing their incomes by serving or selling to individual consumers who are fully informed about services and products and capable of exercising rational, calculated choices designed to minimize their cost. The only way by which a free market can be thought to work to the consumer's advantage lies in full information, for if those offering goods and services are concerned solely with gain, their claims cannot be trusted. Solely for self-protection against the fraudulent claims, inadequate services, defective goods, and overpricing that one might expect from producers, consumers must be knowledgeable, calculating, and free to choose or refuse a good or service.

However, consumers of health care are less well-equipped to protect themselves than consumers in other areas. They can and should be better informed than they are now, but there are serious limitations on what is ultimately possible. In health care the consumer must ultimately rely on trust in the competence and probity of those who provide health services as well as, these days, the third parties who purport to act as their agents (see Barber, 1983). If the free-market model were dominant in organizing health care, the consumer could not trust them. Nor could health workers trust one another.

What about the bureaucratic model? One important contemporary school of economics – the "transaction-cost" approach of Oliver Williamson (1985) – argues that under certain circumstances the dangers and costs of "opportunism" (that is, fraud and malfeasance) in transactions make it more "efficient" to forsake the market and instead to organize transactions and relationships by hierarchical authority. In essence, the bureaucratic model is substituted for the free-market model in order to reduce the dangers of "opportunism" and gain "efficiency." In that model, transactions are routinized and organized, reducing uncertainty by establishing predictable and controllable costs. The thrust is to control performance by formulating specific rules governing responsibilities and uniform standards by which to evaluate it. This reduces discretionary activity as much as possible. Current policy efforts to create a reliable administrative framework for reviewing and controlling medical decisions in hospitals and other practice settings, in conjunction with definite standards to justify such decisions, hope to control costs by such a method.[2]

To evaluate this bureaucratic solution we must note that health services are addressed to the central core of human existence – physical and mental well-being, and the conditions of survival as a human being. The way one conceives of health-care tasks and outcomes reflects the way one conceives of the people being treated. Standardizing the conception of tasks and outcomes for the purpose of measuring and controlling them also standardizes the conception of people and their difficulties. In essence, people are reduced to formally defined categories. They become objects produced by reliable methods at a predictable cost. While the bureaucratic method may solve the problem of trust by its reliability, it undermines the flexible discretionary judgment that is necessary to adapt services to individual needs. If it were to be the dominant goal of policy efforts, it would in essence industrialize consumers in the course of industrializing services.

It is only the professional, or worker-controlled model, I believe, that contains within it potential solutions to the problems of trust and discretion. Unlike the free-market model, its very existence depends on consumer trust. Furthermore, based as it is on collegiality, it is grounded on mutual trust among members, sustained by negotiating the boundaries of competition from other workers and limiting the kind of competition that can take place. Central to its members' commitment is concern with the quality of their work and its evaluation by direct collegial or peer judgment rather than by cost or standardized official categories. In essence, I believe that the overall strategy of social policy should be aimed at keeping the professional model at the center of health care and other human services while checking and correcting the vices of its practitioners by carefully chosen elements of the other models.

THE THREATS TO PROFESSIONALISM

Thus far, my analysis has been based on the underlying logic of ideal typical models without any serious attention to the empirical forms they take today. But a social policy that takes only ideal models for its guide is almost certain to have undesirable consequences. In the case of professionalism we need have no illusions about reality. Where they could, professions have been prone to employ their monopoly to advance the economic interests of their members well past the bounds of necessity, and they have been much too reluctant to judge the performance of their members critically and exercise effective control over them. Trust has been abused and discretion unchecked. The health-care system cannot be left in the hands of physicians without careful checks and balances. Both market and bureaucratic methods should be used to reduce cost and control performance, but only those that do not destroy or seriously weaken what is desirable in professionalism.

   The dangers become apparent when we consider the use of policies based primarily on manipulating economic incentives in an ideological climate that claims professional work to be no different from any other kind of economic activity. Under such circumstances, those who work alone without much contact with colleagues or practice institutions are encouraged to milk the consumer or the paying agent wherever they can. And those who work in a practice network or institution are led either to conspire collectively to maximize income or to disintegrate into unrestrained competition. Surely none of these possibilities is desirable. Policy should discourage those who are inclined to devote their efforts primarily to maximizing their income while encouraging those who assign greater value to doing good work for the benefit of others.

Furthermore, policy that creates the conditions for unfettered individual competition for material rewards cannot but seriously weaken the social network without which the norms and sanctions of competence and service characterizing ideal-typical professionalism cannot be sustained. It runs the risk of destroying what Coleman (1988) calls the "social capital" of professionals. Social capital is defined as the structure of social relations between and among actors engaged in a productive (or economic) activity. An atomized collection of individuals with no definite boundaries is likely to have little social capital. On the other hand, a closed structure of social relations can facilitate the development of norms and sanctions that can lead people to work for the public rather than their individual good. According to Coleman (1988, S107–8), "reputation cannot arise in an open structure, and collective sanctions that would ensure trustworthiness cannot be applied." Without denying the potential usefulness of policies encouraging competition and material incentives in a limited context, therefore, I believe it is important that their effect on the structure of social relations surrounding health care be carefully taken into account.

In contrast to policies designed to maximize the initiatives of the free market based on individual self-interest, it might seem that policies aimed at maximizing the terms of the bureaucratic model would create a social structure (or system of governance) to solve the problem of trust by binding and organizing the behavior of workers through the exercise of hierarchical authority and the systematic institution of formal rules and standards. This is Williamson's solution. However, quite apart from the fact that this discourages discretionary actions adapted to truly individual needs, Granovetter (1985; p. 91) notes that such a policy does not actually

> produce trust but instead is a functional substitute for it .... Substituting [bureaucratic] arrangements for trust results actually in a Hobbesian situation, in which any rational individual would be motivated to develop clever ways to evade them; it is then hard to imagine that everyday economic life [in the organization] would not be poisoned by ever more ingenious attempts at deceit.

Formal bureaucratic devices of control are hostage to the spirit and substance of the social relations of their participants. This is especially the case for health care, where, because the work has not been successfully automated or routinized, supervisors must rely on formal records rather than the direct appraisal of work. The success of the organization depends greatly on the way its members exercise their discretion to choose, perform, and record the outcome of their work. An enormous variety of empirical studies carried out over the past half-century has shown that, when they feel no loyalty to it, people do not passively obey, but instead actively seek ways of "getting around the system" wherever they can. Heavy-handed emphasis on individual material incentives or on conformity with bureaucratized standards can be expected to lead to the manipulation of the system to the detriment of policy intentions and the validity of the records themselves.

SAVING PROFESSIONALISM FROM ITSELF

Let me briefly indicate some of the areas where attention is needed if professionalism in the present-day practice of medicine in the United States is to be advanced and the need for the compensatory use of material incentives or bureaucratic control reduced.

If professionalism is to flourish it is essential that practice be infused with a spirit of openness, infused by the conviction that one's decisions must be routinely open to inspection and evaluation. Competitive advantage gained by trade secrets and property rights has no place in professionalism, where one's obligation is to provide colleagues with all the data upon which one bases a decision or conclusion, and to make public one's results. This norm of openness pervades science and scholarship, but seems to be lacking among practitioners in medicine. Physicians tend to have an individualistic conception of autonomous clinical judgment that leads them to resent examination, evaluation, and commentary on their work by anyone, even colleagues. This notion of individual autonomy of judgment appears to develop during the course of training (see, e.g., Carlton, 1978), and underlies resistance both to peer and administrative review. It surely influences the spirit in which peer review is carried out, and must be changed if peer review is to be effective. In order to encourage a truly professional spirit of openness, the climate of teaching in medical school and teaching hospital, as well as the climate of both practice and review in practice institutions, must be changed to make such openness the norm.

While the spirit of performance is an essential element of fully professional conduct, the way performance is organized either limits or facilitates its expression. Peer review is essential for fully developed professionalism. In health care, peer review requirements have been extended into both practice institutions and administrative review organizations, yet how they are organized and, more important, how they are actually carried out is very poorly understood. Here, the usual academic call for "more research" is certainly justified. An intelligent policy of strengthening peer review (and professionalism) must be well informed. It is essential that direct studies of the organization and operation of the quite varied forms of peer review be undertaken in order to provide a secure foundation for future policy.

Finally, I suggest that considerably more attention must be paid to avoiding circumstances in which practice patterns are inappropriately influenced by organized economic pressures and bureaucratic constraints. Both in health care and in other professionalized areas the formal organization of work has been changing in important ways. More and more physicians are becoming employees of organizations, and many of those organizations are operated for the profit of private investors. Because the health-care system is rooted in professionalism, close attention to the impact of these developments on professionalism is essential, as is reconsideration of some of the law upon which the organization of work is based. What forms of incorporation, for example, are appropriate to organizing and financing work whose prime justification lies in advancing the well-being of the customer? What loyalty do professionals owe to their employers? What right do they have to make ostensible trade secrets public when they bear on the well-being of patients in particular and the public in general? What rights must they have to participate in ostensibly managerial policy-making in order to preserve the integrity of their work while also preserving their right to bargain collectively (see Rabban, 1989; 1990)? Are new forms of incorporation, institutional licensing, chartering and accreditation, and labor law needed to encourage the provision of critical human services in a form that better serves the public good? Answers to questions such as these are essential to the development of policies designed to move our health-care system closer toward the professional ideal.

In sum, policies designed to reduce the cost and maintain and improve the quality of health care by relying primarily on material incentives and individual competition or on the establishment and enforcement of bureaucratic standards are more likely to fail than not. Hope for their success implicitly assumes that the ethics conventionally attached to professionalism will prevent dishonest or cynical manipulation of the system. But without additional policies designed to strengthen the positive elements of professionalism, the social environment that sustains and reinforces those ethics is likely to be damaged. The goal should be to strengthen collective commitment to the quality of work for the benefit of patients, duly tempered by considerations of cost and reliability, and advanced by effective modes of peer discipline – in short, commitment to the maintenance and control of responsible discretion by working colleagues, and to making the professional model more of a reality than an ideal or a promise. Measures designed solely to counteract professional abuse without also strengthening professionalism itself will lead us to an impoverished, and maybe not even cost-controlled, health system that neither physicians nor patients deserve.

NOTES

1 For discussion of this issue and the varied positions of sociologists and economists, see Begun (1986) and Dingwall and Fenn (1987).
2 A useful description of administrative controls now being made possible by both computer technology and the development of quantifiable standards for appraising medical decisions is to be found in Feinglass and Salmon (1990).

12

Nourishing Professionalism

In the United States today, the professions are going through great changes in their composition, numbers, and political influence. At the same time their customary practices and privileges are changing. Law is struggling with both internal changes and vociferous public questioning of its ethics, accountancy is coming under increasing pressure from regulatory authorities, research science faces increasing criticism of its capacity to assure the integrity of its members' work, and engineering is taking its licks. Medicine has been going through the most profound changes, perhaps because it deals with universal needs, and its bills are being paid by the state and a handful of powerful, private "third parties." Its position today exemplifies what is typical about professionalism as a social problem – namely, the tension between the provision of affordable and conscientious service to others, and the economic interest of those who provide it.

Serious as the problem may be, physicians, lawyers, and other professionals continue to hold a special position in our political economy. Unlike many areas of our economy which have been deregulated, the professional arena continues to be characterized by quasi-monopolies over core services, often sustained by exclusive licensing. Only at the margins of their jurisdictional boundaries has competition by other occupations been allowed. However, recent shifts in the ideological winds in the United States have led to pressure to reduce professional control over the way practices are organized and the way professionals compete with one another. Many professionally imposed restrictions on advertising were struck down by the Supreme Court, while other restrictions were whittled away by the Federal Trade Commission's threat of anti-trust action. New forms of ownership and control of the institutions in which professionals practice have been emerging and, while many legal barriers remain,[1] we can now conceive of circumstances in which it is possible for individual professional practices to be drawn into large-scale, non-professional, corporate institutions. Medicine in particular seems likely to undergo such "corporatization," and prominent commentators such as Paul Starr (1982) and Alexander Relman (1980) warn of its consequences.

In this paper I wish to appraise the potential effects of corporatization on professionalism. I shall argue that the simple fact of employment of professionals such as physicians and lawyers by large-scale public or private organizations does not, in and of itself, threaten the spirit and ethos of professionalism. The major threat, I shall argue, comes from more particular policies that are not intrinsic to large-scale organizations and that in fact also influence the professionalism of self-employed practitioners. But first, let me discuss the meaning of professionalism.

PROFESSIONALISM

"Profession" is synonymous with "occupation": it refers to specialized work by which one gains a living in an exchange economy. But it is not just *any* kind of work that professionals do. The kind of work they do is esoteric, complex, and discretionary in character: it requires theoretical knowledge, skill, and judgment that ordinary people do not possess, may not wholly comprehend, and cannot readily evaluate. Furthermore, the kind of work they do is believed to be especially important for the well-being of individuals or of society at large, having a value so special that money cannot serve as its sole measure: it is also Good Work. It is the capacity to perform that special kind of work which distinguishes those who are called professional from most other workers.

The character of professional work suggests two basic elements of professionalism – commitment to practicing a body of knowledge and skill of special value and to maintaining a fiduciary relationship with clients. A relatively demanding period of training is required for learning how to do esoteric and complex work well. That course of training tends to create commitment to knowledge and skill so that the professional's work becomes a central life-interest which provides its own intrinsic rewards. Professionals develop intellectual interest in their work, so they are concerned with extending and refining it and they believe in its value to society. They do not merely exercise a complex skill, but identify themselves with it. What they do is not labor solely for the income but for the pleasure of something more, something that may on occasion be considered to be play.[2]

Second, what professionals do is of special value to their clients. But their knowledge is sufficiently complex and esoteric that clients are not able to evaluate it accurately. Therefore, clients of professionals must place more trust in them than they do in others. A fiduciary relationship must exist between professionals and their clients. Professionals are expected to honor the trust that clients have no alternative but to place in them. The client's needs and benefits must take precedence over the professional's need to make a living.

THE PROFESSIONAL MARKET PROJECT

What I have said so far is singularly unsociological, for I have talked only of knowledge and skill, motives and meanings, values and commitments. In portraying professionals' relations with clients I painted an image of one individual consulting another. It is true that our experience rests primarily on our qualities as individuals and on our interaction with other individuals. Nonetheless, one cannot make adequate sense of that experience without explaining how it is that thousands of individuals can be identifiable members of the same profession, that their interaction with hundreds of thousands of clients has pretty much the same form and content, and that they all share common characteristics. It is the institutions of professionalism that provide that commonality. Furthermore, they produce the circumstances that encourage and reinforce professionalism in individuals.

Remember the distinction holding that, unlike the amateur, the professional does sufficiently good work to warrant getting paid for it. A critical fact about professionals in our day is that they depend on their work for their living. This dependence is neither universal nor inevitable, but in our nation it is the norm. It was made possible during the late nineteenth and early twentieth centuries when the modern professions established their present-day economic position.[3] In the United States they developed institutions designed to control the selection, training, and credentialing of their members, and to gain privileges providing marked advantage in the market-place.

This was not accomplished easily, for both in the United States and elsewhere the political climate opposed constraints on the market for services and goods. Indeed, during the Jacksonian period in the United States, earlier colonial legislation granting privilege to the professions of medicine and law was repealed in many states on the ground that all should be free to practice whatever occupation they wished. The reinstitution of professional privileges by state legislatures came hard for the traditional professions, and similar privileges remain an as yet unful-filled goal for many aspiring occupations today. However, when they *are* legislated, they are typically justified by a series of assumptions about the nature of professional work, the characteristics of the potential con-sumers of that work, and the operation of professional institutions.

The argument supporting professional privilege is fairly standard. On its basis, professions gain a privileged legal position in the market-place which seriously handicaps their competitors even if it does not always completely exclude them. And by their assurances, as well as by their higher education and middle-class status, professions gain general public esteem and trust without which legal support alone would be inadequate. Thus, an implicit contract is made between a profession and both the state and the public: "Protect my members from the unfettered compe-tition of a free market, and you can trust them to put your interest before their own. I will select them carefully and train and organize them to provide competent and ethical service." It is that implicit contract be-tween the corporate profession and society which both allows and requires us to trust the individual professionals we consult.

THE PROFESSIONAL MAINTENANCE PROJECT

The "market project" of the modern professions looks outward to the broader market-place, seeking to establish a secure jurisdiction in the social division of labor,[4] a "labor market shelter," or, in Max Weber's terms, a "social closure"[5] that excludes potential competitors from outside the profession and protects its members from dominance by clients or employers. But they also engage in another necessary project – namely, maintaining sufficient cohesion of the profession as a whole to be able to undertake common action both to sustain its status and privilege and to advance its own "cultural" projects.[6] This might be called its "maintenance project" of adapting to the changing political and economic environment so as to be able to continue to control its own affairs.

A number of things contribute to the maintenance of its cohesion. First, the members of all professions, unlike those of most other occu-pations today, have a distinct public identity that provides a foundation for solidarity and mutual sympathy. Second, when training is attached to the university, lengthened by requiring a college education as a minimum prerequisite, and standardized, all members of a profession share a com-mon socialization experience. Furthermore, the relatively long period of training required to enter the professions encourages their members to commit themselves to a life-long career. Although life-long professional careers are not quite as common as some claim, the very fact of investing a much longer than average part of one's lifetime in training creates a "sunk cost" that encourages commitment to a career in the profession and creates another bond joining its members.

A critical but often ignored method of sustaining the solidarity of the profession lies in norms governing relations among its members and between its members and lay people. They may be written as rules or practiced as unwritten custom. They may be called "etiquette" or even "ethics." Many are designed not so much to *prevent* competition among members as to *control* it. Rules establishing minimum fees, for example, do not prevent price competition among members, for some charge less than others for their services. They are designed to prevent "cut-throat competition" by which a determined price-cutter can literally drive colleagues out of the market. Similarly, rules governing advertising do not prevent competition among members, but rather restrict its content, form, and mode of circulation. Before many of those restrictions were abolished by the Supreme Court, advertising consisted of brief public announcements, the display of a name-plate within prescribed dimensions, speaking out at local community meetings, and socializing at churches, clubs, lodges, and the like, followed by the parting gift of a business card. The rules restricting advertising reflected in part genteel conceptions of professional dignity or status, but their greatest significance lay in their effort to mute the quality and intensity of competition between colleagues and assure a minimum income for all.

In addition to rules designed to reduce the intensity and publicity of competition so as to preserve a modicum of equality and solidarity among them, there are the rules of "etiquette" expected to guide relations between professionals and their clients, and among colleagues. Unlike earlier times, present-day etiquette makes it inappropriate to denigrate the work of a colleague to a client. Even if one feels that a colleague does poor work, it is not proper to inform the client of that. Indeed, one should be reluctant to judge the work of a colleague when one lacks direct experience with the case and its circumstances. "There, but for the grace of God, go I," "Who am I to judge?" or "It may be my turn next," may be heard said to explain the suspension of condemnatory judgment.[7] This reluctance to judge is sustained by an even greater unwillingness to confront apparently erring colleagues, let alone to take any action to punish or otherwise correct them in the interest of the well-being of clients. Even when there is intervention, the dominant rule is confidentiality so as to protect both the reputation and career of the errant colleague and the public face of the profession itself. This etiquette expresses an important part of the ideal-typical spirit of professionalism – namely, collegiality (see Waters, 1989). But because it tends to prevent the use of adequate regulatory procedures which protect the public, it violates the profession's implicit contract with the state and the public. There may be an intrinsic conflict between the profession's efforts to maintain the solidarity of its members and its fiduciary relationship with society.

Finally, I may note a number of devices by which professions attempt to prevent control of their members by lay people. In the United States, professionals may incorporate their practices, but what is legally defined as a professional corporation (PC) requires that only the practitioners themselves may hold stock in the corporation, not lay people or outsiders, and that, should they retire or die, their stock may not be passed on to heirs or sold to those who do not practice. Another device makes it "unethical" for the member of a profession to enter into a partnership agreement to practice with the member of another profession. Still another requires that the executive officer and supervisors of a professional practice organization be members of the profession and not lay people.

The institution of tenure is also employed to protect professionals from external interference with their work. Tenure is similar to seniority rights in conventional union contracts, but there are important differences. In unions, seniority differentiates members only by length of tenure, providing greater security to those with the greatest seniority and specifying that when jobs are to be eliminated the most recently hired go first. By contrast, tenure sharply dichotomizes professionals into those who are on probation and can lose their positions at any time, and those who have tenure and may not lose their positions except under stringently specified circumstances. The justification for union seniority is job security. Tenure also provides professionals with economic security, but its justification is different: it lies in protecting the intellectual independence and discretionary judgment of professional employees. It is assumed that employers could use economic threats to suppress disapproved ideas or actions. Tenure is intended to protect the academic, clinical, or scientific freedom of professionals, whose schooled freedom of judgment is assumed to be of benefit to both clients and society at large.

ORDINARY PEOPLE IN PRACTICE

Thus far I have tried to sketch a synthetic portrait of the various institutional devices by which organized professions have attempted to create a broad set of social and economic circumstances in which the spirit and ethos of professionalism would not be discouraged, even if not necessarily assured. By creating prestigious social identities to which an ideology of high purpose is attached, young people may be led to aspire to them. Extensive hurdles for entry and a demanding course of training, once surmounted, encourage long-term commitment to the profession as a career. Fairly stable and firm jurisdictional boundaries that minimize competition from other occupations and rules that control competition between colleagues create conditions of sufficient economic security (if not necessarily great wealth) to make long-term commitment feasible. And a number of devices are aimed at preserving independence of judgment from the interference of colleagues, clients, and the lay world in general. Running through it all are the threads of the market project to gain collective economic protection from external competition and the maintenance project of preserving solidarity among members, protecting the profession's public face, and deflecting efforts by clients, employers, and others to exercise control over its members' work. With such protection, professionals can afford to be devoted to the integrity of their craft and to use it for the benefit of others.

It may seem inappropriate for an analysis intended to address the ethos of professionalism to devote so much attention to the materialistic aspects of professionalism, dealing more with protectionist devices than with devoted service. I do so, however, in order to establish the nature of the institutions that provide conditions under which it is reasonable to expect ordinary or a bit more than ordinary people to sustain something resembling the high purposes claimed for professionalism. While the extraordinary person may very well rise above discouraging circumstances to be an exemplar, if their very living is threatened it is unlikely that most professionals – which is to say the profession as a whole – will put the good of their clients and the public before their own.

To buttress the plausibility of that statement we need not look to the distant past for complaints about unscrupulous practitioners by such honorable professionals as Sir John Securis (Larkey, 1936) and, much earlier, the writers of the Hippocratic corpus. It also applies to modern times. Carlin's classic studies (1962;1966) of the insecure and sometimes desperate "lower hemisphere" (Heinz and Laumann, 1982) of the legal profession show how the pressure of circumstance degrades practice. The struggle for clients, the need to gain as much income as possible from what "business" they can get, and the shady temptations offered in the lower courts where they work allow us to understand many (though not all) of their ethical lapses. Auerbach (1976) rightly castigates as hypocritical those leaders of the bar from the "upper hemisphere" who, themselves in secure and lucrative practices serving the corporate elite, deplore the behavior of "ambulance chasers" and counsel for personal injury plaintiffs.

I deliberately choose the neighborhood, self-employed lawyer in mid-century Chicago and New York as my example in order to stress that the gross form or organization of practice does not in itself pose a threat to professionalism. However, most who write of the professions labor under an unquestioned prejudice against employment. Self-employment is thought to be the ideal state in which professionalism can flourish. Some anticipate that professionalism will perish when professionals are employed by others. We may think about self-employment this way because the two powerful professions that we tend to keep in mind when we talk of professions, law and medicine, have traditionally been self-employed in the United States, serving individual clients on a fee-for-service basis. Even now, the majority in both professions work either alone or in very small partnerships.

What is true of doctors and lawyers in the United States today is not true of professions in general, however. We need only think of clergymen, military officers, professors, engineers, scientists, schoolteachers, social workers, and most other occupations that have been called professions. From their inception they have been employed, but they have not been any the less professional for that reason. The gross forms of self-employment and fee-for-service payment, or of employment and salary payment, matter far less than the particular circumstances in which they exist. In the case of the self-employed, it is extremely important to remember that history shows how self-employment under unfavorable market conditions discourages professionalism. Nor does fee-for-service or piece-work assure independence when the rates are low. Similarly, the mere fact of employment by large, corporate institutions owned and ultimately directed by non-professionals need not be hostile to professionalism. To show this, let me discuss the characteristics of large-scale institutions in theory and then how in practice those characteristics change when they depend on the skills of professionals.

PROFESSIONALISM AND FORMAL RATIONALITY

Contemporary organizational theory is in a state of flux, but in one way or another both the formal structure of authority within organizations and the "human relations" among their members remain central to it. Max Weber's ideal-typical model of rational-legal administration, or bureaucracy, remains vital to our thinking about large, modern organizaitons. While it has been accurately criticized over and over again for its failure to deal with many of the empirical characteristics of organizations, it continues to serve as an essential intellectual resource for conceiving of the essence of the spirit and structure of both private corporations and the civil service agencies of the state.

The spirit of those organizations is to reduce everything to the predictable and calculable so as to gain a stated set of ends with the greatest possible efficiency. The structure and practices of such rational-legal bureaucracy express that spirit of formal rationality. In the case of private commercial organizations, we might not be too far off the mark to say that the end is the production of saleable goods and services at the lowest possible cost so as either to increase profits or to sustain growth. In the case of public or state organizations, the end is the production of politically acceptable goods or services at the lowest possible cost to the treasury.

Most people have seen the pine-tree-like charts which are meant to portray the formal organization of firms and agencies – who is in charge of what and responsible to whom, the major departments or divisions, the relationships of subordination and superordination, and the "channels." The structure is hierarchical and monocratic, divided vertically into different levels of authority and responsibility, with the ultimate authority held by a single officer who is accountable to those outside the organization itself who own or are otherwise responsible for it. And it is pyramidal, divided not only vertically but also horizontally into a variety of specialized tasks, positions, or jobs which constitute its division of labor.

The structure of rational-legal bureaucracy is designed to create an efficient division of labor, modes of supervision that can effectively control and coordinate a complex variety of specialized tasks, and channels that freely and fully transmit commands, appeals, and information up and down the hierarchy. In constituting that structure, a number of practices are critical for predictable and successful functioning. The personnel of the organization are chosen solely on the basis of their competence to perform a particular kind of work, and they are limited to performing that work alone. Their rights, duties, and responsibilities are delineated fairly precisely, as is their authority over and subordination to others. The authority they are entitled to exercise over others is strictly limited to the position they hold and the tasks they are authorized to perform. Arbitrary authority is proscribed, and all activities are governed by the rules of the organization. Indeed, formal written rules are a major characteristic of rational-legalbureaucracy. Ambiguity of task and arbitrariness of authority are prevented, and rational ordering of a complex division of labor yields the greatest efficiency possible.

Weber's discussion of rational-legal administration was based on the German civil service of his time, and he was concerned more with its difference from patrimonial and charismatic administrative practices than with the actual tasks of its officials. He emphasized staffing practices and the ordering of authority and paid little attention to the way efficiency is connected with the way tasks are formulated. That is what Adam Smith, Karl Marx, and others had analyzed in industrial organizations, showing that, when jobs are made into minute, detailed, repetitive tasks that any normal adult (or even child!) could perform after a short period of training and practice, both greater productivity and greater control over workers could be attained. Tasks of this meaningless and degraded character are the antithesis of professional work.

Those who perform such tasks are by definition the industrial proletariat, and the historic process by which once skilled and independent workers were brought to that position has been labeled proletarianization. Some analysts now believe that the continued development of ever more refined specialization and rationalization of professional work, combined with employment in large-scale bureaucratic organizations, is proletarianizing the professions. Others see the extension of formal rationality as a deprofessionalizing force. If this is so, then surely professionalism is doomed. But is it so?

In Chapter 8 of this volume I argued against the usefulness and accuracy of imputing either proletarianization or deprofessionalization to the professions today, so I shall not repeat myself here. Instead, I wish to suggest that the perceived[8] nature of professional tasks imposes practical political barriers to a continuous movement toward proletarianization or deprofessionalization. In essence, I wish to suggest that, because there has been little inclination to accept the substitution of highly predictable, mechanical activities for the basic professional tasks, managers have had little choice but to expect those tasks to be performed on a discretionary basis and to give professionals the leeway that discretion requires. Thus, they act quite rationally in adapting the organization accordingly.

PROFESSIONALISM AND THE TRUSTED SERVANT

Since the middle of the century a large literature on professionals in organizations has accumulated. Perhaps the earliest studies of importance were of engineers and scientists employed in industry, followed by analyses of physicians in hospitals and clinics, social workers in social agencies, and lawyers in law firms. They may now seem to be out of date, but over the past decade studies of engineers, lawyers in public and private practice organizations, and others, have come to much the same conclusion. By and large, the concrete authority structure and practices by which we characterize rational-legal bureaucracy are systematically modified in organizations devoted to the provision of professional services. Instead we find a hybrid form. In virtually all studies it was observed that professionals had a special position in the organization, either working in units separated from the organization as a whole and headed by a member of the profession, or arrayed in a "staff" or professional hierarchy that was separate from and parallel to the conventional "line" or production and support hierarchy. Furthermore, while some work was structured by "formats" and "standard operating procedures," and all of it (like all work everywhere) limited by available resources, professionals exercised a considerable amount of discretion in the way they performed their work. Indeed, the principal investigator of a recent analysis of a variety of employed professionals had originally formulated it as a study of what he expected to be proletarianization (Derber, 1982). In reflecting on its findings, however, he conceded that, unlike the industrial proletariat, most employed professionals had considerable autonomy in performing their work – "technical autonomy." He sought to salvage the relevance of the concept by pointing to what he called their "ideological proletarianization," their loss of the capacity to determine the policies governing their work. He did not, however, examine critically his unquestioned assumption that in the past the self-employed professional in fact possessed and exercised such a capacity.

I believe that the technical autonomy of professional employees, even when unsupported by strong professional institutions, is most plausibly explained functionally. The core tasks of professionals are thought to *require* discretionary judgment, so that ordinary mechanization or bureaucratic rationalization is not possible. And they are believed to be beyond the capacity of untrained lay people to evaluate, so those who perform them must be supervised by one of their own. In essence, the work of professionals is believed to be such that they must be trusted not only by clients but also by employers. Those who are employees of an organization and serve individual clients therefore have a *double* fiduciary relationship. Peter Whalley's interesting study (1986) of British engineers who, unlike Americans, start at the bottom of the technical worker scale and work their way up to quasi-professional positions, shows how the policies employed by firms lead them to play the role of "trusted employees." And Goldthorpe (1982) suggests a "service class" to which professionals as well as managers belong, in positions of trust by virtue of either their specialized knowledge or their exercise of delegated authority.

By and large, the empirical evidence is that large-scale, bureaucratic organizations do not reduce professional work to the detailed, mechanical tasks that preclude the spirit and ethos of professionalism. Because of the influence of professional institutions, lay conceptions of professional work, consumers' demands of professional work, and perhaps in some instances the intrinsic character of the work itself, professionals are given considerably more leeway than most other employees in deciding what tasks to do and how to do them. However, while both that modified structure of authority and reliance on discretionary judgment are pre-requisites for professionalism, they are not by themselves sufficient.

When we turn from broad issues of organization and overall policies of formulating professional tasks to more concrete internal policies that can very considerably from one organization to another, we gain to fuller understanding of the conditions sustaining professionalism. Indeed, they represent conditions as important to professionalism in individual, self-employed practices as in organized large-scale practices, whether controlled by professionals themselves, by the state, or by private enterprises. Among the most important are policies determining the allocation of resources, defining the obligations of professional employees toward their employing organization, their clients, and the public in general, establishing the standards for evaluating professional work, and the methods of supervising and controlling it. Let me show the relationship of each to professionalism.

SUSTAINING PROFESSIONALISM

Professionalism entails commitment to a particular body of knowledge and skill both for its own sake and for the use to which it is put – that is to say, commitment to preserve, refine, and elaborate that knowledge and skill, to do good work, and, where it has application to worldly problems, to perform it well for the benefit of others – to do Good Works. In order to do good work one must have the nominal freedom to exercise discretionary judgment. And while technical autonomy is perhaps as common among employed professionals as among the self-employed, a critical question is how, in what way, and from what perspective it can be exercised. Without sufficient time, equipment, assistance, and other resources, one cannot do one's work well and one's freedom to employ discretion becomes meaningless.

If there are not enough resources available and the work must be done in any case, it is inevitable that it can be done only by the use of short-cuts and gross formulas that border upon mechanical and only marginally acceptable technique. This threatens the professional character of the work it self. Whatever the nominal right to discretion, severely restricted resources force its use for untoward purposes. Whether they work in private organizations devoted to maximizing profits or growth by minimizing production costs, or publicly supported organizations required to maximize production with minimal resources in order to keep taxes and political pressure low, an overwhelming caseload combined with a poverty of resources by which to handle it will at least discourage if not destroy both the inclination and the capacity to do good work.[9] The same problem can exist in self-employed, individual practices under unfavorable market conditions, when the "free" professional lacks capital for the most basic equipment and assistance, and when a very large caseload is taken on to compensate for the extremely small fees that the market will bear. Under such circumstances "burnout," "cynicism," loss of commitment to the work, and even inclination to leave the profession occur (see Cooper and Marshall, 1980). The resources available to the employing organization, therefore, and its policies in allocating them to working professionals, are critical contingencies for the fate of professionalism.

Yet another critical element of work that nourishes professionalism lies in the nature of the relationship between client and professional. Here, too, the issue is generic to professional work, however it is organized. In the case of employment in large-scale organizations we can put it crudely as whether or not policy is that customers are always right and that the organization and its members exist solely to serve, even cater, to their desires so long as they are willing to pay. Is the policy to provide whatever customers or clients desire, even if their capacity to evaluate the service or product is seriously limited and what they desire contradicts the better judgment of the professional? In short, is it the policy to substitute the discretionary judgment of the consumer for that of the professional?

This crude rhetorical dichotomy only dramatizes the issue, of course, for most would agree that the professional's relationship to clients should sustain a subtle balance between asserting technical authority while respecting the client's right to self-determination. But if the customer (or the citizen, in the case of publicly owned organizations) is to be always right, then professionals are no longer able to exercise the authoritative discretion, guided by their independent perspective on what work is appropriate for their craft, that is supposed to distinguish them. They become mere servants in a cafeteria, doing whatever is demanded of them and seeking above all to please. Professionalism can flourish only when practitioners in organizations have firm but by no means absolute support from their employer for the consequential exercise of judgment that is independent of their clients.[10]

Another source of influence on professionalism that is especially important in organizations is very complex because of the multiplicity of interests involved. Those who are employed, professional or not, are, in traditional legal language, "servants" of their employers. The ideas, services, techniques, and products resulting from their work as employees are the property of their employers. Furthermore, organizations are authorized to conceal from both competitors and the public those of their affairs that are trade secrets (or, in public organizations, "privileged information"). How are professionals to behave if organizational policies establish circumstances in which they cannot create a reasonably safe or reliable product or provide what they believe to be a truly adequate service? Do they have the acknowledged right to protest, resist, and even publicize those circumstances? Can they refuse to obey organizational policies that contradict their professional judgment without fear of being fired?

In short, can employed professionals undertake activities which violate established organizational policies that they believe to be against the best interest or their clients or of the public? Does the fiduciary relationship professionals have with their employers supersede the fiduciary relationship they have with their clients and their profession's fiduciary relationship with the public at large? Goldthorpe delineates the service class to which professionals belong as one that is trusted because the nature of its tasks requires trust, and because it members develop a moral commitment to the organizations that employ them. If that commitment is exclusive, it subverts commitment to the well-being of both clients and society that is part of the ethos of professionalism. It also subverts the independence of the professional's responsibility for the integrity of his or her craft.[11]

Finally, I must address the complex problem of regulating the professional's work, a problem that is particularly prominent in medicine today. When formal rationality is employed, every effort is made to eliminate as much discretion from work as possible, and to employ fixed and objective criteria for evaluating it. A great many industrial, office, and service jobs are formulated by engineers, efficiency experts, industrial designers, and the like, and used both to define the tasks of workers and establish the criteria by which their performance is evaluated. Insofar as possible, those criteria are quantitative or measurable in some objective fashion. As I have already noted, this kind of control over work is not characteristic of organizations employing professionals. In few non-professional jobs is all discretion eliminated, but the difference between the discretion allowed for semi-skilled and professional tasks is marked.[12]

Nonetheless, formal rationality *is* applied to the formulation and evaluation of professional work, though in a special way. It is often visible in the organization of the work of engineers, for example, where at least some assignments are "formatted" or structured in advance. And certainly elements of formal rationality have long been present in law (see, e.g., Engel, 1977), where "boilerplate" – standard forms employed for various purposes – has been an essential work resource made even more pervasive now that computerized word-processing is available. Such rationality is being pressed on medicine by both private and public insurers. Records essential for reimbursement by insurers must employ standard forms in which diagnostic and procedure information is pre-categorized. Quantitative standards are being used to determine whether a physician's performance conforms to statistical as well as absolute norms, and in some cases whether it is appropriate to a stated diagnosis. A significant degree of discretion remains, but its boundaries are becoming more distinct and perhaps more rigid. However, the content of the formats, forms, and standards is created, reviewed, and evaluated not by efficiency experts, industrial engineers, and others outside the profession, but by authorities within the professions. This is one of the circumstances that make the position of professionals quite different from that of the industrial proletariat.

These extensions of formal rationality create a distinct pattern of regulatory procedure, one that in the future is likely to increase in both large-scale organizations and individual practices dependent on public and private third-party payers who attempt to control the cost and quality of professional services. A framework of formal, often quantitative standards for defining tasks and evaluating their outcome is established by members of the profession who serve as cognitive authorities and provide professional legitimacy to hierarchical methods of regulation and control carried out by other members of the profession serving in an administrative capacity. The pressure on practitioners is to restrict the exercise of discretion to the safe limits established by the promulgated norms, which may very well mean, in some cases, forcing the problems of clients into a standardized Procrustean bed. This surely weakens professionalism, for while such standardization may very well be to the benefit of clients in general, it is not likely to be to the benefit of at least some individual clients. Furthermore, such a method of regulating work splits the profession into superior and subordinate, and threatens both collegiality and the cohesion of the corporate body.

The method of regulating work that is most compatible with professionalism is collegiate rather than hierarchical, and is loosely denoted by the term "peer review." As a method, peer review is interactive and, unlike bureaucratic methods, can employ qualitative judgments finely tuned to variable individual circumstances, problems, and clients. It is, furthermore, a method whose use is facilitated by working in a large-scale organization, where all are familiar with the concrete and often idiosyncratic circumstances connected with their work. By contrast, self-employed, solo practice is a form in which professional work is least likely to be amenable to collegial modes of review and regulation. In any case, wherever peer review is practiced, neither the integrity of the craft nor the well-being of clients are advanced if the process is constrained by the self-protecting etiquette to which professionals are prone. To be true to the claims of professional virtue, peer review must be judgmental and demanding even while being supportive.

THE FUTURE OF PROFESSIONALISM

I began this paper by noting that we are living in a time when many are looking closely at the professions, their costs, and their benefits, and when a variety of methods are being considered to make their services more accessible to those who need them, and to provide assurance that they are reliable and well considered. Legal barriers to the development of private, for-profit enterprises attempting to provide services at a reasonable cost have been lowered. In medicine, some types of Health Maintenance Organization (HMO) are examples, as are in law the legal clinics of Hyatt and Jacoby and Meyers. In considering whether the growth of such enterprises threatens professionalism, however, I resisted the inclination to react to gross forms of capitalization, ownership, and organization of professional practice. I have argued that organizations employing professionals have accommodated their structure and procedures to the professional need for discretion. Their potential influence on professionalism, therefore, cannot be inferred from ownership and size alone. What is as critical are a number of internal policies which can vary within the general organizational form.

The policies I discussed bear on generic issues of professionalism and are relevant to all forms of professional practice, including individual, self-employed practice, professionally owned and managed partnerships or organizations, non-profit, community organizations, private, large-scale, for-profit organizations owned by lay investors, and agencies of the state that provide professional services. Focusing primarily on large-scale, quasi-bureaucratic organizations, I have suggested that policies about resource allocation, the organization's and its professionals' relation to clients, the loyalty to organizational interests expected of the professional, and the method of regulating professional work all bear on the viability of professionalism.

I hope the implications of my discussion are clear. Without at all meaning to imply that the individual has no personal responsibility to strive for commitment to craft and the well-being of clients, I have focused on the circumstances which encourage such commitment. I have avoided assuming that professionalism requires heroic self-sacrifice: if that were the case we could not expect to find very much of it, and we certainly could not expect to find it in thousands of institutionally certified professionals. I brought the matter down to the concrete social arrangements which make it likely that ordinary or just a bit more than ordinary people will undertake a relatively long and demanding period of training in a professional pursuit and will not be discouraged from performing their work in the spirit that their profession promises.

Central to all the arrangements I have discussed is the question of how practice institutions are to be governed, and the relationship of working professionals to each other as well as to their clients and the executive boards of their organizations. If they are to be mere passive employees, without a strong organized voice in the allocation of resources that are essential for doing good work, they will find it difficult to remain committed to doing good work. If they are to play the role of merely providing whatever is demanded by consumers and authorized by those who pay for it, they will find it difficult to preserve a sense of the value of their schooled judgment. If they are to be merely loyal servants of the interests of their employers or their own "business," they will have difficulty sustaining any independent commitment to serving the good of both individual clients and the public. And if they are to be required to work within ultimately mechanical, albeit permissive, standards established and enforced by professionals who act as their administrative and cognitive superiors, they will have to forsake the communal or collegiate principle that is distinctive of the professional mode of organizing work.

NOTES

1 For a recent, thorough review of the legal sources of medicine's privileges in the market-place, see Hall (1988).
2 See Pence (1978–9) and Haworth (1977). Haworth's essay is especially valuable for its emphasis on professionalism as devotion to craft for its intrinsic value. For example, "[Ordinary] work, then, exists as a means, unpleasant in itself but useful in view of the results of enduring it. When work is professionalized, the circumstances that make it sensible to construe income as an earned reward for having worked are eliminated. For then the person perceives his occupation as making sense in itself, its own reward, and what is wanted is not a pay-off but the means of carrying it on" (p. 113).
3 For a very influential history and analysis emphasizing the economic and class-based character of the development of the modern professions, see Larson (1977).

4   An important analysis focusing on the struggle with other occupations for jurisdiction is Abbott (1988).
5   Recent works elaborating on Weber's brief discussion of social closures are Murphy (1988) and Waters (1989).
6   The phrase is used for want of a better one. Professions do not merely undertake economic projects. They also encourage research and experimentation to advance their knowledge and skill, disseminate information to their members and the public, and organize projects that they believe benefit society. For a study of some of a bar association's cultural projects, see Halliday (1987).
7   For empirical analyses of physicians in this context, see Freidson (1980) and Bosk (1979).
8   I deliberately phrase this to avoid implying that the tasks professionals perform are *intrinsically* resistant to mechanization. There is no logical reason why a computer cannot diagnose and prescribe treatment for our medical complaints all by itself, nor why *all* legal problems cannot be handled by predetermined formulas. Mechanization or industrialization of all that professionals now do is quite feasible. It does not occur because people are not willing to have their problems and the solutions for their problems simplified and standardized in the fashion that mechanization requires.
9   Perhaps the best general source for discussion of this problem is Lipsky (1980), who is concerned primarily with employees in public agencies that are chronically underfinanced. This problem is also likely to exist among professionals employed by private, for-profit organizations that provide low-cost, mass, professional services, but we know next to nothing about them.
10 Loss of independence is most likely when clients are sophisticated and powerful organizations. For law, see the discussion in Heinz and Laumann (1982, pp. 365–73). A recent appraisal of the architectural profession (Gutman, 1988) notes a marked trend in the importance of such clients and their influence on architectural work.
11 For a sensitive discussion of the conditions that sustain the professional independence of the lawyer, as well as the justification for such independence, see Gordon (1988). It should be remembered that the problem of conflicting loyalties (only some of which is usually labeled "conflict of interest") also exists among the self-employed. It is an especially thorny problem for lawyers and accountants, but physicians and other professionals are by no means free of it. What is special about employed professionals is the addition of yet another fiduciary relationship, with the employing organization likely to have considerably more immediate power to enforce its claim for loyalty than individual clients or the public at large.
12 Conversely, in few professional jobs is discretionary judgment *always* required, for there is much virtually mechanical routine in all everyday professional work. The difference between the qualities of professional and non-professional work is one of degree, with the professional, much more than the non-professional, having to be prepared to forsake routine and exercise schooled judgment whenever that necessity becomes apparent.

References

Abbott, Andrew (1988): *The System of Professions: An Essay on the Division of Expert Labor*. Chicago: University of Chicago Press.

Abel, Richard L. and Lewis, Philip S. (eds) (1988a): *Lawyers in Society*, vol. 1: *The Common Law World*. Berkeley: University of California Press.

—— (1988b): *Lawyers in Society*, vol. 2: *The Civil Law World*. Berkeley: University of California Press.

—— (1989a): *Lawyers in Society*, vol. 3: *Comparative Theories*. Berkeley: University of California Press.

—— (1989b): Putting law back into the sociology of lawyers. In *Lawyers in Society*, vol. 3: *Comparative Theories*, ed. Richard L. Abel and Philip S. Lewis. Berkeley: University of California Press, pp. 478–526.

Akers, Ronald L. (1968): The professional association and the legal regulation of practice. *Law and Society Review*, 3, pp. 463–82.

Alford, Robert (1975): *Health Care Politics: Ideological and Interest Group Barriers to Reform*. Chicago: University of Chicago Press.

Argyris, Chris (1972): *The Applicability of Organizational Sociology*. Cambridge: Cambridge University Press.

Aronowitz, S. (1973): *False Promises: The Shaping of American Working Class Consciousness*. New York: McGraw-Hill.

Auerbach, Jerrold S. (1976): *Unequal Justice: Lawyers and Social Change in Modern America*. New York: Oxford University Press.

Avineri, Shlomo (1968): *The Social and Political Thought of Karl Marx*. Cambridge: Cambridge University Press.

Barber, B. (1962): *Science and the Social Order*. New York: Collier.

Barber, Bernard (1983): *The Logic and Limits of Trust*. New Brunswick, NJ: Rutgers University Press.

Becker, Howard S. (1970a): The nature of a profession. In Howard S. Becker, *Sociological Work*. Chicago: Aldine, pp. 87–103.

—— (1970b): *Sociological Work*. Chicago: Aldine.

Becker, Howard S. and Carper, James (1956): The elements of identification with an occupation. *American Sociological Review*, 21, pp. 341–8.

Begun, James W. (1986): Economic and sociological approaches to professionalism. *Work and Occupations*, 13, pp. 113–29.

Bell, Daniel (1967): Notes on the post-industrial society. *The Public Interest*, 6, pp. 24–45; 7, pp. 102–18.

—— (1968): The measurement of knowledge and technology. In *Indicators of Social Change*, ed. E. B. Sheldon and W. E. Moore. New York: Russell Sage Foundation, pp. 145–246.

—— (1976): *The Coming of Post-Industrial Society*. New York: Basic Books.

Ben-David, J. (1964): Professions in the class system of present-day societies. *Current Sociology*, 12, pp. 247–330.

—— (1977): *Centers of Learning: Britain, France and the United States*. New York: McGraw Hill.

Bendix, Reinhard (1956): *Work and Authority in Industry: Ideologies of Management in the Course of Industrialization*. New York: Harper & Row.

Bennis, W. G. and Slater, P. E. (1968): *The Temporary Society*. New York: Harper & Row.

Berg, Ivar (1970): *Education and Jobs: The Great Training Robbery*. New York: Praeger.

Berkley, G. E. (1971): *The Administrative Revolution*. Englewood Cliffs, NJ: Prentice-Hall.

Berlant, J. (1975): *Profession and Monopoly: A Study of Medicine in the United States and Great Britain*. Berkeley: University of California Press.

Björkman, James Warner (1989): Politicizing medicine and medicalizing politics: physician power in the United States. In *Controlling Medical Professionals: The Comparative Politics of Health Governance*, ed. Giorgio Freddi and James Warner Björkman. London: Sage, pp. 28–73.

Blau, Peter and Schoenherr, Richard A. (1971): *The Structure of Organizations*. New York: Basic Books.

Blumer, Herbert (1969): *Symbolic Interaction*. Englewood Cliffs, NJ: Prentice-Hall.

Bosk, Charles L. (1979): *Forgive and Remember*. Chicago: University of Chicago Press.

Braverman, H. (1974): *Labor and Monopoly Capital: The Degradation of Work in the Twentieth Century*. New York: Monthly Review.

Bregger, J. E. (1963): Self-employment in the U. S., 1948–1962. *Monthly Labor Review*, 76, pp. 37–43.

Bücher, Carl (1907): *Industrial Evolution*. New York: Henry Holt.

Bucher, Rue and Stelling, Joan (1969): Characteristics of professional organizations. *Journal of Health and Social Behavior*, 10, pp. 3–16.

Bucher, Rue and Strauss, Anselm (1961): Professions in process. *American Journal of Sociology*, 66, pp. 325–34.

Building Trades Employers' Association of the City of New York (1973): *Handbook*. New York: Building Trades Employers' Association.

Burnham, James (1960): *The Managerial Revolution*. Bloomington: Indiana University Press.

Burrage, Michael and Torstendahl, Rolf (eds) (1990): *Professions in Theory and History: Rethinking the Study of the Professions*. London: Sage.

Cairnes, J. E. (1887): *Some Leading Principles of Political Economy Newly Expounded*. London: Macmillan.

Caplow, Theodore (1964): *The Sociology of Work*. New York: McGraw-Hill.

Carlin, Jerome (1962): *Lawyers on Their Own*. New Brunswick, NJ: Rutgers University Press.

—— (1966): *Lawyers' Ethics*. New York: Russell Sage Foundation.

Carlton, W. (1978): *"In Our Professional Opinion . . .": The Primacy of Clinical Judgment over Moral Choice*. Notre Dame, IN: Notre Dame University Press.

Carr-Saunders, A. M. (1928): *Professions: Their Organization and Place in Society*. Oxford: Clarendon Press.

Carr-Saunders, A. M. and Wilson, P. A. (1933): *The Professions*. Oxford: Clarendon Press.

Child, John and Falk, Janet (1982): Maintenance of occupational control: the case of professions. *Work and Occupations*, 9, pp. 155–92.

Childers, Grant W., Mayhew, Bruce H., Jr., and Gray, Louis N. (1971): System size and structural differentiation in military organizations: testing a baseline model of the division of labor. *American Journal of Sociology*, 76, pp. 813–30.

Churchward, L. G. (1973): *The Soviet Intelligentsia: An Essay on the Social Structure and Roles of the Soviet Intellectuals*. Boston: Routledge & Kegan Paul.

Clark, Burton R. (ed.) (1987): *The Academic Profession: National, Disciplinary and Institutional Settings*. Berkeley: University of California Press.

Clemente, Frank (1972): The measurement problem in the analysis of an ecological concept: the division of labor. *Pacific Sociological Review*, 15, pp. 30–40.

Cocks, Geoffrey and Jarausch, Konrad H. (eds) (1990): *German Professions, 1800–1950*. New York: Oxford University Press.

Cohen, M. D. and March, James G. (1972): *The American College President*. New York: McGraw-Hill.

Coleman, James S. (1988): Social capital in the creation of human capital. *American Journal of Sociology*, 94, S95–120.

Collins, Randall (1971): Functional and conflict theories of educational stratification. *American Sociological Review*, 36, pp. 1002–19.

—— (1979): *The Credential Society: An Historical Sociology of Education and Stratification*. New York: Academic Press.

Cooper, C. L. and Marshall, J. (eds) (1980): *White Collar and Professional Stress*. New York: John Wiley & Sons.

Davies, C. (1980): Making sense of the census in Britain and the USA. *Sociological Review*, 28, pp. 581–609.

Derber, Charles (1982): Toward a new theory of professionals as workers: advanced capitalism and postindustrial labor. In *Professionals as Workers:*

Mental Labor in Advanced Capitalism, ed. Charles Derber. Boston: G. K. Hall, pp. 193–208.

Derber, Charles, Schwartz, William A. and Magrass, Yale (1990): *Power in the Highest Degree: Professionals and the Rise of a New Mandarin Order*. New York: Oxford University Press.

Désrosières, A. (n.d.): Elements pour l'histoire des nomenclatures socio-professionelles. In F. Bédarida et al., *Pour un histoire de la statistique*. Paris: Institut National de la Statistique et des Etudes Economiques, pp. 155–94.

Dibble, V. K. (1962): Occupations and ideologies. *American Journal of Sociology*, 68, pp. 229–41.

DiCesare, C. B. (1975): Changes in the occupational structure of U.S. jobs. *Monthly Labor Review*, 93, pp. 23–34.

Dingwall, Robert (1976): Accomplishing profession. *Sociological Review*, 24, pp. 331–49.

Dingwall, Robert and Fenn, Paul (1987): "A respectable profession"? Sociological and economic perspectives on the regulation of professional services. *International Review of Law and Economics*, 7, pp. 51–64.

Dingwall, Robert and Lewis, Philip (eds) (1983): *The Sociology of the Professions: Lawyers, Doctors, and Others*. London: Macmillan.

Doeringer, Peter B. and Piore, Michael J. (1971): *Internal Labor Markets and Manpower Analysis*. Lexington, MA: Heath Lexington Books.

Dubin, Robert (1956): Industrial workers' worlds: a study of the "central life interests" of industrial workers. *Social Problems*, 3, pp. 131–42.

Dubin, Robert, Headley, R. Alan and Taveggia, C. (1976): Attachment to work. In *Handbook of Work, Organization and Society*, Robert Dubin. ed. Chicago: Rand McNally, pp. 281–341.

Durkheim, Emile (1957): *Professional Ethics and Civic Morals*. London: Routledge & Kegan Paul.

—— (1964): *The Division of Labor in Society*. New York: Free Press.

Edwards, Richard (1979): *Contested Terrain: The Transformation of the Workplace in the Twentieth Century*. New York: Basic Books.

Edwards, Richard C. (1975): The social relations of production in the firm and labor market structure. In *Labor Market Segmentation*, ed. Richard C. Edwards et al. Lexington, MA: D. C. Heath, pp. 3–26.

Ehrenreich, Barbara and Ehrenreich, John (1977): The professional-managerial class. *Radical America*, 2 (March-April), pp. 7–31; (May-June), pp. 7–22.

Elbaum, Bernard and Wilkinson, Frank (1979): Industrial relations and uneven development: a comparative study of the American and British steel industries. *Cambridge Journal of Economics*, 3, pp. 275–303.

Elliott, P. (1972): *The Sociology of the Professions*. London: Macmillan.

Ellul, Jacques (1964): *The Technological Society*. New York: Vintage Books.

Emerson, Robert M. and Pollner, Melvin (1976): Dirty work designations: their features and consequences in a psychiatric setting. *Social Problems*, 23, pp. 243–54.

Engel, David M. (1977): The standardization of lawyers' services. *American Bar Foundation Research Journal*, pp. 817–44.

Engel, Gloria (1973): Social factors affecting the work satisfaction of the physician's assistant. *Sociological Review Monograph*, no. 20, pp. 245–61.

Esland, Geoffrey (1980): Professions and professionalism. In *The Politics of Work and Occupations*, ed. Geoffrey Esland and Graeme Salaman. Toronto: University of Toronto Press, pp. 213–50.

Etzioni, Amitai (1968): *The Active Society*. New York: Free Press.

—— (1969): Preface. In *The Semi-Professions and their Organization*, ed. Amitai Etzioni. New York: Free Press, pp. v–xviii.

Feinglass, Joe and Salmon, J. Warren (1990): Corporatization of medicine: the use of medical management information systems to increase the clinical productivity of physicians. *International Journal of Health Services*, 20, pp. 233–52.

Field, Mark G. (1957): *Doctor and Patient in Soviet Russia*. Cambridge: Harvard University Press.

Flexner, A. (1915): Is social work a profession? In *Studies in Social Work*, no. 4. New York: New York School of Philanthropy.

Fores, M. and Glover, I. (1978): The British disease: professionalism. *Times Higher Education Supplement*, 24 February, p. 15.

Form, William M. (1968): Occupations and careers. *International Encyclopedia of the Social Sciences*, 11, pp. 245–53.

Form, William H., and Huber, Joan A. (1976): Occupational power. In *Handbook of Work, Organization and Society*, ed. Robert Dubin. Chicago: Rand McNally, pp. 751–806.

Fortescue, Stephen (1987): *The Communist Party and Soviet Science*. Baltimore: Johns Hopkins University Press.

Foucault, Michel (1975): *The Birth of the Clinic*. New York: Vintage Books.

—— (1979): *Discipline and Punish: The Birth of the Prison*. New York: Vintage Books.

—— (1980): *Power/Knowledge: Selected Interviews and Other Writings, 1972–1977*. New York: Pantheon.

Freddi, Giorgio and Björkman, James Warner (eds) (1989): *Controlling Medical Professionals: The Comparative Politics of Health Governance*. Newbury Park, CA: Sage.

Freedman, Marcia (1976): *Labor Markets: Segments and Shelters*. Montclair, NJ: Allanheld, Osmun.

Freidson, Eliot (1970): *Professional Dominance: The Social Structure of Medical Care*. New York: Atherton Press.

—— (1976): The division of labor as social interaction. Chapter 3 in this volume.

—— (1977): The futures of professionalisation. Chapter 7 in this volume.

—— (1980 [1976]): *Doctoring Together: A Study of Professional Social Control*. Chicago: University of Chicago Press.

—— (1982): Occupational autonomy and labor market shelters. Chapter 5 in this volume.

—— (1983): The theory of professions: state of the art. Chapter 1 in this volume.

—— (1986a): *Professional Powers: A Study of the Institutionalization of Formal Knowledge*. Chicago: University of Chicago Press.

—— (1986b): Les professions artistiques comme défie à l'analyse sociologique. *Revue française de sociologie*, 27, pp. 431–43.

—— (1987): Professionals and amateurs in the welfare state. In *Applied Research and Structural Change in Modern Society*, ed. Lise Kjølsrød et al. Oslo: Institute of Applied Social Research, pp. 13–31.

—— (1988 [1970]): *Profession of Medicine: A Study in the Sociology of Applied Knowledge*. Chicago: University of Chicago Press.

—— (1990): Labors of love: a prospectus. In *The Nature of Work: Sociological Perspectives*, ed. Kai Erikson and Steven Peter Vallas. New Haven: Yale University Press, pp. 149–61.

Frieden, Nancy M. (1981): *Russian Physicians in an Era of Reform and Revolution, 1856–1905*. Princeton: Princeton University Press.

Friedman, Milton (1962): *Capitalism and Freedom*. Chicago: University of Chicago Press.

Fuchs, Victor R. (1966): The first service economy. *Public Interest*, 2, pp. 7–17.

Galbraith, J. K. (1968): *The New Industrial State*. New York: New American Library.

Gawalt, Gerard W. (ed.) (1984): *The New High Priests: Lawyers in Post-Civil War America*. Westport, CT: Greenwood Press.

Geison, Gerald L. (ed.) (1983a): *Professions and Professional Ideologies in America*. Chapel Hill: University of North Carolina Press.

—— (1983b): *Professions and the French State, 1700–1900*. Philadelphia: University of Pennsylvania Press.

Gella, A. (1976): An introduction to the sociology of the intelligentsia. In *The Intelligentsia and the Intellectuals: Theory, Method and Case Study*, ed. A. Gella. London: Sage.

Gibbs, Jack C. and Martin, Walter T. (1962): Urbanization, technology, and the division of labor: international patterns. *American Sociological Review*, 27, pp. 667–77.

Giddens, Anthony (1975): *The Class Structure of the Advanced Societies*. New York: Harper Torchbooks.

Gilb, Corrine Lathrop (1966): *Hidden Hierarchies: The Professions and Government*. New York: Harper & Row.

Gispen, Kees (1988): German engineers and American social theory: historical perspectives on professionalization. *Comparative Studies in Society and History*, 30, pp. 548–72.

Goldner, Fred and Ritti, R. R. (1967): Professionalism as career immobility. *American Journal of Sociology*, 72, pp. 489–502.

Goldthorpe, John (1982): On the service class, its formation and future. In *Social Class and the Division of Labour*, ed. A. Giddens and G. Mackenzie. Cambridge: Cambridge University Press, pp. 162–85.

Goode, William J. (1957): Community within a community. *American Sociological Review*, 22, pp. 194–200.

Goode, William J., Jr. (1960): Encroachment, charlatanism, and the emerging profession: psychology, medicine and sociology. *American Sociological Review*, 25, pp. 902–14.

—— (1969): The theoretical limits of professionalization. In *The Semi-Professions and their Organization*, ed. Amitai Etzioni New York: Free Press, pp. 266–313.

Gordon, David M. (1977): Capitalist efficiency and socialist efficiency. *Monthly Review*, 29, pp. 19–39.

Gordon, Robert W. (1988): The independence of lawyers. *Boston University Law Review*, 68, pp. 1–83.

Gordon, Robert W. and Simon, William H. (1992): The redemption of professionalism? In *Lawyers' Ideals/Lawyers' Practices: Transformations in the American Legal System*, ed. Robert L. Nelson, David M. Trubek and Rayman L. Solomon. Ithaca, NY: Cornell University Press, pp. 230–57.

Gorman, R. A. (1976): *Basic Text on Labor Law: Unionization and Collective Bargaining*. Minneapolis: West.

Goss, Mary (1961): Influence and authority among physicians in an outpatient clinic. *American Sociological Review*, 26, pp. 39–50.

Gouldner, Alvin W. (1979): *The Future of the Intellectuals and the Rise of the New Class*. London: Macmillan.

Granovetter, Mark (1985): Economic action and social structure: the problem of embeddedness. *American Journal of Sociology*, 91, pp. 481–510.

Gyarmati, G. (1975): Ideologies, roles and aspirations: the doctrine of the professions: basis of a power structure. *International Social Science Journal*, 27, pp. 629–54.

Habenstein, Robert (1963): Critique of "profession" as a sociological category. *Sociological Quarterly*, 4, pp. 291–300.

Hafferty, Frederic W. and McKinlay, John B. (eds) (1993): *The Changing Medical Profession: An International Perspective*. New York: Oxford University Press.

Hall, Mark A. (1988): Institutional control of physician behavior: legal barriers to health care cost containment. *University of Pennsylvania Law Review*, 137, pp. 431–536.

Hall, Richard H. (1968): Professionalization and bureaucratization. *American Sociological Review*, 33, p. 97.

—— (1969): *Occupations and the Social Structure*. Englewood Cliffs, NJ: Prentice-Hall.

—— (1975): *Occupations and the Social Structure*, 2nd edn. Englewood Cliffs, NJ: Prentice-Hall.

Halliday, Terence C. (1985): Knowledge mandates: collective influence by scientific, normative and syncretic professions. *British Journal of Sociology*, 36, pp. 421–47.

—— (1987): *Beyond Monopoly: Lawyers, State Crises, and Professional Empowerment*. Chicago: University of Chicago Press.

—— (1989): Legal professions and politics: neocorporatist variations on the pluralist theme of liberal democracies. In *Lawyers in Society*, vol. 3: *Comparative Theories*, ed. Richard L. Abel and Philip S. Lewis. Berkeley: University of California Press, pp. 375–426.

Halmos, P. (1966): *The Faith of the Counsellors*. New York: Schocken.

—— (1970): *The Personal Service Society*. New York: Schocken.

Harries-Jenkins, G. (1970): Professions in organizations. In *Professions and Professionalisation*, ed. J. A. Jackson. Cambridge: Cambridge University Press, pp. 53–107.

Haug, Marie R. (1973): Deprofessionalization: an alternative hypothesis for the future. *Sociological Review Monographs*, no. 20, pp. 195–211.

—— (1975): The deprofessionalization of everyone? *Sociological Focus*, 8, pp. 197–213.

—— (1977): Computer technology and the obsolescence of the concept of profession. In *Work and Technology*, ed. M. R. Haug and J. Dofny. Beverly Hills, CA: Sage, pp. 215–28.

Havighurst, Clark C. and King, N. M. P. (1983): Private credentialing of health care personnel: an antitrust perspective, parts 1 & 2. *American Journal of Law and Medicine*, 9, pp. 131–334.

Haworth, Lawrence (1977): *Decadence and Objectivity*. Toronto: University of Toronto Press.

Heidenheimer, Arnold J. (1989): Social scientific discourse, professional knowledge and public policies. *International Social Science Journal*, 41, pp. 529–53.

Heydebrand, Wolf V. (1979): The technocratic administration of justice. *Research in Law and Society*, 2, pp. 29–64.

Holzner, B. (1968): *Reality Construction in Society*. Cambridge, MA: Schenkman.

Horn, Joshua (1969): *Away with all Pests*. New York: Monthly Review Press.

Hughes, E. C. (1958): *Men and their Work*. New York: Free Press.

—— (1971): *The Sociological Eye: Selected Papers*. Chicago: Aldine.

Illich, Ivan (1980a): *Toward a History of Needs*. New York: Bantam Books.

—— (1980b): Useful unemployment and its professional enemies. In Ivan Illich, *Toward a History of Needs*. New York: Bantam New Age Books.

Jackson, J. A. (ed.) (1970): *Professions and Professionalization*. Cambridge: Cambridge University Press.

Jaffe, Abraham J. (1968): Labor force: definitions and measurement. *International Encyclopedia of the Social Sciences*, 8, pp. 469–74.

Jamous, H. and Peloille, B. (1970): Changes in the French university-hospital system. In *Professions and Professionalisation*, ed. J. A. Jackson. Cambridge: Cambridge University Press, pp. 111–52.

Jarausch, Konrad H. (1990): *The Unfree Professions: German Lawyers, Teachers, and Engineers, 1900–1950*. New York: Oxford University Press.

Jewson, N. D. (1974): Medical knowledge and the patronage system in eighteenth century England. *Sociology*, 8, pp. 369–85.

Johnson, Terence (1972): *Professions and Power*. London: Macmillan

—— (1973a): Imperialism and the professions. *Sociological Review Monographs*, no. 20, pp. 281–309.

—— (1973b): Professions, In *Human Societies: An Introduction to Sociology*, ed. G. Hurd. London: Routledge & Kegan Paul, pp. 131–2.

Jones, Anthony (ed.) (1991): *Professions and the State: Expertise and Autonomy in the Soviet Union and Eastern Europe*. Philadelphia: Temple University Press.

Kanter, Rosabeth Moss (1977): *Work and Family in the United States: A Critical Review and Agenda for Research and Policy.* New York: Russell Sage Foundation.

Katz, M. B. (1972): Occupational classification in history. *Journal of Interdisciplinary History*, 3, pp. 63–88.

Kemper, Theodore D. (1972): The division of labor: a post-Durkheimian analytical view. *American Sociological Review*, 37, pp. 739–53.

Kerr, Clark (1950): Labor markets: their character and consequences. *American Economic Review*, 40, pp. 278–91.

—— (1954): The balkanization of labor markets. In *Labor Markets and Economic Opportunity*, ed. E. W. Bakke. New York: John Wiley & Sons, pp. 92–110.

Kissam, Phillip C. (1980): Antitrust law, the First Amendment and professional self-regulation of technical quality. In *Regulating the Professions*, ed. R. D. Blair and S. Rubin. Lexington, MA: Lexington Press, pp. 143–83.

Klegon, D. A. (1978): The sociology of professions: an emerging perspective. *Sociology of Work and Occupations*, 5, pp. 259–83.

Kornhauser, William (1962): *Scientists in Industry: Conflict and Accommodation.* Berkeley: University of California Press.

Krause, Elliott (1971): *The Sociology of Occupations.* Boston: Little, Brown.

Kreckel, Reinhard (1980): Unequal opportunity structure and labor market segmentation. *Sociology*, 14, pp. 525–50.

Kronus, Carol L. (1976): The evolution of occupational power. *Sociology of Work and Occupations*, 3, pp. 3–37.

Kuhn, T. S. (1962): *The Structure of Scientific Revolutions.* Chicago: University of Chicago Press.

Kusterer, Ken C. (1978): *Know-How on the Job: The Important Working Knowledge of "Unskilled" Workers.* Boulder, CO: Westview Press.

Labovitz, Sanford and Gibbs, Jack P. (1964): Urbanization, technology and the division of labor: further evidence. *Pacific Sociological Review*, 7, pp. 3–9.

LaCapra, Dominick (1972): *Emile Durkheim – Sociologist and Philosopher.* Ithaca, NY: Cornell University Press.

Lane, R. E. (1966): The decline of politics and ideology in a knowledgeable society. *American Sociological Review*, 31, pp. 649–62.

Larkin, Gerald V. (1983): *Occupational Monopoly and Modern Medicine.* London: Tavistock.

Larson, Magalí S. (1977): *The Rise of Professionalism: A Sociological Analysis.* Berkeley: University of California Press.

—— (1989): The changing functions of lawyers in the liberal state. In *Lawyers in Society*, vol. 3: *Comparative Theories*, ed. Richard L. Abel and Philip S. Lewis. Berkeley: University of California Press, pp. 427–77.

—— (1990): In the matter of experts and professionals, or how impossible it is to leave nothing unsaid. In *The Formation of Professions: Knowledge, State and Strategy*, ed. Rolf Torstendahl and Michael Burrage. London: Sage, pp. 24–50.

Laski, H. L. (1931): The limitations of the expert. *Fabian Tract*, no. 235.

Laumann, Edward O. and Heinz, John P. (1977): Specialization and prestige in the legal profession: the structure of deference. *American Bar Foundation Research Journal*, pp. 155–216.
—— (1979): The organization of lawyers' work: size, intensity and co-practice of the fields of law. *American Bar Foundation Research Journal*, pp. 217–46.
Layton, E. T. (1971): *The Revolt of the Engineers*. Cleveland: Case Western Reserve University Press.
Lees, D. S. (1966): *Economic Consequences of the Professions*. London: Institute of Economic Affairs.
Lewis, Roy and Maude, Angus (1952): *Professional People*. London: Phoenix House.
Lieberman, J. K. (1970): *The Tyranny of the Experts: How Professionals are Closing the Open Society*. New York: Walker.
Lipset, S. M. and Schneider, W. (1983): *The Confidence Gap: Business, Labor and Government in the Public Mind*. New York: Free Press.
Lipset, Seymour Martin, Trow, Martin and Coleman, James (1962): *Union Democracy: The Internal Politics of the International Typographical Union*. Garden City, NY: Anchor Books.
Lipsky, Martin (1980): *Street-Level Bureaucracy: Dilemmas of the Individual in Public Service*. New York: Russell Sage Foundation.
Machlup, F. (1962): *The Production and Distribution of Knowledge in the United States*. Princeton: Princeton University Press.
Mallet, Serge (1975): *The New Working Class*. Nottingham: Spokesman Books.
Mann, Michael (1973): *Consciousness and Action Among the Western Working Class*. London: Macmillan.
Marcson, S. (1960): *The Scientist in American Industry*. Princeton: Industrial Relations Section, Princeton University.
Marcus, P. M. (1973): Schoolteachers and militant conservatism. In *The Professions and their Prospects*, ed. Eliot Freidson. Beverly Hills, CA: Sage, pp. 191–216.
Marglin, Stephen (1974): What do bosses do? The origins and functions of hierarchy in capitalist production. *Review of Radical Political Economics*, 6, pp. 60–112.
Marshall, T. H. (1939): The recent history of professionalism in relation to social structure and social policy. *Canadian Journal of Economics and Political Science*, 5, pp. 325–40.
Marx, Karl (1963): *The Poverty of Philosophy*. New York: International Publishers.
Maurice, M. (1972): Propos sur la sociologie des professions. *Sociologie du Travail*, 13, pp. 213–25.
McKinlay, John B. (1973): On the professional regulation of change. *Sociological Review Monograph*, no. 20, pp. 61–84.
McKinlay, John B. and Stoeckle, J. D. (1988): Corporatization and the social transformation of doctoring. *International Journal of Health Services*, 18, pp. 191–205.
Metzger, Walter P. (1987): A specter is haunting American scholars: the specter of "professionalism". *Educational Researcher*, 16, pp. 10–19.

Millerson, Geoffrey (1964): *The Qualifying Associations: A Study in Professionalisation*. London: Routledge & Kegan Paul.

Mills, C. W. (1942): The professional ideology of social pathologists. *American Journal of Sociology*, 49, pp. 165–80.

—— (1951): *White Collar: The American Middle Classes*. New York: Oxford University Press.

Mincer, Jacob (1968): Labor force participation. *International Encyclopedia of the Social Sciences*, 8, pp. 474–81.

Montagna, P. (1968): Professionalization and bureaucratization in large professional organizations. *American Journal of Sociology*, 74, pp. 138–45.

Moore, W. E. (1970): *Professions: Roles and Rules*. New York: Russell Sage Foundation.

Morris, Richard and Murphy, Raymond J. (1959): The situs dimension in occupational structure. *American Sociological Review*, 24, pp. 231–9.

Morse, Dean (1969): *The Peripheral Worker*. New York: Columbia University Press.

Murphy, Raymond (1988): *Social Closure: The Theory of Monopolization and Exclusion*. Oxford: Clarendon Press.

Navarro, Vicente (1977): *Social Security and Medicine in the USSR: A Marxist Critique*. Lexington, MA: Lexington Books.

Nelson, Robert L. and Trubek, David M. (1992): Arenas of professionalism: the professional ideologies of lawyers in context. In *Lawyers' Ideals/Lawyers' Practices: Transformations in the American Legal System*, ed. Robert L. Nelson, David M. Trubek and Rayman L. Solomon. Ithaca, NY: Cornell University Press, pp. 177–214.

Oakley, Ann (1974): *The Sociology of Housework*. New York: Pantheon Books.

Olesen, Virginia L. and Katsuranis, Frances (1978): Urban nomads : women in temporary clerical services. In *Women Working: Theories and Facts in Perspective*, ed. Ann H. Stromberg and Shirley Harkness. Palo Alto, CA: Mayfield, pp. 316–38.

Oppenheimer, M. (1973): The proletarianization of the professional. *Sociological Review Monograph*, no. 20, pp. 213–27.

Orzack, Louis H. (1959): Work as a "central life interest" of professionals. *Social Problems*, 7, pp. 125–32.

—— (1977): Competing professions and the public interest in the European Economic Community: drugs and their quality control. In *Perspectives in the Sociology of Science*, ed. Stuart S. Blume. London: John Wiley, pp. 95–129.

Parkin, Frank (1979): *Marxism and Class Theory: A Bourgeois Critique*. New York: Columbia University Press.

Parsons, Talcott (1939): The professions and social structure. *Social Forces*, 17, pp. 457–67.

—— (1951): *The Social System*. New York: Free Press.

—— (1964): A sociologist looks at the legal profession. In Talcott Parsons, *Essays in Sociological Theory*. New York: Free Press.

—— (1968): Professions. In *International Encyclopedia of the Social Sciences*, 12, pp. 536–47.

—— (1969): "The intellectual": A social role category. In *On Intellectuals*, ed. Philip Rieff. New York: Anchor Books, pp. 3–26.

Pavalko, R. M. (1971): *Sociology of Occupations and Professions*. Itasca, IL: F. E. Peacock.

Peterson, M. Jeanne (1978): *The Medical Profession in Mid-Victorian London*. Berkeley: University of California Press.

Pettigrew, Andrew M. (1973): *The Politics of Organizational Decision-making*. London: Tavistock.

Piore, Michael J. (1975): Notes for a theory of labor market stratification. In *Labor Market Segmentation*, ed. Richard C. Edwards et al. Lexington, MA: D. C. Heath, pp. 125–50.

Platt, Anthony M. (1969): *The Child Savers: The Invention of Delinquency*. Chicago: University of Chicago Press.

Price, D. K. (1965): *The Scientific Estate*. Cambridge: Harvard University Press.

Rabban, David (1989): Distinguishing excluded managers from covered professionals under the NLRA. *Columbia Law Review*, 89, pp. 1775–1860.

—— (1990): Can American labor law accommodate collective bargaining by professional employees? *Yale Law Journal*, 99, pp. 689–758.

Ramsey, Matthew (1983): Review essay: history of a profession. Annales: the work of Jacques Léonard. *Journal of Social History*, 17, pp. 319–38.

—— (1988): *Professional and Popular Medicine in France, 1770–1830*. Cambridge: Cambridge University Press.

Ray, R. N. (1975): A report on self-employed Americans in 1973. *Monthly Labor Review*, 98, pp. 49–54.

Reader, W. J. (1967): *Professional Men: The Rise of the Professional classes in Nineteenth Century England*. New York: Basic Books.

Relman, Arnold S. (1980): The new medical-industrial complex. *New England Journal of Medicine*, 303, pp. 963–70.

Ringer, F. K. (1979): The German academic community. In *The Organization of Knowledge in Modern America 1860–1920*, ed. A. Oleson and J. Voss. Baltimore: Johns Hopkins University Press.

Ritti, R. R. (1971): *The Engineer in the Industrial Corporation*. New York: Columbia University Press.

Roth, J. (1974): Professionalism: the sociologist's decoy. *Sociology of Work and Occupations*, 1, pp. 6–23.

Rothman, David J. (1971): *The Discovery of the Asylum*. Boston: Little, Brown.

Rothschild, Joyce and Russell, Raymond (1986): Alternatives to bureaucracy: democratic participation in the economy. *Annual Review of Sociology*, 12, pp. 307–28.

Rueschemeyer, Dietrich (1964): Doctors and lawyers: a comment on the theory of professions. *Canadian Journal of Sociology and Anthropology*, 1, p. 17.

—— (1973): *Lawyers and their Society: A Comparative Study of the Legal Profession in Germany and in the United States*. Cambridge: Harvard University Press.

—— (1986): Comparing legal professions cross-nationally: from a professions-centered to a state-centered approach. *American Bar Foundation Research Journal*, pp. 415–46.

Rushing, William A. (1968): Hardness of material as related to division of labor in manufacturing industries. *Administrative Science Quarterly*, 13, pp. 229–45.

Salaman, Graeme (1974): *Community and Occupation*. Cambridge: Cambridge University Press.

Schneyer, Theodore (1992): Professionalism as politics: the making of a modern legal ethics code. In *Lawyers' Ideals/Lawyers' Practices. Transformations in the American Legal System*, ed. Robert L. Nelson, David M. Trubek and Rayman L. Solomon. Ithaca, NY: Cornell University Press, pp. 95–143.

Schnore, Leo F. (1958): Social morphology and human ecology. *American Journal of Sociology*, 63, pp. 620–34.

Schriesheim, J., von Glinow, M. A. and Kerr, S. (1977): Professionals in bureaucracy: a structural alternative. *TIMS Studies in Management Science*, 5, pp. 55–69.

Scott, W. Richard (1965): Reactions to supervision in a heteronomous professional organization. *Administrative Science Quarterly*, 10, pp. 65–81.

—— (1966): Professionals in bureaucracies – areas of conflict. In *Professionalization*, ed. H. M. Vollmer and D. L. Mills. Englewood Cliffs, NJ: Prentice-Hall, pp. 265–75.

—— (1981): *Organizations, Rational, Natural and Open Systems*. Englewood Cliffs, NJ: Prentice-Hall.

Scoville, J. G. (1965): The development and relevance of U. S. occupational data. *Industrial and Labor Relations*, 19, pp. 70–9.

Sharlin, A. (1979): From the study of social mobility to the study of society. *American Journal of Sociology*, 85, pp. 338–60.

Shils, Edward (1982): Great Britain and the United States: legislators, bureaucrats and the universities. In *Universities, Politicians, and Bureaucrats: Europe and the United States*, ed. Hans Daalder and Edward Shils. Cambridge: Cambridge University Press, pp. 437–87.

Shimberg, Benjamin (1982): *Occupational Licensing: A Public Perspective*. Princeton: Educational Testing Service.

Shimberg, Benjamin, Esser, Barbara F. and Kruger, Daniel H. (1973): *Occupational Licensing: Practices and Policies*. Washington: Public Affairs.

Shryock, Richard (1947): *The Development of Modern Medicine*. New York: Knopf.

Simborg, D. W. (1981): DRG creep: a new hospital-acquired disease. *New England Journal of Medicine*, 304, pp. 1602–4.

Simon, William H. (1985): Babbitt v. Brandeis: the decline of the professional ideal. *Stanford Law Review*, 37, pp. 565–87.

Smigel, Erwin O. (1964): *The Wall Street Lawyer: Professional Organization Man?* New York: Free Press.

Solomon, Rayman L. (1992): Five crises or one: the concept of legal professionalism. In *Lawyers' Ideals/Lawyers' Practices: Transformations in the American*

Legal System, ed. Robert L. Nelson, David M. Trubek and Rayman L. Solomon. Ithaca, NY: Cornell University Press, pp. 144–73.

Spence, A. M. (1974): *Market Signalling: Informational Transfer in Hiring and Related Screening Processes*. Cambridge, MA: Harvard University Press.

Spence, Gregory E. (1978–9): Towards a theory of work. *Philosophical Forum*, 10, pp. 306–20.

Spencer, H. (1914 [1896]): *The Principles of Sociology*, vol. 3, part 7. New York: Appleton.

Starr, Paul (1982): *The Social Transformation of American Medicine: The Rise of a Sovereign Profession and the Making of a Vast Industry*. New York: Basic Books.

Stebbins, Robert A. (1992): *Amateurs, Professionals, and Serious Leisure*. Montreal: McGill–Queen's University Press.

Stewart, Phyllis L. and Cantor, Muriel G. (eds) (1974): *Varieties of Work Experience*. Cambridge: Schenkman.

Stinchcombe, Arthur L. (1959): Bureaucratic and craft administration of production: a comparative study. *Administrative Science Quarterly*, 4, pp. 168–87.

Strauss, Anselm et al. (1964): *Psychiatric Ideologies and Institutions*. New York: Free Press.

Tausky, Curt (1978): *Work Organizations*. Itasca, IL: Peacock.

Tawney, R. H. (1920): *The Acquisitive Society*. New York: Harcourt, Brace.

Thrupp, S. L. (1963): The gilds. In *The Cambridge Economic History*, 3, pp. 230–80. Cambridge: Cambridge University Press.

Torstendahl, Rolf and Burrage, Michael (eds) (1990): *The Formation of Professions: Knowledge, State and Strategy*. London: Sage.

Touraine, A. (1971): *The Post-Industrial Society*. New York: Random House.

Turner, C. and Hodge, M. N. (1970): Occupations and professions. In *Professions and Professionalisation*, ed. J. A. Jackson. Cambridge: Cambridge University Press, pp. 19–50.

Vladeck, Bruce (1984): Medicare hospital payment by diagnosis-related groups. *Annals of Internal Medicine*, 100, pp. 576–91.

Vollmer, H. M. and Mills, D. L. (eds) (1966): *Professionalization*. Englewood Cliffs, NJ: Prentice-Hall.

Waters, Malcolm (1989): Collegiality, bureaucratization, and professionalization: a Weberian analysis. *American Journal of Sociology*, 94, pp. 945–72.

Webb, Sidney and Webb, Beatrice (1917): Special supplement on professional associations. *New Statesman*, no. 211, p. 9.

Weber, Max (1947): *The Theory of Social and Economic Organization*. New York: Oxford University Press.

—— (1968): *Economy and Society*, vol. 1. New York: Bedminster Press.

Weick, Karl (1976): Educational systems as loosely coupled systems. *Administrative Science Quarterly*, 21, pp. 1–19.

Wilensky, Harold L. (1964): The professionalization of everyone? *American Journal of Sociology*, 70, pp. 137–58.

—— (1967): *Organizational Intelligence*. New York: Basic Books.

Williamson, Oliver E. (1985): *The Economic Institutions of Capitalism*. New York: Free Press.

Willis, Evan (1989): *Medical Dominance: The Division of Labour in Australian Health Care*, 2nd edn. Sydney: Allen & Unwin.

Wilsford, David (1991): *Doctors and the State: The Politics of Health Care in France and the United States*. Durham, NC: Duke University Press.

Woodward, Joan (1958): *Management and Technology*. London: HMSO.

Wright, Erik Olin (1978): Race, class, and income inequality. *American Journal of Sociology*, 83, pp. 1368–97.

—— (1985): *Classes*. London: Verso.

Zeitlin, Jonathan (1979): Crafts control and the division of labor: engineers and compositors in Britain, 1890–1930. *Cambridge Journal of Economics*, 3, pp. 263–74.

Znaniecki, F. (1968): *The Social Role of the Man of Knowledge*. New York: Harper.

Index